Paying the Premium

**Recent Titles in
Contributions in Military Studies**

The Laws of Land Warfare: A Guide to U.S. Army Manuals
Donald A. Wells

Raiders or Elite Infantry? The Changing Role of the U.S. Army Rangers from Dieppe to Grenada
David W. Hogan, Jr.

The U.S. Military
John E. Peters

Unconventional Conflicts in a New Security Era: Lessons from Malaya and Vietnam
Sam C. Sarkesian

"Mad Jack": The Biography of Captain John Percival, USN, 1779–1862
David F. Long

Military Helicopter Doctrines of the Major Powers, 1945–1992: Making Decisions about Air-Land Warfare
Matthew Allen

Joint Military Operations: A Short History
Roger A. Beaumont

Iron Brigade General: John Gibbon, A Rebel in Blue
Dennis S. Lavery and Mark H. Jordan

Looking Back on the Vietnam War: A 1990s Perspective on the Decisions, Combat, and Legacies
William Head and Lawrence E. Ginter, editors

The Search for Strategy: Politics and Strategic Vision
Gary L. Guertner, editor

PAYING THE PREMIUM

A Military Insurance Policy for Peace and Freedom

Edited by WALTER HAHN
and H. JOACHIM MAITRE

Prepared under the auspices of the Potomac Foundation and the Center for Defense Journalism of Boston University

Contributions in Military Studies, Number 140
COLIN GRAY, Series Adviser

Greenwood Press
Westport, Connecticut • London

Library of Congress Cataloging-in-Publication Data

Paying the premium : a military insurance policy for peace and freedom
 / edited by Walter Hahn and H. Joachim Maitre.
    p. cm.—(Contributions in military studies, ISSN 0883-6884
; no. 140)
    Includes index.
    ISBN 0-313-28849-6
    1. United States—Military policy. I. Hahn, Walter.   II. Maitre,
Hans Joachim.   III. Series.
UA23.P374   1993
355'.0335'73—dc20   92-35552

British Library Cataloguing in Publication Data is available.

Copyright © 1993 by the Center for Defense Journalism

All rights reserved. No portion of this book may be
reproduced, by any process or technique, without the
express written consent of the publisher.

Library of Congress Catalog Card Number: 92-35552
ISBN: 0-313-28849-6
ISSN: 0883-6884

First published in 1993

Greenwood Press, 88 Post Road West, Westport, CT 06881
An imprint of Greenwood Publishing Group, Inc.

Printed in the United States of America

The paper used in this book complies with the
Permanent Paper Standard issued by the National
Information Standards Organization (Z39.48-1984).

10 9 8 7 6 5 4 3 2 1

Contents

ILLUSTRATIONS		vii
PREFACE		ix
1.	IN SEARCH OF AN AMERICAN "DEFENSE INSURANCE POLICY" **Walter Hahn**	1
2.	RISKS AND UNCERTAINTIES IN A CHANGING WORLD **Gen. Donn Starry, USA (Ret.)**	13
3.	ARMY FORCES FOR THE FUTURE **Lt. Gen. John W. Woodmansee, Jr., USA (Ret.)**	33
4.	NAVAL FORCES FOR THE FUTURE **Adm. Harry Train II, USN (Ret.)**	55
5.	TACTICAL AIR FORCES FOR THE FUTURE **Gen. John L. Piotrowski, USAF (Ret.)**	71
6.	MARINE FORCES FOR THE FUTURE **Gen. George Crist, USMC (Ret.)**	93
7.	STRATEGIC FORCES FOR THE FUTURE **Gen. Larry D. Welch, USAF (Ret.)**	111

8.	COPING WITH GLOBAL MISSILE PROLIFERATION	
	Gen. John L. Piotrowski, USAF (Ret.)	123
9.	THE PIVOTAL ELEMENTS: AIRLIFT AND SEALIFT	
	Gen. Duane Cassidy, USAF (Ret.), and Vice Adm. Albert Herberger, USN (Ret.)	141
10.	THE NEED FOR FORWARD PREPOSITIONING	
	Gen. Joseph Went, USMC (Ret.)	159
11.	THE U.S. DEFENSE–INDUSTRIAL BASE	
	Gen. Alfred G. Hansen, USAF (Ret.)	173
12.	CONCLUSION: HOW THE CHALLENGES AND DANGERS OF THE POST-CONTAINMENT ERA CAN BE MASTERED	
	H. Joachim Maitre	185
INDEX		191
ABOUT THE EDITORS AND CONTRIBUTORS		197

Illustrations

FIGURES

8.1.	Strategic Defense Initiative (SDI) Planned Architecture	131
8.2.	Brilliant Pebble, in Life Jacket	132
8.3.	Brilliant Pebble, without Station-keeping Fuel Tanks and Life Jacket	133

TABLES

4.1.	The United States Navy of the Mid-1990s	69
5.1.	Projected United States Air Force Tactical Air Forces under the Base Force Concept	77
7.1.	Strategic Force Modernization Expectations	114
7.2.	Survivability of U.S. Strategic Forces under START	116
7.3.	Strategic Nuclear Warheads in Central Eurasia, January 1992	117
8.1.	Ballistic Missile and Spacecraft Launches, 1987–89	125
8.2.	Third World Ballistic Missiles	127
8.3.	Comparing the Strategic Defense Initiative (Phase I) with the Global Protection against Accidental Launch System (GPALS)	136
9.1.	Four-Engined Airlift Aircraft, Excluding Support Aircraft	144
9.2.	Military Airlift Command, Gained Aircraft Inventory	145
9.3.	Government-owned and Chartered Fleet as of May 1, 1990	147

9.4.	Privately Owned Merchant Fleet, Active Ships, as of May 1, 1990	149
9.5.	Effectively U.S.-controlled Fleet	150
9.6.	Airlift in Desert Shield/Storm/Sortie	151
9.7.	Desert Shield/Desert Storm Delivery	153

Preface

The Potomac Foundation and the Center for Defense Journalism at Boston University jointly conceived the project that resulted in this book. This undertaking was born out of the need to design a new military strategy for the emerging post–Cold War era. The emergence of new configurations of power in the world is characterized by uncertainty and instability. No one knows where these realignments of national interests will lead. Therefore, it is imperative that the strategy, posture, and force structure of the military force adapt to the demands and challenges of this new, and probably no less dangerous, era. This can only be accomplished by making sure that the war-fighting and deterrence capabilities of the U.S. armed forces remain tailored to the threats and opportunities of the radically altered international environment and by maintaining these high standards of modernization and readiness.

There is a danger that the United States might embark on a politically and financially driven course that would result in dismantling military assets that have been of the utmost importance in recent successful military campaigns. These assets will unquestionably be needed in the future, perhaps even more than they have been needed so far. Therefore, based on the changing geopolitical landscape and the necessity of maintaining military strength in this "new" world, what is needed can be best described as an insurance policy intended to cope with the unforeseen, as contrasted with the foreseen. To formulate this mechanism we sought the views of senior military leaders who have experienced first hand the waxing and waning of support for adequate forces. Events that have taken place since the beginning of this project have proven this approach to be a sound one.

Major cuts in defense spending were on the horizon, and plans for substantial reductions in U.S. force structure were on the drawing board even before the Gulf War erupted. In the face of these cuts there is a need to discuss and debate the future shape of the U.S. forces. The Cold War has ended, which means that the force structure must be geared more toward meeting regional threats and other contingencies on the lower end of the spectrum of conflict, rather than confronting the former Soviet threat. But questions remain: How should the forces be restructured, and how much is actually enough in the post–Cold War era?

No sooner had the chairman of the Joint Chiefs of Staff, General Colin Powell, attempted to answer that question with the Pentagon's Base Force Concept, based on a 25 percent reduction in forces, than the crisis in the Persian Gulf erupted in August 1990. Taking the Base Force Concept as a starting point, we reached out to a group of seasoned military men who were all well qualified to debate the type of force structure the United States needs to maintain its national security.

While the Gulf crisis and the ensuing Gulf War pointed to some of the strengths and weaknesses of the current force structure, they did not provide answers to all questions on what might be needed to meet the spectrum of challenges to U.S. interests in the future.

As the project progressed, Communist hard-liners attempted a coup in the Soviet Union; a civil war broke out in what had been Yugoslavia; and the U.S. president, George Bush, proposed two successive and dramatic cuts in the U.S. and former Soviet Union's nuclear arsenal, the first matched by the then Soviet president, Mikhail Gorbachev and the second matched by the new leader of Russia, President Boris Yeltsin. Further progress in reducing the nuclear arsenals was achieved when presidents Bush and Yeltsin agreed in June 1992 to go beyond the Strategic Arms Reductions Treaty (START) agreeing in principle to warhead and weapon ceilings that were the equivalent of both countries' arsenals in the 1950s. Meanwhile, the two countries withdrew all nonstrategic nuclear weapons from their land and sea forces worldwide. In terms of conventional arms control, the Treaty on Conventional Forces in Europe (CFE) was concluded in November 1990, with the effect of virtually eliminating the Soviet, and now Russian, capability of overrunning Europe in a few days or weeks. Moreover, agreements among the former Warsaw Pact members were reached, dictating that the Red Army will withdraw from Central and Eastern Europe by 1996 at the latest. The Soviet Union retreated with breathtaking speed, which resulted in the pacification of war-torn regions. National governments resumed power in their countries, or international agreements paved the way for peaceful resolutions of conflicts among warring factions. With President Yeltsin assuming power in Russia, a westward-looking leader began proposing "friendship" rather than "hostile competition" with the United States.

All of these events have contributed to a public perception that the U.S. military budget can be cut substantially and safely. We think the lessons of history suggest

Preface

otherwise. The contributors to this book have all had to train and fight during periods of higher and lower defense spending. Most recently, they served through the so-called decade of neglect in the 1970s and the Reagan buildup of the 1980s. Given today's budget constraints and the demise of the central threat of the past four decades, a military restructuring for the 1990s and beyond will not require the scale of effort it took to rebuild the military in the 1980s. However, it should also avoid the path that led to "hollow forces," a consequence of insufficient investment in the 1970s.

The point of any insurance policy is to prepare for what is unexpected but possible. People do not expect their houses to burn down, but they hold fire insurance, paying premiums in the hope that they will never need to collect. The same goes for life insurance; few people want to pay for it, but by doing so they buy security for themselves and those who depend on them.

Providing for the common defense has always been one of the most basic guarantees of American governments. Yet Americans also have a history of reluctance to invest heavily in their national defense. The perennial debate over guns versus butter attests to this proclivity. In spite of this inclination toward minimal investment, the United States has been able to survive, but it narrowly avoided disaster in two world wars, for which it was largely unprepared.

Curiously, the investments made, or premiums paid, during the 1980s were never expected to be used against an Iraqi dictator bent on controlling the flow of oil to the West. But for the first time, in the Gulf War, the United States was well prepared to defend its interests.

Given the pace of change in the world, including the chaos among the member states of the fragile Commonwealth of Independent States (CIS); the proliferation of nuclear, biological, and chemical arms among Third World countries; the continuing adherence to communism by China, North Korea, and Cuba; the instability in the Middle East; and the eruption of a war among the former Yugoslav republics, planning against a well-defined threat seems futile.

In this situation, a flexible insurance policy is needed, to guide U.S. military strategy into and through the post-containment era. Insurance policy options are exercised, renewed, canceled, and closed. Insurance policies are different in type, amount, form, and duration, and can be for cars, homes, or human life. The authors of this volume, in their collective wisdom, have pieced together a combination of options and provisions that constitutes an insurance policy for the nation—one that will help, we believe, to ensure peace in freedom, an order that only the United States is capable of fulfilling—if it has the willpower to do so.

Established in 1988 as an independent, nonprofit research organization, the Potomac Foundation undertakes activities dedicated to improving the quality of public dialogue and policy in the areas of national security, economic development, and education. To date, these programs have been concentrated on national defense, the influence of technology in the economy, and education and training.

The Center for Defense Journalism at Boston University was founded in January 1988 with a twofold mission: to provide a concerted program designed to prepare current and future journalists to report and write competently about military affairs, national security issues, and strategic problems; and to train military officers and government officials to appreciate the role of the journalist in our society. With the help of this program there will be improved communication among the military, the media, and the defense industry.

Stanley E. Harrison
President, The Potomac Foundation

H. Joachim Maitre
Director, Center for Defense Journalism

Paying the Premium

1

In Search of an American "Defense Insurance Policy"

Walter Hahn

The United States has once again arrived at one of those turning points in its uneven history of foreign policy involvement and abstinence—a turning point that is crucial for determining the nation's position in the world for the next decade and perhaps the next century. A national debate about the nation's strategic choices has unfolded since 1989, when a wildfire of revolutionary change began to transfigure the erstwhile Soviet empire—and with it the image of a pervasive threat which had sustained the nation's historically most protracted engagement in the global arena.

In its early phase, until August 1990, the debate had almost exclusively focused on the future of the U.S. defense budget—on how far, how rapidly, and how "safely" defense outlays might be slashed to reap the promises of a "peace dividend" for domestic spending. The initial debate resulted in a congressional "budget agreement" that essentially called for reductions in defense expenditures on the arbitrary order of some 25 percent over a five-year period.

The debate was interrupted by the shock of the Gulf War and its warning that the collapse of the Soviet superpower may signal, not the idyll of a new and peaceful world order, but an ever more uncertain global scenario, rife with unpredictable dangers. The shock has worn off, and the national debate has flared anew, with greater intensity and sweep.

Indeed, sharpened by partisan politics and the pressures of domestic economic problems, the debate seems to be proceeding in a virtual vacuum of agreed-upon premises about where the future lines of the nation's security should be drawn. In the process, the U.S. defense posture, painstakingly established over some four decades, is being dismantled or consigned to attrition. And, absent a consensus on fundamental national interests and objectives in a dramatically changing global environment, not to mention the requirements for safeguarding those interests and furthering those objectives—in other words, absent a national "strategic conception,"—the whole issue of future security threatens to be preempted by parochial politics and short-term fiscal considerations.

Given the lead times applying to the implementation and fruition of defense planning and investments in the modern age, the urgency of the "defense restructuring" task confronting the United States militates against the luxury of awaiting the guiding light of a comprehensive new "strategy design," not to mention a national consensus behind it, welcome though those might be. At a minimum, what can be aspired to in the critical short term are the basic terms of a "defense insurance policy," based on a realistic assessment of the salient "risks" in the unfolding world environment and of the needed resources, even if substantially reduced ones, for meeting those risks.

The purpose of this book is to adduce such an "insurance policy" and to invoke in that quest the judgments of those best qualified by training and experience to relate perceived security requirements to military means—namely, military professionals.

A NEW AMERICAN ISOLATIONISM?

The opening sentence in this chapter referred to a historic "turning point." Any projection of future "security architecture" for the United States, to be meaningful, calls for a larger historical canvas.

The ongoing debate in the United States putatively is over more than defense and budget, even if those issues seem to dominate the immediate agenda. More fundamentally, the debate is a symptom of the nation's search for renewed self-definition and reorientation in the new world order. Increasingly the term "neo-isolationism" echoes in the debate. It tends to be applied to lines of advocacy rising from disparate parts of the American political-ideological spectrum. One analyst has described the phenomenon as follows:

With the death of Communism and the waning of the Cold War, a three-sided strategic debate over the future course of U.S. foreign policy has emerged. The anti-Communist coalition that won the "long, twilight struggle" has splintered. . . . Traditional isolationism, long associated with the Old Right, has been resuscitated through a Hatfields-and-McCoys wedding to the neo-isolationism of the Vietnam-era New Left. And as if that were not enough, a new argument has erupted about the viability of realism . . . as a guide for American action in the world. The parallels to the 1930s are unmistakable: "back to the future" may well define the foreign policy debate in the 1990s. Perhaps the most curious of these related phenomena has been the isolationist renaissance. Once regarded as having been consigned to the murkier nether regions of our public discourse, isolationism (or, as its proponents prefer, the new nationalism or "non-interventionism") has once again become a significant voice in the argument over the national interest and the national purpose.[1]

An American "Defense Insurance Policy"

In short, we are witnessing the reemergence of forces that were paralyzed, or frozen, during the Cold War era. What accounts for their existence and their seemingly cyclical appearance and disappearance?

Students of American history have long grappled with this question.[2] It is worth noting that in 1952, in the initial phase of the Cold War, one historian, Frank L. Klingberg, pioneered the fashion of quantitative measurement of societal trends in probing successive historical epochs of American "introversion" and "extroversion." He concluded that those alternating cycles generally lasted some twenty-five years. On that basis, he predicted a new U.S. retrenchment from the global arena sometime in the late 1960s.[3]

Hindsight may lend some credibility to Klingberg's projection by marking the years of the Vietnam War as the acme of America's post–World War II "global commitment," with a subsequent retreat, notwithstanding a "spasm" of recommitment in the "Reagan era" of the 1980s. Still, even with such a broad interpretation of past developments, Klingberg's cyclical formula does not seem to be holding up. According to it, the nation should be reentering the world arena in the 1990s, rather than retrenching.

The effort of precise cyclical measurements aside, there is little question about a tidal pattern in America's historic ventures onto the larger world stage. Klingberg based his thesis primarily on the play of U.S. domestic forces. While stereotypes related to a nation's makeup, and internal dynamics, may be suspect guides to its external behavior, they do carry greater weight in the case of our relatively sheltered society.

Thus, some generalizations about the "American ethos" seem to have passed the test of history. As settlers fleeing the conflicts, social injustice, and economic privations of the societies they left behind, Americans forged a social order not only disparate from, but in large measure in defiance of, the Old World. They established formal nationhood on the operative principle of "no entangling alliances." Preoccupied for over a century following the birth of their nation with the conquest of a continent, and protected by two oceans, they paid scant attention to the world beyond the hemisphere. The building of the nation cost them a civil war, but they were rewarded with a dynamic society, burgeoning industrial power, and a stable political system. These accomplishments, fired by the engine of a unique "progressivism," served to lengthen the psychological distance between the New World and the Old.

Virtually every episode of American involvement in conflict abroad has been a story of national leadership (enlightened or not) overcoming deep-seated popular reluctance. The prods of involvement have invariably been those of self-defense and/or aggrieved-ness ("remembering" the Maine, the Lusitania, and Pearl Harbor). Just as invariably, the slogans of involvement have evinced a zealous sense of mission—in World War I to "make the world safe for democracy" and in World War II to make it safe for the United Nations. It is above all this pronounced moralism that has long puzzled observers of the American phenomenon, from Alexis de Tocqueville to (putatively) Saddam Hussein.

Perhaps the moralism draws from the religious principles that impelled the early settlers and founding fathers. Or it may reflect more generally an outward projection of societal values. Robert W. Tucker writes persuasively:

Every nation is disposed to interpret the world in light of the interpretation it has given to its domestic experience. America is no exception to this pattern. Our interpretation of the world beyond our borders is clearly a reflection of the interpretation we have given to our own rise and development as a nation. The freedom we find in our own historical development has been transformed into a general view of history.[4]

The ideal of freedom, of the "open society," clearly is central to the American world view. The late Walter Lippmann took the proposition one step further. He wrote of the American

refusal to admit, to take as the premise of our thinking, the fact that rivalry and strife and conflict among states, communities and factions are the normal conditions of mankind. ... In the American ideology the struggle for existence, and the rivalry for advantages, are held to be wrong, abnormal and transitory.[5]

Tucker spoke of the "interpretation we have given to our own . . . development," and Lippmann referred to an "American ideology." Skeptics will contend that the American worldview has little in common with the actual workings of American society itself, in which harsh competition, the "rivalry for advantages," has constituted the very lifeblood of a dynamic socioeconomic order. Still, the contradiction between idealized self-image and reality is probably at the root of any "ideology." It is also consistent with the meaning of that term that the yardsticks of ideals are more easily applied to societies other than one's own.

There is no question, in any event, of "moral messianism" as a traditional spark plug of U.S. excursions into world politics, and as a conditioning force behind the flow and ebb of those engagements. Also consistent with history is the proposition that the "flipside" of the idealism that the nation has brought to bear in foreign adventures is popular impatience. As a nation, America has consistently been slow to respond to external challenge. Once we have responded, we have tended to do so with a starkly dichotomized view of forces of good arrayed against forces of evil. Moreover, we have tended to enter the arena in the self-arrogated role of umpire rather than that of a permanent player, and with the desire to get the particular match over with as quickly as possible.

The U.S. failure in Vietnam, and the lingering Vietnam "syndrome," can be attributed not least to the fact that by historical experience and idealistic inclination the American people were not prepared to stay the course of a protracted conflict in which the moral issues had become diffused. Impatience, disillusionment, and demobilization followed not only in the wake of this military defeat, but also after the victory in the Gulf War.

LESSONS OF THE COLD WAR

Questions may legitimately be raised: Even if the above general treatment of "American national traits" in foreign policy is historically plausible, does it still apply as forcefully as in the past? American isolationism was the logical product of the nation's geographical isolation during its formative first century. Has not the intervening experience of two world wars, followed by four decades of "American empire," imposed a "learning curve"? That is perhaps the key question hanging over the current debate on the nation's future course over a convulsively changing globe. A "learning curve" relevant to a nation's evolution is at best difficult to identify, let alone to plot. In terms of recent history, moreover, even on a generalized level the evidence is moot.

America is often said to have "come of age" after World War II. It is true that in the Cold War, coming so shortly on the heels of victory in World War II, the United States seemed to break with past isolationist tradition and patterns. Yet the phrase "coming so shortly on the heels" is in need of qualification.

There is neither the space nor the intent here to rehearse the history of the critical years between the end of World War II and America's ascent to "global posture." Suffice it to note that students of the period of America's mobilization for the Cold War, from roughly 1946 to the early 1950s, come away with certain general conclusions. The major one concerns the uniqueness of the post–World War II American leadership generation. It was a generation of "realist" practitioners of foreign policy under President Harry S Truman—men such as George C. Marshall, Dean Acheson, James Forrestal, and others. They were united in a view of history honed by their witness to the developments spanning two disastrous conflicts, and by the determination that the nation could not risk repeating the tragic mistake of post–World War I in a return to isolation. That historic view also conditioned them to discern alertly the signals of a newly emergent danger of global scale.

A searching examination of U.S. policy evolution in the immediate postwar years, particularly via the testimony of those who were, in Acheson's phrase, "present at the creation," yields some intriguing conclusions. Essentially, the story of America's mobilization for the Cold War is a chronicle of policy salesmanship in a democracy—and even of "bureaucratic conspiracy." A small band of policy makers, led by Acheson, not only recognized the signals of a rising threat to the postwar order, and to the direct security of the United States, but spliced the evidence into a comprehensive "threat assessment." They were able, early on, to persuade President Truman of the validity of the threat assessment and the urgency of the danger. They then set about, patiently and methodically, to shape a consensus at the top levels of government, thereupon extending it into the legislative branch and finally to the populace at large.

A pivotal point in that "salesmanship" process came in late February 1947. Against the background of Soviet takeovers in Eastern Europe, a Communist "fifth-column" offensive in Western Europe, and a campaign of pressures and insurgency against Greece and Turkey in the Mediterranean, President Truman invited congressional leaders to the White House. Acheson gave a comprehensive briefing of the threat assessment, with emphasis on the Mediterranean area, and of its implications. Truman asked the congressional leaders for their reaction and advice. The Republican leader in the Senate, Arthur Vandenberg, responded that if Truman wanted an aid program for Greece and Turkey, he had no choice but to appear in person before Congress and "scare the hell out of the country." On March 12, 1947, in his famous enunciation of what became known as the Truman Doctrine, President Truman did just that.

This episode is recounted here in order to illustrate several points about the traditional themes in the U.S. response to external challenge. It attests, first of all, to the chronic laggardness of that response. The Truman Doctrine of March 1947 marked the birth of a unique bipartisan consensus, essential to the prosecution of the Cold War. In retrospect, it can also be said to mark the true start of the popular mobilization for that struggle. Still, it took another four years and an explicit act of aggression—the invasion of South Korea in 1950—for that popular mobilization to be translated into military remobilization.

Moreover, the subsequent four decades of the Cold War by no means traced an epoch of steadfast U.S. engagement in the global arena. Rather, there were sharp fluctuations in that engagement, accompanied by intensifying domestic debate and climaxed in the breakdown of the bipartisan consensus during the Vietnam conflict. Reference was made earlier to the question of whether the reengagement and military buildup during the Reagan years represented a revival of national resolve or a temporary interruption of the drift of retrenchment after the Vietnam War. The subsequent collapse of the Soviet Union serves to withhold a clear verdict. Hence the case can be made for the proposition that the "regeneration" of the 1980s reflected less a national reawakening to global role and purpose, and more a typical American response to a specific stimulus—in this case, the wounding of national pride in the Iran hostage crisis.

IMPLICATIONS OF THE GULF WAR

History's verdict is also pending with respect to the Gulf War of 1991 and how it reflects upon America's "self-definition" and future role. Was Operation Desert Storm basically a reflexive reaction of the "new nationalism" marshalled during the Reagan era? Did it thus connote a detour on the road toward retrenchment following the "end of the Cold War?" Or did it signify an inchoate national recognition of the imperative of leadership by the United States, in a time of global transition to the "new world order" prescribed by its president?

Answers to those questions are obscured by a number of factors and circumstances. Prominent among them is the fact that the Gulf War in many respects defined the typical conditions under which historically the United States has gone into battle. The national leaders discerned a threat to the (extended) interests of the nation. They were able to evoke popular support regardless of the divided

Congress, by appealing to relatively clear-cut moral principle, as well as to a particularly repellent image of the "enemy." The undertaking had the sheen of moral approbation by the international community, resplendent in the United Nations, along with the attribute of "collective action." Finally, the needed forces and weapons were available, having been amassed during the long confrontation with a much more powerful adversary.

If the conditions for going to war thus were "typical" in meeting the historic criteria for U.S. military engagement abroad, the outcome of Desert Storm, measured by those same criteria, was ideal. It was the epitome of the "quick punitive action," resulting in the decisive defeat of the transgressor and achieved at a stunning minimum of American casualties. It was thus in sharp contradistinction to the Vietnam War; indeed, it served as an antidote to the "Vietnam syndrome," which had festered for some twenty years.

If the Gulf War thus extended a tradition of U.S. engagement, however, its aftermath seems also to be exemplifying the other side of that tradition, namely, a popular desire to evacuate the field of battle as rapidly as possible in order to return attention and energy to domestic problems. Not only has the Gulf War failed to brake the schedule of deep U.S. military reductions that were in train before Operation Desert Shield, but it has occasioned an even steeper decline in defense spending and an even more indiscriminate process of defense dismantlement.

A POST-CONTAINMENT STRATEGY?

Let us return here to the subject of "national strategic conception." In Chapter 7 of this book, Gen. Larry D. Welch posits an "orderly and rational" process of military construction. He describes it as a process of "defining national objectives and the threat to those objectives, formulating a strategy, and identifying the military tasks, capabilities and forces required to underwrite the strategy." The nexus in the process is "strategy." As was suggested earlier, a chronic misunderstanding of that term has served to compound the confusion of the American debate.

What is "military strategy"? There is no need to invoke treatises on strategy, from Sun Tsu to Sir Basil Liddell Hart, to get at its basic meaning. Quite simply, "strategy" describes an overall plan of action—the harnessing of available means toward the achievement of explicit objectives. This elementary meaning of strategy has been distorted in the American dialogue by indiscriminate application of the term, particularly confusion of the concept with its components, such as military posture, tactics, doctrine, concept of operations, and even "policy."

To relieve the confusion, let us posit here some basic definitions of those components. If "strategy" describes an overall plan of action, "posture" denotes the physical means to carry it out—basically, the "order of battle" of military forces, and the weaponry at their command, and the disposition of their deployment. "Force structure" describes the organization of forces and weapons.

"Tactics" and "operational art" cover the moves and stratagems adopted in the employment of those forces and weapons for maximum advantage on the various levels of combat on the battlefield. "Doctrine" embraces the optimal harnessing of forces and tactics toward the desired end. A thin line separates "doctrine" from "concept of operations," a term that basically means the adaptation of doctrine and strategy to meet variable contingencies of battle. And somewhat apart from the process is "military policy," which generally embraces the procurement and management of all the component parts of strategy and the marshalling of resources to sustain them.

The meaning of "national strategy" can best be assayed in the context of a nation's security endeavors. Ideally, the highest authorities of a nation, reflecting a consensus of the governed, would set the nation's fundamental security goals and priorities. An overall plan of action would be devised—a national or "grand" strategy—toward the securing of those goals, with "military strategy" as one of its components, the others being diplomatic and economic strategies. The requirements of the chosen military strategy, in military forces, their deployment, and their support, would then yield the outlines of "military posture." "Doctrine" and "concepts of operations" would be contrived for the effective employment of those forces in combat. "Policies" would be adopted for the management of available means. It needs to be added that, again ideally, only at the end of this architectural process of strategy formulation would there be constraints, particularly constraints on available resources, which would be addressed for the extent to which they might delimit the given strategy.

Historically, grand strategy expresses the outward projection of a nation's perceived needs and objectives. Its design and durability reflect an essential consensus within the given society regarding those needs and objectives. Probably the classic example in the modern era is the strategy that was followed by Great Britain in Europe for over two centuries. That strategy was based on a consensual recognition within Britain's ruling establishment that the nation's fundamental security rested on a balancing of power on the Continent. In practice this meant the prevention of shifts in the Continental balance in favor of a predominant power or alliance that could challenge Britain's supremacy. This "balancing strategy" entailed frequent changes of alliances—even relatively abrupt changes—along with direct applications of British military power.

Given America's "inward"-looking foreign policy tradition, the United States, in the four decades after World War II, followed the classical process of national strategy formulation and implementation, even if fuller elements of that strategy evolved over time. Mention was made earlier of the overall perception of the external threat to the nation and its interests by Acheson and his band of policy makers in the Truman Administration. A transcendent national goal was fixed upon, which became the basis of a national and bipartisan consensus. The Soviet Union was identified as the principal threat to international order and to the United States itself. The American national goal was set: to prevent the extension

An American "Defense Insurance Policy"

of Soviet hegemony over Eurasia, let alone other continents. In pursuit of that goal, a grand strategy evolved: the strategy of "containment."

The military salient of this strategy rested on two pillars: (1) direct deterrence of Soviet aggression and expansion, and (2) the application of "containing" U.S. military power in a wide arc along the peripheries of the Eurasian "heartland." A military posture for that strategy was developed over time; it embraced strategic nuclear forces (for deterrence), forward-deployed general purpose forces (for immediate defensive purposes), and their support in the form of strategic reserves and an infrastructure of global mobility, including long-range strategic transport capabilities and a comprehensive network of overseas bases.

The "containment strategy" endured notwithstanding periodic adjustments in the U.S. military posture. These adjustments were made primarily in response to fluctuations in threat perception and budget constraints.

THE QUANDARY OF U.S. DEFENSE PLANNING

With the collapse of the Soviet empire, the "containment strategy" has lost relevance. Notwithstanding the Gulf War and vague references by national leaders to a "new world order," nothing resembling a comprehensive strategic conception, let alone strategic consensus, has yet taken its place to anticipate the nation's future course and requirements.

In the early 1990s, planners of America's future defenses confront not only massive uncertainty (a term that will recur with great regularity in this book) but a huge quandary. A planner's task is to "reconstruct" the wherewithal for safeguarding his nation's fundamental security and underwriting its vital interests and objectives. But he has little in the way of a compass, let alone guidance from the nation's leaders, in projecting those national interests at stake within a "world in uncertain transition."

In effect, the defense planner is compelled to approach the process of strategy design "in reverse": to begin with a projection of available means (or better, the constraints upon them). Then he has to find for those prospective means a viable concept for their use. Next he must discover the reach of the military posture he has created, to arrive at the contribution this makes in terms of designing a "residual strategy." But if he is mindful of the historic inconsistencies in his nation's engagement on the global stage, he will know better than to venture a confident, longer-range projection of the national interests, objectives, and means.

TOWARD A "DEFENSE INSURANCE POLICY"

So here we come back to the points made at the outset of this discussion. Perhaps all that can be undertaken at the present juncture of "transition" and uncertainty is not a new, comprehensive design—that is, "strategy"—to guide

U.S. defense planning in the post–Cold War era, but the more practical alternative of some measure of agreement on the minimum requirements of a "defense insurance policy" against potential risks to its security. Those best qualified to draw up at least the initial outlines of such an "insurance policy" are professional military men who have devoted substantial parts of their careers to the task of translating basic defense requirements into military missions and capabilities.

That is the purpose of the dialogue that follows in this book. The emphasis is on "dialogue." The effort is not directed toward putting together a comprehensive and detailed blueprint for defense. Rather, each author has undertaken, from the vantage point of his professional experience and knowledge, to project his view of likely future U.S. defense requirements. These projections are undertaken with a strong recognition of the constraints already imposed by recent decisions as they will affect the likely availability of military resources. Salient among these constraints are the future "end strengths" in U.S. military forces that have been postulated under the "Base Force Concept" developed by the U.S. Department of Defense in 1990–91.

The basic questions to be addressed are the following:

1. What are the principal, looming "risks" to the nation's security, and its extended interests, in the unfolding global environment—risks that may call for military responses? Such risks range from the potentially resurgent threat from the successor states to the former Soviet Union (with emphasis on the nuclear dimension), to a "militarization" of conflict in broad reaches of the Third World, as heralded by the Gulf War, and to a general trend of proliferation of weapons of mass destruction.

2. Given the already decreed constraints bearing upon the sizing of U.S. military forces, whether land, sea, or air, how might the remaining forces, both active and reserve, best be configured for coping with those risks? What are the "management" and planning implications and priorities, in terms of these restraints, for each of the U.S. military services?

3. The experience of the Gulf War is a generally acknowledged platform for such projections. The war demonstrated the high caliber of the U.S. fighting forces, the excellence of U.S. operational doctrine, and the effectiveness of U.S. weaponry. Nevertheless, the lessons of the conflict call for closer scrutiny. Operations Desert Shield and Desert Storm were aided by unique circumstances that may not occur in future contingencies. They also bared gaps and shortcomings.

4. Five to ten years from now, will the United States be able to respond to external challenges as effectively as it did in the Persian Gulf? A large part of that ability will depend upon whether the United States can modernize its forces rapidly enough to keep pace with technological advances on a global scale.

5. There is general agreement that the United States is in the process of shifting its military posture from a "forward-deployment" into a "power-projection" mode. Will the means be available for projecting military power to distant battlefields in needed volume and in requisite time?

6. Will the nation have the ability to mobilize its industrial resources in response to a major threat to its security, as it has managed to do in the past? Is that American industrial capacity (or "strategic reserve") still extant? Could it be mobilized in time?

Those are some of the fundamental questions reflected in the dialogue in this book. It may well be that the progressive tumult of international developments, combined with the caprices of domestic U.S. politics, will intrude further into the framework of assumptions, analyses, and conclusions presented here. What is aspired to at the very least, however, is a basic framework upon which this "insurance policy" can be made a reality. If this is not done, the debate over the wherewithal of the nation's future security seems destined to become an exercise in irrelevance at best, and disastrous futility at worst.

NOTES

1. George Weigel, "On the Road to Isolationism?" *Commentary*, January 1992, p. 36.
2. Some of the points in this chapter were treated by the author in another context, in "American Introversion Post-Vietnam," *Strategic Review*, Fall 1975, pp. 26–34.
3. Frank L. Klingberg, "The Historical Alternation of Moods in American Foreign Policy," *World Politics*, January 1952, pp. 261–72.
4. Robert W. Tucker, *The Just War: A Study of Contemporary American Doctrine* (Baltimore, Md.: Johns Hopkins University Press, 1960), p. 233.
5. Walter Lippmann, "The Rivalry of Nations," *Atlantic Monthly*, February 1948, p. 18.

2

Risks and Uncertainties in a Changing World

Gen. Donn Starry, USA (Ret.)

> We cannot know when or where the U.S. Army will again be ordered into battle, but we must assume the enemy we face will possess weapons generally as effective as our own. And we must calculate that he will have them in greater numbers than we will be able to deploy, at least in the opening stages of a conflict. Because the lethality of modern weapons continues to increase sharply, we can expect very high losses to occur in short periods of time. Entire forces could be destroyed if they are not properly employed.

This is how the 1976 Field Manual FM 100-5 describes the risks and uncertainties U.S. forces could expect to encounter in modern battle. The doctrinal treatise goes on to describe the nature of that battle and project how U.S. Army forces should fight, organize, and train, and with what kinds of weapons they should be equipped in order to cope with the uncertainties of modern war. It reflects the traditional and characteristic way the "military mind" goes about solving the complex problems of operational concepts, tactics, organization, training, and equipment for the nation's military forces. While the citation is from an Army publication, it could as well have been an Air Force, Navy, or Marine Corps document.

In this case the doctrine writers also acknowledged what may be the most perplexing uncertainty of their trade: that of describing risks and uncertainties—in other words, "the threat"—without specifying the geography, region, country, and actual forces so closely that their entire undertaking may be rendered irrelevant by even the slightest change in one or more of those elements. Therefore, in this case as in other such works, the authors have wisely sought to set forth a generic description of the risks and uncertainties of the modern battlefield. Their description is general enough to frame the mix of forces and supporting infrastructure within the broader parameters of national military strategy. At the same time, it is specific enough to elicit relevant and more detailed operational and tactical schemes, organizational structure, quantitative and qualitative equipment requirements, and training systems when they are needed to bring the whole together for battle.

The lines that open this chapter were written at a time of great change for the U.S. armed forces. The Vietnam War was over, at least for the United States, although its wounds would fester for decades; the national treasure sacrificed in young lives would scar generations; and the revolt of youth against all authority that so characterized the war years would irrevocably change American society. Withal, our direct military involvement in Southeast Asia was ended. Accordingly, those responsible for shaping national military strategy set about their task of protecting a world that had, in so many ways, changed dramatically in but a few brief years.

As we take stock on the threshold of the final decade of our century, the landscape ahead appears to be somewhat like the one confronted by military planners after Vietnam, as they set out to discern and redefine the playing field, plays, and players in the world as it had changed then. The purpose of this chapter is to project the most challenging risks and uncertainties we can expect to encounter, in order to erect a suitable frame of reference for the dialogue in later chapters, over the requisite U.S. military posture, strategy, and force structure for the 1990s and beyond.

The Gulf War illuminated the road ahead, but it would be both myopic and unwise to regard that conflict as the definitive guide to the future: we face far greater uncertainties and deeper complexities in this post–Cold War era.

THE SHIFTING SOVIET EQUATION

As this is written, the world reflects on several years of tumultuous, dramatic, and continuing change in the former Soviet Union and Eastern Europe. For more than four decades, the standoff between the North Atlantic Treaty Organization (NATO) and the Warsaw Pact, under the long shadow of nuclear and conventional armaments, dominated the strategic arena and captivated strategic thinking. Recent developments, particularly the retreat of the Soviet empire from Eastern Europe, along with disintegrative economic and political trends and the collapse of the Soviet Union itself, have sharply affected the outward expression of what is now Russian military power and its threatening potential vis-à-vis the vital interests of the United States and its allies. At the same time, new instabilities and flashpoints of conflict are emerging, as the European continent passes through a spasmic transition, heralded by war in what was Yugoslavia and by ethno-nationalist forces and stresses elsewhere in the "liberated" part of the continent.

No one can predict with any confidence the trajectory, let alone the ultimate

Risks and Uncertainties in a Changing World 15

outcome, of these complex trends. Yet in looking five to ten years into the future, a prudent planner of the U.S. military posture and strategy cannot permit himself to become mesmerized by the drama of immediate events. Instead, he must proceed from some "fail-safe" assumptions.

One of those assumptions, validated by the longer light of history, applies to Russia. The centuries of Russia's emergence as a nation, and then as a major actor on the Eurasian stage, have been marked by recurrent internal crises and convulsions, as well as by ebbs and flows in external power. Again in the historical span, those fluctuating fortunes have been both weathered by, and also contributed to, a remarkable and stoic resilience on the part of the Russian people, along with a "messianic spirit" that, according to chroniclers of Russia's history, is endemic to the nation's cultural legacy.

That resilience has been exemplified in this century. The de facto defeat of Russian armies on the battlefields of World War I, compounded by revolution in 1918 and the ravages of the ensuing civil war, was soon followed by the "forced march to industrialization" under Stalin in the 1930s. The devastation inflicted by World War II gave way, within a decade, to the Soviet Union's ascent to superpower. Throughout this turbulent period, with its sharp ups and downs in Soviet external power and expansionist drive, economic malaise and systemic inefficiencies were steady, chronic facts of internal Soviet life. Even before the recent crisis, it was apparent that this system, whether called Soviet or Russian, was highly proficient in only one pursuit: the building of a war machine.

Moreover, the drama of crisis tends to obscure the fact that at its core the Russian war machine remains essentially intact. True, the cutting edge of the Russian offensive threat on the ground in Central Europe has been blunted by developments since the 1980s, particularly a retraction of what had been imperial control over East European polities and the disbanding of the Warsaw Pact. Still, during the tense confrontation in Europe, the satellite armies, with the possible exception of East German formations, never figured heavily in NATO threat assessments. The spotlight was always on the modernized Soviet armies, employed under the doctrine of mass momentum and continuous land combat, and under ever more demanding operational time lines.

Some of those Russian armies are now being pared down in the wake of the Conventional Forces in Europe (CFE) Treaty. Yet it is easy, perhaps even convenient, for some to forget that in the 1950s the Soviet Union, under Nikita Khrushchev, demobilized more than a million men-under-arms, only to follow in subsequent decades with a buildup and modernization of deployed forces that substantially widened the preponderance of Soviet conventional power in Europe.

That preponderance is now qualified. Nevertheless, a U.S. military planner, in projecting the emerging military balance in Europe allowing for future uncertainties, must place the unfolding trends into broader perspective. First, he must distinguish between military power withdrawn and even demobilized, and military power permanently dismantled. The CFE agreement on mutual force reductions apply only to the geographical span from the Atlantic to the Ural Mountains; Russia is therefore free to amass military forces in its Asian expanses. In this context, the flow of Soviet material, notably heavy armor, from Europe eastward across the Ural Mountains in anticipation of the CFE concords triggered concern, particularly in Asian countries, faced with a growing shadow of "displaced" Soviet military power. It should also be viewed with concern by Europeans, as military potential that could easily be "replaced."

Second, in terms of overall military balance, force reductions are relative in their military meaning. The CFE limits on weapons represent, at best, ceilings; it is already more than evident that the "slippery slope" of reductions will lead NATO force levels substantially below those sanctioned by the CFE agreement. That prospect is sharpened by the political uncertainties surrounding a unified Germany as a continuing, major contributor to the alliance's conventional forces and as territorial host to its multinational formations, particularly those with a U.S. component. Existing plans call for reductions in the total U.S. force stationed in Western Europe, down to 75,000 by 1996. Prevalent trends in the U.S. Congress make it doubtful that even this "floor" will be maintained.

Third, in the modern era of "force multipliers" provided by relevantly directed technology, quantitative reductions do not necessarily equate to a lowered combat potential. It is instructive to recall that, well before the Soviets entered serious negotiations for large-scale mutual force reductions in Europe, in the late 1970s and early 1980s, Marshal Nikolai Ogarkov and other Soviet military thinkers foresaw a "revolution in military affairs"—one that would fundamentally alter conventional battlefields, shifting the premium to mobility and firepower, rather than massed formations of overwhelming numbers of soldiers and equipment.

Increasingly, the key to relative strength and combat effectiveness in conventional arms lies in modernization—more specifically, in a sustainable rate of modernization. According to published intelligence findings, the Russian pace of modernization of conventional armaments continued under Mikhail Gorbachev, nor has Boris Yeltsin shown any inclination to change course. Under Yeltsin, however, the production of conventional weaponry has dropped slightly. As a salient example, even while agreeing to substantial mutual reductions in the armor systems deployed in the European theater, the Soviets were busily replacing older-model tanks with the more capable T-80 and M1989 series.

The Cold War decades offered ample testimony that, while the technological base of the United States in particular, and of the West more generally, was in some ways superior to that of Russia, the latter demonstrated greater alacrity in seizing upon technological advances and incorporating them into fielded equipment. Moreover, while U.S. exploitation of technological opportunity tended to be sporadic, and chronically at the mercy of Pentagon politics and budget battles in Washington, the former Soviets and now the Russians have exhibited a steady pace of modernization spanning the full spectrum of military capabilities.

Nuclear weapons cannot be ignored from that equation. Notwithstanding mutual reductions in the intermediate-range nuclear forces stationed in Europe as a consequence of the Intermediate-Range Nuclear Forces (INF) Treaty of 1987, the Russians retain a massive inventory of modernized, theater-level nuclear weapons of both long and short range. The prospect of further, even drastic reductions in force levels and inventories of such weapons, spurred by President Bush's nuclear disarmament initiative of September 1991, cannot obscure the inherent advantage of pure geography that the Russians enjoy in the European theater. In the meantime, as Gen. Larry D. Welch of the United States Air Force points out in Chapter 7, no matter how deeply START cuts into the intercontinental nuclear arsenals of both sides, Russia will certainly remain the only country capable of directly and significantly threatening the territory of the United States.

Thus it seems accurate, on the basis of current trends, to describe the Russian military threat as being "in recession." That judgment applies to Russian military withdrawals from the heart of Europe, amid dramatic political change. Still, history cautions against prematurely judging the "irreversibility" of a trend. As long as military power remains, it stands ready to be used. Moreover, the temptation to use it conceivably may be sharpened in a period of convulsive crisis.

If today's U.S. military planner must include the contingency of a "resurgent Russian threat" in possible scenarios of the future, how must he weigh the implications of this "risk" for the U.S. force posture, which also is in a process of "recession"? On the hard assumption of substantial U.S. military withdrawals from Europe, the central question becomes one of likely warning time and exploitation thereof. What would be the signs of a resurgent Russian threat?— massive remilitarization efforts, abandonment of troop withdrawals from Central and Eastern European countries, and reemerging ambitions for territorial aggrandizement? Would such "signals" be read correctly in time to permit an effective U.S. military response?

Perhaps reflective of a general pessimism surrounding potential answers to these questions is the notion in U.S. professional military circles that U.S. military forces might have to face a replay of a scenario reminiscent of the one on the eve of World War II. Having virtually disengaged from Europe, U.S. forces would then have to be brought back into the European theater.

Whether or not that pessimism is warranted, the specter of largely unpredictable contingencies, in Europe and elsewhere, emphasizes one imperative U.S. military planning has to take into consideration in the future: The United States, in framing an "insurance policy" against global risks and uncertainties, cannot look to forces-in-being alone. Central to such an "insurance policy" is the maintenance of a requisite mobilization base of manpower and industrial resources that can meet, in requisite time, the demands of the "large challenge."

MILITARIZATION OF CONFLICT IN THE THIRD WORLD

As statesmen in Europe were readying the final drafts of treaties sealing the unification of Germany and promising an end to the Cold War and to the partition of the continent, Saddam Hussein sent Iraqi forces into Kuwait. Not only did he thereby plunge the Middle East, and the broader international community, into crisis, but he also offered a stark preview of what has been called, prematurely or not, the "post-containment era."

Perhaps the only surprising aspect of Saddam's action was its timing. The trend to which he gave expression has been in evidence for some time; it may be described as militarization of conflict in the so-called Third World. What gives that trend new and ominous dimensions is its progressive employment of modern weapons systems, from armored vehicles, to ballistic missiles, to, increasingly, weapons of mass destruction. The trend is pervasive throughout the Third World, but most ominously evident in an arc extending from Northeast Asia (North and South Korea), through the Asian Subcontinent (India and Pakistan), into the Middle East and North Africa (Libya).

Nowhere, however, is the trend more dramatically in evidence than in the Middle East. Some simple comparisons can be invoked to put it into perspective. In the early 1960s there were, in the entire Middle East region, no more than 500 first-line armored ground combat vehicles, about 150 first-line fighter aircraft, and a handful of naval vessels, mostly coastal patrol craft. However, before the Gulf War in 1991, as a consequence of extensive arms imports, principally from the United States and the USSR, those combined regional inventories included some 15,000 modern armored vehicles, perhaps as many as 5,000 first-line fighter aircraft, and several hundred ships, including frigate-class combatants and submarines. While those total inventories were reduced by Iraq's losses in Desert Storm, they may be replenished in the future. Meanwhile, Syria, as one example, continues to field tank formations more numerous than those commanded by the German Wehrmacht on the eve of Operation Barbarossa, the invasion of the Soviet Union in 1940.

A widespread belief that much of the weaponry in the hands of Middle East states is largely obsolete—an image reinforced by the Gulf War—is contradicted by the facts. While some older equipment remains in place, in many cases the countries supplying the weapons have provided upgraded models in pace with their own weapons programs. The Soviets in particular were generous in their export of "the next to the most modern" version of equipment in their inventories. A salient example is the special export model of the Soviet T-72 tank. As will be brought out below, the fact that Iraqi forces failed to exploit the capabilities of the T-72, as well as of other modern weapons in their inventory, during the Gulf War should not be accepted as an argument against the high quality of the equipment as such.

Indeed, one of the urgent questions regarding Russian intentions relates to the fate of their programs of supplying arms to client states. In July 1990, President Gorbachev announced a review of the Soviet role as a world arms supplier, in order to "determine what we can afford." There has been some speculation that this announcement, with its implication of a possible cessation of Soviet arms assistance to Iraq, played a part in the timing of Saddam Hussein's invasion of

Kuwait. He may have been determined to exploit his fleet of some 5,000 tanks and supportive weapons before an interruption of the flow of Soviet spare parts, ammunition, and other assistance would compromise operations in the field. In July 1992 Yeltsin supported plans to increase arms sales to other countries in open defiance of requests by the United States and Germany that Russian arms sales be reduced. Undoubtedly, arms export policies constitute a critical test of Moscow's professed shift to a cooperative stance in the world arena. The question assumes even greater urgency at a time when arms reductions in Europe, along with increased pressures for hard-currency earnings, presumably will make ever greater quantities of modern Russian military hardware available for "diversion" and export.

Notwithstanding its significance, however, the Russian factor, by this time at least, is by no means the only one in the equation of proliferation of modern weaponry and militarization of conflict in the Third World. Moreover, the proliferation is entering a new and more ominous stage. According to some authoritative projections, by the turn of the century as many as twenty Third World countries will have deployed, or be in the process of deploying, ballistic missile systems.

The proliferation of ballistic missiles, dramatically demonstrated by the use of Iraqi Scuds in the Gulf War, will be addressed more specifically in Chapter 8. Nonetheless, the significance of this trend and its implications merits prominent inclusion in any general assessment of the emergent global threat. The proliferation process began in the 1960s, when possession of ballistic missiles was limited to the superpowers and several of their allies and clients. In the ensuing decades, a widening demand for ballistic missile capabilities, and thus for missile-related technologies, led to a dramatic increase in suppliers. Their numbers now include the industrial nations of Europe, private consortia based in Europe, and even some "second-tier" suppliers in the Third World. Today this proliferation is accelerating and expanding globally.

Unfortunately, this trend is again concentrated in the region that has been the main arena of militarization in the past: the area embracing the Levant and North Africa and including Iran, Iraq, Saudi Arabia, Syria, Yemen, Israel, and Libya. Yet the proliferation trail leads elsewhere, as well. In South Asia, both India and Pakistan have added ballistic missiles to their military capabilities. Before its collapse, the Soviet-installed regime in Kabul fired ballistic missiles against the Afghan resistance. In Northeast Asia, the possessors include both Communist China and the Republic of China on Taiwan, as well as North and South Korea, while Japan unquestionably has the capacity to achieve those capabilities. In Southeast Asia, Indonesia is testing sounding rockets. In Central America, Cuba commands ballistic missiles. In South America, missile development programs are underway in Brazil and Argentina. South Africa has tested a ballistic missile system.

The missile proliferation picture gains sharper perspective when the capabilities in question are grouped in terms of their ranges: long range (greater than 1,000 km), medium range (200–1,000 km) and short range (less than 200 km). India, Iraq, and Saudi Arabia have tested long-range systems; the Saudis apparently have already deployed the Chinese CSS-2 system in that category.

Long-range systems are relatively difficult to produce, require fairly complex electronics, and thus are not readily available in the arms marketplace. Once deployed, however, they provide their owners with, in effect, an intercontinental, or at least transregional, capability.

Medium-range ballistic missile systems are deployed in Afghanistan, Egypt, Iraq, Iran, Syria, Yemen, and Libya, as well as in Pakistan and both Koreas. These systems provide their owners with a theater-level capability—one that may plausibly be described as "strategic" in their contexts of these countries because the missiles can be targeted across the breadth of regional territories at airfields, ports, and installations, as well as population centers and economic infrastructure. As the Iraqi Scuds so starkly demonstrated in the Gulf War, there is a broad availability of systems in this range category in the international arms market.

Even more readily available, of course, are short-range missiles. Not only is it fairly easy for aspiring nations to find salesmen for such weapons abroad, but their manufacture is within the grasp of those states that have mustered reasonably modern industrial-technological establishments of their own. For instance, short-range missiles are known to be in the inventories of Algeria, Egypt, Iraq, Iran, Israel, Yemen, Pakistan, Taiwan, North Korea, South Korea, and Cuba.

Superimposed on this globe-spanning picture of proliferating missile capabilities is the even more fearsome prospect of the warheads that can be fitted onto them. Among the nations listed above, three—India, Pakistan, and Israel—are believed to have nuclear warheads already in storage, or to have the capability to assemble them in fairly rapid order. Four others—Iraq, Argentina, Brazil, and South Africa—are managing programs that could yield nuclear weapons, probably by the end of the century.

The list is longer with respect to chemical and biological weapons. Ten states—Egypt, Iran, Iraq, Israel, Libya, Syria, North Korea, South Korea, Taiwan, and South Africa—are credited with the possession of stockpiles of chemical weapons. Four of them—Iran, Iraq, Syria, and North Korea—are also believed to be storing biological weapons.

The picture and its interconnections can be overdrawn, however. The possession or pursuit of missile capabilities does not necessarily mean that each of the countries mentioned above will acquire the nuclear, chemical, or biological warheads to go with them. For that matter, modern conventional explosives have a level of potency that makes them fearsome in their own right.

Besides that, two conditions make the picture particularly worrisome. First, the militarization of conflict in the Third World involves deeply rooted regional ambitions, and rivalries that are far less subject to the "rational" restraints that have tended to bound the competition and confrontation in mass-destruction weapons between the two superpowers. Second, as Iraq's use of chemical weapons against Iran and against its own Kurdish population has already demonstrated, what draws developing states toward weapons of mass destruction is their "cost effectiveness"—the promise of a "short-cut" to military power and regional hegemony.

GEOECONOMIC FAULT LINES OF CONFLICT

Saddam Hussein's Iraq serves as a microcosm of all of the Third World trends sketched above. But the Gulf War highlighted one other fact: Those trends are relevant to the national interests of the United States. More specifically, it has demonstrated why the passing of the era of containment cannot mean withdrawal of the United States into isolation or a "Fortress America."

It is a truism that the world has become economically interdependent, to the extent that no nation can look to self-sufficiency in economic resources and no part of the globe is shielded from the effects of dysfunctions, for whatever reasons, in other parts. Conflict in regions once considered "remote," which in bygone days could comfortably be allowed to "play itself out," today sends instant tremors throughout the international structure.

Global geography, or better, geology, has provided a disturbing imbalance in the modern international system. The unhappy fact is that virtually all the Third World states mentioned above in one or another context of weapons proliferation happen to be situated astride resources that are heavily, in some cases critically, relied upon by the ever-expanding industrial infrastructures of the more advanced nations. The relationship between this geological bounty and the "militarization of conflict" phenomenon is by no means coincidental.

First, it is revenues derived from these resources and flowing into the treasuries of developing states—revenues often inflated by cartels—that are providing the principal purchasing power for importation of modern arms. The incentives for authoritarian leaders, besides their hegemonic ambitions, are economic considerations. The paths toward industrialization taken by developing countries are at best incremental; irrespective of the availability of funds, there is a limit to the investments that can be absorbed, at a given time, by any country's modernization process. By contrast, modern weapons systems can be purchased whole, along with the technical and training assistance to operate them. They thus offer a "broad jump" toward military modernization.

Second, while the arms thus purchased feed and often inflame regional rivalries and conflicts, those rivalries themselves tend to be exacerbated by the struggle among those nations for control of riches. Iraq's invasion of Kuwait was a salient demonstration of this vicious circle of destabilization and conflict. Saddam Hussein made his bid for the oil fields of Kuwait after some eight years of devastating conflict with Iran (waged in large part over disputed oil reserves in the Shatt al-Arab) had depleted the treasury of even oil-rich Iraq. Adding to this incentive was the fact that the capture of Kuwait also promised virtual Iraqi control over the flow of oil from the Persian Gulf.

Arguably, it was this latter prospect that compelled a direct military response from the United States, even though the United States is less dependent on Middle Eastern oil than are other industrialized nations, notably those of Western Europe and Japan. Yet dependency cannot be measured in terms of percentage of imports alone.

Conceivably the United States may now finally be persuaded to pursue seriously programs of energy conservation and search for alternative energy sources. Even under the best assumptions, however, the road to reasonable self-sufficiency in essential raw materials for a vibrant U.S. industrial economy is problematic. That applies not only to oil, but also to other critical minerals at stake in conflict-rife regions of the Third World. For instance, substitutes are unlikely to be found for nickel, cadmium, cobalt, and chromium.

Many of the potential regional conflicts would threaten the vital natural resources of the interlocking world economy, from which the United States cannot stand apart. The Gulf War can be regarded as neither unique nor conclusive. The coming years can be expected to bring new contingencies and new challenges, requiring the projection of U.S. military power into regions that in the past were considered "remote" and far less critical to U.S. interests than is the case today.

THE BROADER IMPACT OF ECONOMIC FACTORS

If economics have thus become a principal goad of conflict in an ever more interdependent world, they impact upon defense planning in another significant way. At the same time that the potential for military conflict is heightened, the means for dealing with it are becoming progressively constrained.

Economic factors have been a key driving force behind the changes taking place in the former Soviet Union and its erstwhile empire in Eastern Europe. It was above all the dire economic failures and shortcomings of the communist system, accentuated by the challenges of the new technological era, that prodded Gorbachev onto his path of fundamental systemic reforms under the banner of perestroika. Gorbachev's departure was not unprecedented; the impulse toward reform had motivated his predecessors in the Kremlin, prominently Nikita Khrushchev in the 1960s. What distinguished Gorbachev's changes was their ambitious reach, along with the power of the forces unleashed in their wake.

Gorbachev, a consummate tactician, showed a tendency to improvise, pressing ahead in his reforms while manipulating the forces of political power. Despite the best efforts of expert observers of the Soviet Union, and even with the benefit of hindsight, it is difficult to see a comprehensive game-plan that guided Gorbachev's strategy and its objectives, beyond the imperative of economic and systemic reform as such. Still, one fundamental aspect of that strategy stands out in retrospect: the recognition that the faltering Soviet economy could no longer shoulder the burdens of empire in Eastern Europe, and that the satellite states therefore had to be cast off, to fend largely for themselves. Implicit in that decision was also the expectation that a "devolution of empire" would have the effect of clearing away obstacles to the massive economic help needed by the Soviet Union from the western nations.

It is not known whether Gorbachev anticipated the full force of revolutionary change that would grip the satellite states once Soviet control was loosened, let alone the backlash of developments in Eastern and Central Europe and in the Soviet Union itself, particularly the awakening of aspirations for independence in the non-Russian republics of the former USSR. Yeltsin, for his part, has continued where Gorbachev refused to move on. While Yeltsin's record of encouraging the establishment of a market system is more encouraging than Gorbachev's, it remains to be seen whether he will be able to complete this transformation successfully. Yeltsin and his economic advisors have undertaken great efforts to liberalize the price system, but certain prices of key goods remain set by the state. The privatization efforts have been completely aborted. Collectivist thinking, particularly countryside, hampers private initiatives. Also, measures to achieve full convertibility of the ruble will remain insufficient so long as Yeltsin seeks to accommodate certain "reactionary" interest groups by simply printing more money. Apparently, Russia has not yet reached the critical point of success in its transformation from socialism to capitalism.

The changes in Russia have given even greater primacy to economic factors and forces in Europe and the trans-Atlantic alliance. Those effects can be summarized as follows:

First, the remission of the most immediate military threat to Western Europe has spurred a trend that was evident even before the dissolution of the Soviet empire. This trend has been a downward curve in defense expenditures by all the NATO countries in comparison to their increase in wealth.

Second, the decreasing defense budgets in the West have been abetted by the developments in Eastern Europe. The economy of the unifying European Community (EC) is challenged by the burden of reviving, and ultimately integrating, the virtually bankrupt economies of Eastern European states that have become, in effect, wards of the West. The problem is epitomized by the united Germany; West Germany, once the vibrant core of the EC, faces an economic drainage of huge proportions in absorbing the former GDR.

The overall prospect is that the Western Alliance, in particular, and the industrialized nations more generally, will be increasingly preoccupied with economic challenges—and increasingly divided by economic competition. Economic concerns will overshadow security concerns. In fact, there will be a progressive tendency to define "security" in primarily economic terms. Expenditures for defense by the industrialized nations, not least the United States, will continue to decline. This general trend is likely to prevail regardless of temporary reactions to crises and military challenges in the Third World, and even in those instances the impact will be uneven among the nations affected. The problems encountered by the United States in its efforts to elicit a more equitable sharing of the military and financial burdens of the Gulf crisis, particularly from nations whose interests were more directly and more profoundly at stake than those of the United States, clearly show how difficult it will be in the future to maintain the "harmony of interests" the West was used to during the Cold War.

The only contingency that might prompt significant change in this evolving picture of the last decade of the twentieth century would be the one discussed in the opening section of this analysis: a clearly and generally recognized resurgence of the Russian military threat. The qualifying emphasis, however, is on "clearly and generally recognized." If the past is any guide, this would have to entail more than "merely" a return of dictatorial rule, a reconsolidation of the Soviet Union, or even a "remilitarization" of the Russian society; it would also have to signify a reassertion of Russian military power in behest of clearly aggressive, expansionist aims.

The Gulf War experience suggests that in future military challenges, the United States will not be able to look to the direct support and burden sharing provided by multilateral alliances. It will be increasingly reliant on (1) its own resources, (2) bilateral alliance ties, and (3) whatever ad hoc international coalitions may be organized in the given case. In that context as well, the Persian Gulf crisis provided a telling preview.

HEIGHTENED REQUIREMENTS FOR COMPREHENSIVE INTELLIGENCE

It is difficult at best to assess the overall impact of these projected risks and uncertainties on U.S. defense planning. Still, some general implications readily come into view. One is the logical requirement for enhanced and expanded intelligence capabilities. The emergence of a diversified "threat environment" of truly worldwide dimensions dictates a broadening of U.S. intelligence surveillance from its focus on Russia and the Commonwealth of Independent States (CIS) to a more comprehensive coverage of potential crisis areas and flash points of conflict. At the same time, the urgent need for timely power projection calls for more incisive intelligence, to provide the requisite warning time for decision making and response. This is a large, complex, and necessarily shrouded subject, and moreover, one that lies not entirely within the purview of the defense planner, embracing as it does the total array of U.S. intelligence capabilities, especially those of the Central Intelligence Agency and the National Security Agency. Nor is it the intent here to belittle or to document shortcomings in these agencies. But over the past decade knowledgeable observers of the U.S. intelligence establishment have pointed to a trend away from "human" ("traditional") intelligence gathering to greater reliance on more remote "electronic" means. Far from dichotomous, the two categories of intelligence gathering are, or should be, complementary. Beyond the general merits of "electronic eavesdropping," the technical means of intelligence are most relevant to observation of physical phenomena, such as the existence, quantity, deployment, and movement of military resources. "Traditional" intelligence is more relevant to the far less tangible area of the political context of decision making. In the main, technological intelligence focuses on capability; traditional intelligence illuminates intent.

An authoritative assessment of U.S. intelligence relevant to the Gulf War may never be made public. In its absence, some general conclusions, and questions, are warranted. Electronic intelligence obviously was a key element of success on the battlefield, although there were at least some indications of prior shortcomings in assessments of the Iraqi order of battle, such as those relating to the number of Iraqi Scud missiles available to be fired. More controversial, in any event, is the question of the degree to which the United States was forewarned of Saddam Hussein's intent to move into Kuwait. This is clearly a question involving "traditional" means of intelligence.

Whatever may be the intelligence lessons of the Gulf War, however, they are somewhat obscured by the fact that the United States and its allies enjoyed a lead time of some five months to respond to the crisis with appropriate force. Future contingencies may not allow so much lead time between warning and action. A priority is thus for comprehensive U.S. intelligence capabilities, which at the same time should be incisively targeted at the political, economic, religious, and other societal factors that may yield warning of impending crises, particularly in regions in which U.S. interests and commitments are at stake. What is called for is a "situation awareness" where, in the main, none has existed before.

SMALLER U.S. FORCES

The U.S. force planner must proceed under the almost certain assumption that there will be sharp reductions in U.S. standing forces, both those making up a "residual" military presence overseas and those deployable from the continental United States. Barring the reappearance of a central, massive threat of global dimensions, comparable to that generated by the Soviet Union in the post–World War II period, the trend toward an ever more quantitatively constrained U.S. military posture seems inexorable. As was suggested earlier in this chapter, the trend is determined by two mutually reinforcing factors: (1) economic pressures on defense budgets, and (2) reduced perceptions of a global threat. Even to the extent that it may affect the United States directly, the global threat requires less "standing" military power than it did in the past. Even the experience of Desert Storm appears to have spelled little difference in prevailing congressional attitudes toward the defense budget, which attests to the strength of the political mind-set that is involved. The military planner, in any event, has to assume that the relative downward trend in U.S. expenditures for defense is not likely to be reversed.

The defense planner must also proceed from the assumption of a progressive retrenchment in the U.S. military posture from its erstwhile strong points overseas, in both Europe and Asia, over the next several years. This applies not only to the forward-deployed U.S. military presence, but also to the global logistical network of bases and facilities that supported that forward-deployed power in the past.

Increasingly, therefore, the United States, in meeting potential challenges to its vital interests, will have to depend on (1) quantitatively fewer forces than in the past, and (2) forces projected from the United States. In the process, moreover, it will have to look less confidently to the "force multipliers" provided by allied capabilities overseas, in terms of both actual forces and logistical support. As was noted earlier in this chapter, Desert Shield/Desert Storm provided a strong indication of the trend away from multilateral alliances. Instead of drawing on allies already bonded by common purpose and automaticity of response, in contemplating future contingencies, particularly in the wide expanses of the Third World, the United States will have again to look to whatever nations are willing to share the burden, the risks, of a common military action. In the worst case, the United States will have to be prepared to "go it alone."

The U.S. military planner, in short, confronts the problem of "accomplishing more with less" and over greater distance. A larger premium is inevitably placed on the flexibility, effectiveness, and responsiveness of those forces likely to be available—and it is to these areas that the planner must direct his energy and his innovative ideas.

Military effectiveness is a compound of many factors. One of these, particularly during a period of constrained resources, is the efficient marshaling and management of those resources. If Desert Shield/Desert Storm yielded one generally applicable lesson, it is that modern warfare is an "all-arms" task; that is, it calls for the combined and synchronized actions of all military arms and services, and of all the elements within the individual services. The intensity of modern battle, the density of weapons systems over and on the battlefield, the compressed decision time in face of the risk of staggering losses—all these attest to the heightened significance of the combined-arms concept. In the Gulf War this concept was implemented in exemplary fashion against a sluggish adversary—one, moreover, who permitted the United States some five months to put in place the intricate command, control, and communications system that lay at the heart of success. There is no guarantee that the United States will prevail with the same ease against a similarly well armed but tactically more sophisticated (and forewarned) enemy in the future. The concept needs to be further honed and, more important, institutionalized in the organization of U.S. armed services and unified command structures.

Another conspicuous lesson of the Gulf War is the need for well-trained, ready, and rapidly responsive forces. "Well-trained" and "ready" primarily describe the products of operations and maintenance budgets designed to provide optimal training. A singular advantage enjoyed by the U.S. Army forces in Desert Storm was the realistic training they had undergone at the National Training Center (NTC) at Fort Irwin, California, against a simulated opponent, in an environment not unlike what they were to encounter in the North Arabian Desert.

Smaller forces, if they are to shoulder the roles and missions previously assigned to larger formations, must by definition be transformed into "elite forces"—units trained to operate, and interact, in a fashion that allows little margin for error.

IMPLICATIONS FOR POWER PROJECTION

"Rapidly responsive" forces are rapidly deployable forces. Phrased in strategic terms, above all, "projection of power" means the timely transport of fighting forces and their wherewithal. As will be pointed out in much greater detail in a subsequent chapter, it is here that the "success story" of Desert Storm tends to obscure what is perhaps the greatest shortcoming—call it even the "missing link"—in the proposed transition by the U.S. armed forces from a forward-deployed posture to one dependent primarily to power projection from the continental United States. This shortcoming is the inadequacy in military lift capabilities, especially sealift. The inadequacy was shaded by a number of relative luxuries the United States enjoyed in the contingency: the luxuries of time for the buildup, of easily accessible and friendly regional ports and airfields, of foreign-flag commercial shipping willing to join in the effort, of regional sources of supply (e.g., in food and water), and so forth. There is absolutely no assurance that any, let alone all, of such luxuries of time and resources will be granted in future contingencies.

The critical factor is sealift for heavy forces. As was stressed above, the heavy-armored threat wielded by Saddam Hussein's Iraq was by no means atypical; today there are fourteen nations with tank inventories that include more than one thousand vehicles. The units of the 82nd Airborne Division initially deployed to Saudi Arabia, and the U.S. Marine detachments that early reinforced them, were no match for the heavy armor of the Iraqi army. Had Saddam Hussein ordered the invasion of Saudi Arabia in August 1990, they could not have stopped the Iraqi advance.

Especially with the retraction of forward-deployed U.S. formations from Europe and Asia, there is thus a mounting need for "power-projection forces," including heavy forces, with the ability to transport them over long distances in short periods of time. That means sealift, but sealift is expensive and so far the nation has shown little disposition to make the requisite investments. Indeed, special-purpose sealift—fast-deployment, roll-on/roll-off ships—are a commodity not likely to be affordable, certainly not in adequate number. Moreover, funding for fast seaborne lift inevitably competes with investment in combat ships. Force designers thus face the challenge of finding some acceptable scheme for moving forces rapidly by sea, but doing it in increments that are affordable in the context of a more generally robust national maritime capability. If power projection is to become more than merely a declaratory strategy, there is no way around that challenge.

IMPLICATIONS FOR MODERNIZATION

Smaller standing forces call, logically, for the insurance of backup capability—in forces, in technology, and in production base. In the popular perception, Operation Desert Storm was a demonstration of U.S. prowess in military technology, a "video war" of battlefield surveillance and target-acquisition systems pinpointing targets, and of precision-guided munitions striking with uncanny accuracy. This image is justified up to a point, even though it was exaggerated via the (understandable) policy of the military command to display success while shading failures.

Even though the Gulf War featured, in the aggregate, a successful demonstration of military technology, that picture is a dangerous guide to the future unless the lessons of the war are considered in proper context. Let us put aside for the moment the later claim by the Soviets, the principal suppliers and one-time advisers of Iraq's armed forces, that the war did not yield an accurate test of the contending merits of military hardware on the battlefield because of a combination of the tactical surprise achieved by the coalition forces and Iraqi ineptitude. Be that as it may, there is another important point to consider. Most of the "modern" weapons systems displayed by the United States in Desert Storm represented technologies essentially dating back to the 1970s.

Even after discounting for disparities in tactical employment, the Gulf War essentially involved a contest between some of the most modern equipment in the U.S. inventory against Soviet equipment marked for export, which by definition did not reflect the very latest in the Soviet arsenal.

The unhappy reality is that the United States had been laggard in military modernization—in the rate of translating technological advance and innovation into fielded equipment and systems. By comparison, the Soviet Union, notwithstanding its systemic problems and shortcomings, had demonstrated in the past a modernization rate in fielded conventional arms systems—in tanks, artillery, infantry, and other components—at least four times that generated by the U.S. research and development and acquisition process.

Moreover, the "flip side" of technological success in the Gulf War is intelligence and the lessons it holds out to other contenders in the technological arena. The Russians, according to reports, have been engaged in an intense effort to sort out the bountiful intelligence yielded by the war regarding U.S. weapons and their employment. More generally, the nature of the conflict and its outcome are bound to spur the trend to military modernization by other countries.

Particularly in the technological arena, therefore, celebration of success needs to be tempered by recognition of demands for the future. The Gulf War demonstrated beyond doubt the wisdom of the U.S. investment in military technology in the early 1980s, notwithstanding the relative slowness of the U.S. modernization rate. Today the certainties of dwindling defense budgets demand an even more urgent focus on the way we exploit our technology to achieve the best advantage on the field of battle. Surely, given the hard budgetary trends, there will be fewer new start-ups in military systems, and substantially less military equipment will be produced in the aggregate. Two priorities, long subjects of U.S. debate, thus become ever more compelling: (1) the creation and maintenance of an adequate military-technological industrial base capable of meeting flexibly the modernization demands of the immediate and longer-term future, and (2) a more disciplined and efficient method than the nation has mustered in the past for moving advanced technology out of the laboratory and into fielded products and systems.

IMPLICATIONS FOR NUCLEAR WEAPONS

Modernization requirements also apply to nuclear weapons. A major problem confronted by U.S. defense planners is how to factor the "nuclear element," long considered to constitute the nation's "first line of deterrence and defense," into their projection of the risks, and thereby priorities, of the future.

The problem is compounded by prevalent political trends attendant upon the presumed advent of the "post-containment era." Nuclear weapons epitomized the U.S.-Soviet confrontation. With a defusing of that confrontation—a process spearheaded by U.S.-Soviet arms agreements affecting nuclear weapons—that "first line of deterrence and defense" seemingly has receded in importance. The trend is exacerbated by an understandable popular desire, in the United States and abroad, to dispel entirely the oppressively overhanding clouds of a nuclear "balance of terror." The drive for "denuclearization" is progressively eroding the political ground under forward deployments of U.S. nuclear power in Europe and in Asia. In the budget battles in Congress, nuclear programs, especially the "big-ticket" ones related to strategic forces and strategic defense, have become prominent targets for cutbacks. That trend is bound to be reinforced by START, followed by President Bush's unilateral initiative calling for withdrawal of land- and sea-based theater and battlefield weapons from abroad.

The trend contradicts realities spelled out earlier in this chapter. Nuclear weapons are here to stay. Their number and deployment may well be increasingly restricted, especially in the direct U.S.-Russia context, but still, residual Soviet strategic nuclear capabilities—whether they remain under a central command, in the control of the Russian Federation, or are placed in some other arrangement among the increasingly sovereign entities that have made up the former Soviet Union—continue as a direct threat to the territorial United States. Russian strategic forces, moreover, have been undergoing constant modernization. The same applies to Russian theater nuclear forces, which, while retracted by treaty and in political retreat from forward positions of empire, remain ready to be put into the field.

U.S. defense planners, in any event, must hedge their projections of the future threat environment, and future uncertainties, with these realities and assumptions, especially as they affect the irreducible priority of the planners' endeavors, which is the direct defense of the nation itself. At the same time, the planner confronts the reality of proliferation of nuclear weapons and the means of their delivery to other actors on the world stage—actors predictably less subject to the "rules" of restraint and rationality that have tempered the nuclear confrontation between the superpowers.

These implications above all apply to the future cast of residual U.S. theater-level nuclear capabilities. To put the implications into sharper perspective, let us imagine a replay of the Persian Gulf crisis scenario, but this time under the assumption that Iraq possesses nuclear weapons, in whatever number, that are deliverable by aircraft or ballistic missiles. How would that fact affect U.S. decision-making in the crisis? What would provide a credible deterrent to Saddam Hussein's use of such weapons, especially at the critical juncture when he contemplated the defeat of his forces on the conventional battlefield? In that scenario, and absent the availability of such a deterrent, would the decision have been made to mount Desert Shield in the first place, thereby placing many thousands of U.S. service men and women under direct threat of nuclear attack?

There can be no confident, certainly no definitive, answer to the question of "credible deterrence" in such a scenario. Perhaps, as Gen. John L. Piotrowski argues in Chapter 8, antimissile defenses point to a promising solution in the broader context of the problem. Yet comprehensive defenses against missiles will require lead time of development and procurement, and the scenario sketched above may be ominously close at hand. Moreover, such defenses, no matter how effective and rapidly deployable they may turn out to be, cannot offer the solution, if only because nuclear munitions can be delivered by means other than ballistic missiles, notably air-breathing delivery means.

In short, countervailing U.S. nuclear forces remain essential to any strategy for coping with the global proliferation problem in its new and ominous setting. New and urgent demands are thereby imposed on U.S. theater nuclear capabilities. What do these demands call for in the technological arena, in terms of requisite types of weapons and their rapid deployability? What might be appropriate operational and tactical doctrines to guide the employment of the weapons?

Here we have what may be the hardest questions confronting U.S. defense planners. They are all the more difficult to address in the prevalent climate of nuclear disarmament initiatives and popular-political antipathy to all things nuclear. The questions, nevertheless, demand answers.

THE UNCERTAINTIES OF TRANSITION

The "nuclear dimension" is an appropriate subject with which to conclude this inventory of the uncertainties confronting U.S. defense planners. An era of transition, such as the one in which we find ourselves, is by definition rife with uncertainty. From the vantage point of the military planner, however, there is not only uncertainty, but also a compounding of risk and threat.

The risk and threat are compounded because they partake of both old and emergent dangers in the transition. Historian Arthur M. Schlesinger, Jr., noted in his 1986 book, *The Cycles of American History*, that nuclear weapons "introduce a qualitatively new factor into the historical process. For the first time in the life of humanity the crack of doom becomes a realistic possibility."[1] Schlesinger was referring, of course, to the threat of a U.S.-Soviet nuclear exchange. At least in terms of old scenarios of crisis confrontations, that threat may now be receding, but nevertheless, the threat remains—in the eyes of some even more disturbingly so in light of a diffusion of control in Central Eurasia. At the same time, the fuses of mass destruction are being spread almost unpredictably elsewhere, into environments less subject to the reins of mutual restraint—and less subject, for that matter, to the broader (and in many respects stabilizing) effects of the traditional superpower standoff.

This chapter began with a reference to the uncertainties that faced a U.S. military planner following the Vietnam war. Those uncertainties were great, and they were attended at the time by the prospect of shrinking defense budgets. Still, they were bounded by a framework of explicit strategy, the strategy of "containment," and by a broad national consensus that served to cushion any truly precipitous decline in the means to effect that strategy. Today's planner can no longer look to an explicit, stable framework of national strategy, nor can he confidently look to available means. He faced the task, if you will, of drawing up a comprehensive national insurance policy against multiple and largely unpredictable risks, without assurance that the premiums will be paid. It is an unenviable task, but it must be carried forward.

NOTE

1. Arthur M. Schlesinger, Jr., *The Cycles of American History* (Boston: Houghton Mifflin, 1986).

3

Army Forces for the Future

Lt. Gen. John W. Woodmansee, Jr., USA (Ret.)

As Gen. Donn Starry suggests in Chapter 2, probably never before in the nation's history have U.S. defense planners confronted as rapidly shifting scenarios of global change and national defense requirements and priorities. On the one hand, developments such as the dissolution of the Soviet empire, followed by the unraveling of the Soviet Union itself, along with the trends of militarization and conflict in the Third World, signal a world in volatile transition, with largely unpredictable implications for U.S. security. On the other hand, the reality of a shrinking defense budget and substantial reductions in the armed forces call for clear vision and painful choices.

It is with a view to the prospect of limitless potential for conflict on our small, warring planet and the reality of constrained resources that we must go about developing a long-range defense program that can provide an adequate "insurance policy" against future risks to our security. History teaches us that the last war is rarely a reliable guide to the requirements of the next one. Still, any projection of future security requirements must heed recent experience—in this case, the Gulf War.

DESERT STORM AND AIRLAND BATTLE

The victory achieved by the U.S.-led coalition forces in Operation Desert Storm unquestionably will go down as one of the most decisive, with fewest casualties for the victorious side, of any campaign of comparable magnitude in history. It ranks with Gen. Douglas MacArthur's Inchon invasion and breakout of the Pusan perimeter in 1951 as the best in America's rich military heritage.

Desert Storm was a stunning demonstration of the synergism of combined arms on the modern battlefield. It revalidated the importance of technological superiority on that battlefield. The final act was an exquisitely executed lightning maneuver and attack throughout the depth of the battle area. The circumstance of a poorly led enemy who had relinquished operational and tactical initiative does not detract substantially from the overall achievement—even though it does warn strongly against a sweeping and uncritical drawing of lessons for future battles, against opponents who not only will be less accommodating, but will have absorbed lessons of their own from Saddam Hussein's operational and tactical failures.

Some of the Gulf War's specific lessons, as they apply particularly to the U.S. Army's future requirements, will be noted in this chapter. First, however, we should take a more focused look at the role played in Desert Storm by doctrine—the AirLand Battle. Even in the wake of the war, there has been widespread misconception of that doctrine's fundamental content, and therefore its abiding relevance for the future.

We must gain clearer understanding of what AirLand Battle is and what it is not. The doctrine is not a recipe for victory. It does not explain how to blend electronic warfare with precision-guided munitions, stir in deep fires, add some command and control, and then maneuver violently for 100 hours and expect victory. Rather, AirLand Battle is a doctrinal description for the application of combat power across the depth and breadth of a modern battlefield.

Some historical background is needed to place the doctrine in its proper context. Although its roots extend farther back, the doctrine was developed in the late 1970s and early 1980s. It was addressed primarily to the European theater and to the challenge of defeating the superior forces of a Soviet-led Warsaw Pact attack against NATO's Central Region. That, however, was not the doctrine's exclusive preoccupation. Its evolution was also strongly influenced by analyses of conflict scenarios in Southwest Asia and by lessons drawn from modern Arab-Israeli wars. Quite early in that evolution, in the late 1970s, the then U.S. Army chief of staff, Gen. Edward C. "Shy" Meyer, went so far as to establish the 9th Division as a high-technology "test bed" in order to stimulate identification of the organizational, doctrinal, and matériel requirements of a highly mobile force optimized for desert warfare.

From Arab-Israeli battles, we learned of the need to seize the initiative and shift rapidly from defensive to offensive operations. Similarly, we perceived the limitations, in the absence of a combined arms approach, of using armor and tactical air power in the face of defense antitank defenses supported by a Soviet-style forward air defense umbrella. Beyond a renewed emphasis on the combined arms team, the doctrinal studies yielded other design imperatives. The need to upgrade the firepower of artillery with the Multiple Launch Rocket System (MLRS) became startlingly clear, as did the importance of "smart" munitions and the electronic battlefield.

Two main theories emerged from this intellectual effort, which were validated

Army Forces for the Future 35

by the outcome of Desert Storm. The first was an integrated conception of tactical operations that recognized the importance of delaying and disrupting the enemy's uncommitted echelons in order to set the stage for the decisive defeat of his forces in piecemeal fashion. The conception thus extended the battlefield from the start, putting a premium on deep strikes against high-value targets with precision-guided munitions. The second development generated by the early studies was the United States Army's commitment to a sizable Army aviation structure of a brigade in each division and corps, along with a modernization effort aimed at providing the Army with an advanced attack helicopter (Apache) and scout (OH-58D), both capable of operating in limited visibility while firing long-range, precision anti-tank weapons.

The AirLand Battle Doctrine, published in 1982 as a field manual, FM 100-5 Operations, dealt with many conceptual problems: How to defend forward in Europe; how to add depth to the battlefield; how to transition from defense and rapidly seize the initiative; how to take the battle to the enemy's territory; how to exploit our inherent technological advantage; and how to be prepared for both the conventional and the nuclear/chemical battlefield.

The nascent AirLand Battle Doctrine also codified a dimension of battle between the tactical and strategic levels of war: this was described as the "operational" level. The impetus behind this three-level conception (indeed, behind AirLand Battle more generally) owed much to the influence of General Starry, then the commander of the Army's Training and Doctrine Command (TRADOC). In early 1982, in a communication from the Army chief of staff to all his general officers and senior civilian executives, Col. Don Holder, who was to command the 2nd Armored Cavalry Regiment in Desert Storm, ascribed to the new doctrine the following distinctive features:

[AirLand Battle] views battles as nonlinear and enlarges the geographical area of conflict, stressing unified air and ground operations throughout the theater. . . . This operational level recognizes the non-quantifiable elements of combat power, especially maneuver, which is considered equal and complementary to firepower. It acknowledges the importance of electronic warfare as well as nuclear and chemical weapons and details their effect on operations. Most important, [the new doctrine] keeps the human element prominently in the foreground. . . . This operational concept applies to all our forces operating anywhere in the world.

FM 100-5 was revised in May 1986. Meanwhile, a new adaptation of the doctrine, called AirLand Battle Future, has been in development. A further variant, AirLand Operations, was approved in principle by the outgoing chief of staff, Gen. Carl Vuono, in the summer of 1991. In essence, four features remain fundamental to the AirLand doctrine: initiative, depth, agility, and synchronization. Perhaps the best way to weigh the relevance of AirLand Battle to Desert Storm is to discuss each of these tenets in light of that battle.

Initiatives

As has been noted, AirLand Battle was addressed primarily, though not exclusively, to the European Theater. Coloring the doctrine, therefore, was the most threatening scenario of a massive Warsaw Pact attack against NATO Europe, requiring U.S. and allied forces to absorb that initial onslaught before shifting to the offensive. Against that background, the 1986 version of FM 100-5 defines "initiative" as "setting the terms of battle as a result of action."

In Operation Desert Storm, the U.S. and coalition forces certainly set the terms of battle as a result of action, once the air campaign commenced in the night of January 17, 1991. The pressure of the campaign was maintained without pause, with air dominance maintained over the battlefield continuously, day and night. When the ground campaign was set in motion, the coordinated sledgehammer blows by the heavy force and the sealing of retreat routes by the 101st Airmobile Division ensured that once the Iraqi forces were reeling, they would undergo constant pressure and swift pursuit until termination of the battle. At the strategic level, President Bush contributed significantly by permitting no diplomacy-imposed pauses once the air campaign began.

Depth

AirLand Battle conceives a single battle waged in three realms: deep battle, to ensure that the enemy cannot mass and execute his plan; close battle, to defeat selected enemy forces decisively; and rear battle, to protect one's own forces and retain freedom of initiative and plan-execution.

In Desert Storm, the air campaign and air operations during the ground campaign were the main instruments of deep battle. Never before had a more devastating demonstration of air power been exercised throughout the full depth of a battlefield. The rapid achievement of air superiority—indeed, air dominance—conditions all three realms of the AirLand Battle. The only problem was the Iraqi Scud missiles. The Patriot antimissile defenses, through their superb performance, limited the potentially disastrous impact—politically and militarily—of those weapons on the outcome of the war. A strong warning signal for the future, however, is that the toll, and impact on the rear battle, would have been substantially higher had the Iraqi missiles been more accurate and armed with chemical, let alone nuclear, warheads.

The United States Army's contribution to the battle-in-depth was modest in comparison with that of tactical air power. Still, Desert Storm underscores the utility of an organic capability that the Army has been seeking for a decade. The availability of some 100-plus Army Tactical Missile System (ATACMS) missiles, combined with their Guardrail electronic-eavesdropping aircraft and targeting data from prototype Joint Surveillance and Target Attack Radar System (JSTARS) airborne radar, gave the ground commander the ability to locate

Army Forces for the Future

moving and emitting targets accurately beyond 100 kilometers, and to attack them with high precision and lethality. This capability was originally justified within the explicit context of the European Theater, as a means of delaying and disrupting follow-on Soviet echelons. Desert Storm clearly demonstrated the broader value inherent in "seeing" deeply over the battlefield, and in engaging high-value targets with aircraft, air and surface missiles, naval gunfire, attack helicopters, and ground forces.

Agility

According to FM 100-5 (1986 version), agility is the ability of friendly forces to act faster than the enemy. The stress is on the mental and organizational flexibility required to gain a step on the opponent. Both versions of the manual speak to the need to continuously frustrate the enemy's plans and engender the piecemeal defeat of his forces.

What is missing in the discussion of agility in both manuals, but is being addressed in AirLand Operations, is the benefit of (and therefore requirement for) a dominant reconnaissance and counter-reconnaissance capability. Years of experience at the Army's National Training Center (NTC) have shown that the battalion that wins the local reconnaissance/counter-reconnaissance battle is the heavy favorite to win the engagement. The force with the superior situational awareness, the ability to see the battlefield, has the inherent advantage in the agility to move without wasted energy and achieve mass and surprise on the enemy force. In this sense, agility is not so much a function of speed and maneuver as it is the product of a dominant command, control, communications, and intelligence (C3I) system.

In Desert Storm, this agility advantage was decisively demonstrated by Gen. H. Norman Schwarzkopf's ability to position his swing corps undetected off to the west and to launch it upon the enemy's exposed flank before the Iraqi Republican Guards could react. A dominant C3I system had been put in place combining overhead satellites, human observation teams deep in the enemy rear, remotely piloted vehicles, and JSTARS radar. in the final ground campaign, the system literally allowed the coalition forces to perceive the full depth of the battlefield, while the enemy was blinded to the point where he could not even process targets rapidly enough to bring effective artillery to bear on the inrushing armored forces.

The point to be made is that, while agility is frequently associated with a "miles-per-hour" advantage at the tactical level, it is more appropriately described at the operational level as the function of a higher-order central nervous system. It embraces a better capability of "reading" the battle, issuing orders, and taking action, thus achieving the definition of "acting faster" than the enemy.

Synchronization

FM 100-5 (1986) defines synchronization as "the arrangement of battlefield activities in time, space and purpose to produce maximum relative combat power at the decisive point." The discussion of the subject ends with the following thoughtful observation: "To achieve this requires anticipation, mastery of time-space relationships, and a complete understanding of the ways in which friendly and enemy capabilities interact. Most of all, it requires unambiguity of purpose throughout the force."

It is an understatement that the air campaign in Desert Storm required, and received, substantial centralized control in order to integrate the air assets of U.S. and coalition forces into a coherent plan, all of which had to be focused on established priorities. Reportedly the joint air tasking order, issued daily, was nearly 70 pages long. The magnificent management of this effort, involving many thousands of sorties flown by variously configured aircraft and cruise missiles across the full spectrum of missions, was a credit to the air component commander, Lt. Gen. Charles A. "Chuck" Horner, and his staff. Their accomplishment unquestionably redefined the term "synchronization" for the air portion of AirLand Battle.

Desert Storm also made vivid the fact that the land portion of AirLand Battle is synchronized differently from the air portion. True, the major subordinate operations of the land forces were all guided by the commander-in-chief's concept and were coordinated with respect to the areas of advance and objectives. But the execution was decentralized in nature, requiring leadership at all levels to achieve the decisive "operational" outcome as the aggregation of innumerable "tactical" successes. The staging of the marine amphibious threat; the prepositioning of VII Corps to the west and its earlier-than-planned commitment; the assault by the Marine forces and coalition units through the breach into Kuwait; the airmobile execution by the 101st Division and link-up with the 24th Mechanized to seal off the routes of retreat; the coordinated moves by the British 1st Armored Division and the French 6th Light Armored Division, plus all the logistical activities involved across the board—such a spread and magnitude of efforts, moves, and activities, along with the associated tactical options, could not possibly be compressed into a single operational blueprint, much less fine-tuned by a daily, central tasking order. The nature of ground force operations simply is different from the nature of air force operations.

One of the significant improvisations made by General Schwarzkopf in synchronizing the land battle deserves fuller study: namely, the spreading of Army capabilities across all the land forces, to ensure that the entire formation enjoyed the benefits of the technology contributed by the U.S. ground forces. To the 2nd Marine Division and its antiquated M-60 tanks was assigned the Tiger Brigade, with 120 M1A1 tanks and 60 Bradley Infantry Fighting Vehicles. The brigade took with it two battalions of direct-support, self-propelled 155 mm artillery and a battery of nine MLRS, plus Firefinder radars for locating enemy artillery. On the return side of the technology-sharing story was the provision by the Marines and Navy of unmanned aerial vehicles (Pioneer and Pointer systems) to the Army forces.

More generally, a detailed study of Desert Storm will show that the United States Army "leavened" the entire force, not just with its technology, but also with its talent. U.S. engineer units served with French forces; U.S. Special Forces were assigned to the pan-Arab forces. Herein lies a lesson in synchronization, particularly with respect to coalition warfare, that future drafters of joint doctrine should not treat lightly.

The technological lessons of the Desert Storm land campaign can also be dangerously deceptive, however, especially as they apply to the modernization requirements for the United States Army. More will be said on this point later in this chapter.

IMPERATIVES FOR THE FUTURE

There is no sign that the victory in Desert Storm, and even the surge of patriotism it called forth, will have an appreciable impact in slowing, let alone reversing, the shrinkage of U.S. allocations for defense and the cutbacks in overall U.S. military strength. In fact, in paradoxical ways the ostensible ease of that victory has encouraged the notion, particularly in the corridors of the U.S. Congress, that such cutbacks can safely be undertaken. The principal questions still under debate seem to concern their extent and speed.

A painful dilemma thus challenges all the U.S. military services. As the defense budget declines, the services are ever more hard pressed to decide on the basic distribution of scarcer funds between operating accounts (salaries, training, spare parts, base operations, etc.) and investment accounts (research and development, procurement of new weapons systems, ammunition storage, product improvements, etc.).Therefore, a fundamental choice is to be made between force structuring and modernization.

Arguably the dilemma bears most sharply on the United States Army, given the clear prospect that it will have to accept the largest share of cutbacks overall. Albert Einstein once observed, "Perfection of means and confusion of ends seem to characterize our age." Mindful of that caveat, let us attempt to list the enduring, core issues before postulating the specifics.

Personnel requirements. The Army must continue to attract and retain high-quality young men and women for voluntary service, as well as for leadership roles.

Force requirements. The size and composition of our active United States Army force, the modernization of its equipment, and the ability to deploy it to battle to meet time-sensitive contingencies and to present a forward presence in critical areas—all these must be considered as a whole and not as separate issues. The size, composition, and modernization of our reserve force, and its ability to meet required readiness levels, must be geared as well to the potential challenge of a reemergent land threat of global dimensions.

Technological requirements. We must as a nation sustain a leading edge in military research and development—and do so as a fielded capability rather than just in our laboratories or in our rhetoric. We must also maintain an industrial base to provide the requisite sinews and muscle of sustained modern war-fighting capabilities.

Training requirements. Leaders and their units must be physically, mentally, and emotionally prepared for battle, with demanding and realistic training.

Infrastructure requirements. Our general support infrastructure must provide decent living and working conditions for military personnel and high-quality medical, educational, and community services for their families.

PROJECTED ARMY FORCES

Residual Forward Deployments

In a speech delivered on August 2, 1990, shortly after having been informed that Iraq had invaded Kuwait, President Bush announced that by 1995 U.S. security needs can and will be met with forces 25 percent smaller than today's. The president cited three broad requirements for those forces: "to demonstrate a forward presence in key areas, to respond effectively to crises, [and] to retain the national capacity to rebuild our forces should this be needed." He also stressed readiness, rapid response, and research as key principles guiding the restructuring of the armed forces.

Taking the active strength of the United States Army at its 1990 level of 746,000, a 25 percent cut would yield a force of approximately 560,000. The six-year defense program submitted in the President's FY 1992–93 budget request to Congress called instead for a reduction in U.S. Army forces down to 535,000, almost a 30 percent "drop beneath the drop." This end-strength figure, along with others that have emerged in the budget negotiations, provides at least a starting point for projecting force composition and assessing the implications for the investment accounts.

Let us begin with forward-stationed Army forces. The European theater remains the key arena of such forward deployments. The dramatic changes that have reshaped the political landscape of Central and Eastern Europe—including the disbanding of the Warsaw Pact, large-scale Soviet force withdrawals, and dissolution of the USSR itself—have substantially blunted the erstwhile Soviet offensive threat against NATO. Nevertheless, as General Starry suggested in Chapter 2, a responsible U.S. military planner, whose task it is to project in lead-times of five years or longer, has to look at both the contingency of resurgent Russian military threat and other potentially destabilizing forces in the increasingly chaotic scenario of Eurasia.

All things considered, two heavy divisions and an armored cavalry regiment could constitute the maneuver forces around which a 70,000-strong U.S. Army corps could be constituted in the Central Region of NATO. Additional theater assets, composed of air defense and intelligence units, of a support base that would permit backup logistical capabilities, and of a base for rapid expansion ("reconstitution"), would add another 15,000 to the United States Army forces stationed within the Central Region.

The rising importance of NATO's Southern Flank, both in its relevance to Europe's defenses and in its potential as a forward staging area for U.S. contingency operations in the Middle East and beyond, argues logically for enhancement of the U.S. force presence and logistics in that region. An expanded presence might entail some 15,000 troops, comprising an airborne regimental combat team and several brigades of long-range artillery and anti-air/missile defense. Headquarters for these units would remain with the Southeastern Task Force (SETAF), functioning as a forward command post for the residual U.S. corps and also capable of rapid deployment with the airborne regimental combat team.

Called for in the same context is implementation of the long-standing idea of establishing in Turkey an instrumented training facility for air and ground maneuver exercises, similar to those conducted in the United States at the NTC. The training center in Turkey might also be the site for stockpiling a full division's equipment, for use by U.S. forces stationed in the Central Region or those deploying from the continental United States.

In Asia, U.S. forces will continue to be committed to the defense of the Republic of Korea, pending any conclusive change in the political-military situation on the divided peninsula. That commitment argues for retention of the existing U.S. division in Korea, reinforced with an MLRS/ATACMS battalion, an anti–tactical ballistic missile capability, and selected combat service support and command and control capabilities. With the emphasis on firepower rather than manpower, the forces thus allocated should number around 20,000.

With respect to residual forward emplacements elsewhere, a strong case can be made for maintaining a brigade of U.S. ground forces (some five thousand troops) in Panama, both on political-military grounds and for continued operation of the Jungle Training School there. If the current plan for removing all U.S. forces from Panama by 1996 remains in effect, however, an alternate site will have to be found for the training of forces and testing of equipment in tropical-jungle conditions.

The aggregate of forward-deployed United States Army forces, as outlined above, would come to approximately 125,000. They would comprise one corps, three divisions, and three brigade-size organizations, plus their supporting forces.

Contingency Forces

The remainder of active United States Army forces will be keyed, in keeping with the emphasis of the Base Force concept developed by the Joint Chiefs of

Staff, to dealing with major and minor regional contingencies. The requirement the Base Force concept is built on calls for rapidly deployable insertion forces and follow-on forces. They will have to be highly modernized, with a mix of heavy and light units attuned both to tactical requirements and available strategic airlift and sealift.

Light insertion forces must be capable of forced (airborne) entry and of establishing a lodgment for the buildup of follow-on forces. Where tactical conditions call for close combat with predominantly dismounted forces, any reinforcement requirements can be satisfied by additional light infantry units, as well as Marine units deployed to the scene.

The requirements for insertion forces change substantially, however, in a scenario featuring heavy armor and artillery. In that context, a clear "what might have happened" lesson emerged from Operation Desert Shield. The 82nd Airborne Division was the first to arrive in Saudi Arabia to signal American intervention and to "draw a line in the sand." Notwithstanding the legendary fighting caliber of that force, however, such "signalling" was about all it could be expected to do in the critical early days, even weeks, of Desert Shield, when it would have been virtually defenseless against an Iraqi armored thrust across the Kuwait–Saudi Arabia border. The obvious lesson is that light insertion forces, if committed to a similar high-intensity combat environment in the future, must be equipped with the most advanced antiarmor weapons and reinforced with other capabilities to defend their lodgement pending the arrival of heavy reinforcing forces.

The heavy forces must link with the light insertion forces in time to protect them and to bring decisive combat power to bear on enemy armored formations. The stress is on "timely" and "decisive." It means requisite strategic airlift, primarily for the rapid deployment of light insertion forces and their equipment, and strategic sealift, for the timely commitment of heavy forces. The pivotal role of strategic lift in the new emphasis on "power projection" is treated in Chapter 9, but it needs to be underlined from the vantage point of a United States Army "customer."

Operation Desert Shield once again spotlighted fast sealift as the critical conveyor of heavy combat power. The eight SL-7 fast sealift ships performed according to general expectations. The first Army heavy forces, the 24th Mechanized Division, reached port in Saudi Arabia in early September 1990. Yet units of the Army's second deployed heavy force, the 1st Cavalry Division, did not arrive until early November, some three months after the start of Desert Shield. As in the case of inadequate weaponry in the hands of the 82nd Airborne, the penalties of delay in the deployment of requisite heavy forces and their equipment were obscured, fortunately, by luxuries of time in the buildup. The scenario could easily, and disastrously, have turned otherwise.

There is a graphic way to define the sealift problem from an Army planner's point of view. Maintaining a respectable capability of four U.S.-based Army divisions in a reinforcing role, with a full component of active-duty support

Army Forces for the Future

forces and two additional corps headquarters, would entail some 130,000 personnel. In order for this force to be "projected" expeditiously abroad in response to a large-scale contingency and to meet the Army's stated timeliness, the nation's sealift capacity would have to be expanded to at least twice, and possibly three times, what it is today.

In addition to the main body of U.S.-based Army light and heavy divisions earmarked for the contingency role, six separate brigade-size formations should be retained for special functions and missions. These would include: (1) a brigade of heavy forces at the NTC as the "sparring partner" for units being trained; (2) the 3rd Armored Cavalry Regiment at Fort Bliss, Texas, to serve as the mounted cavalry regiment for the heavy reinforcing corps, and also as the "test bed" for the doctrinal and matériel components of desert warfare; and (3) a separate brigade maintained in Alaska to meet some of the same training, doctrinal, and matériel-testing requirements in extreme cold weather conditions. Ancillary brigade-sized forces, finally, would embrace Special Forces, Rangers, and Special Operating Forces, to carry out special tactical missions in contingency and antiterrorist operations.

The importance cannot be overemphasized of retaining brigade-sized formations for training and as test beds for combat in desert, jungle, and arctic conditions. Wars are rarely fought in temperate climates these days, and failure of familiarity with, and adaptability to, such special climatic and terrestrial conditions can exact an inordinately high price on the battlefield.

The roster of Army contingency forces, as outlined above, reads as follows: four light divisions, four heavy divisions, three corps headquarters, three separate brigade organizations, and the equivalent of three brigades of Rangers, Special Forces, and Special Operating Forces. Together, those forces would total 275,000. Adding forward-deployed forces of 125,000, the overall strength of active Army tactical formations would come to 400,000. It would comprise eleven flag divisions, with the six separate maneuver brigades providing additional fighting power measurable in terms of two divisions, giving the Army a thirteen-division equivalent of force on active duty.

Regeneration of Forces

The potential requirement of "reconstitution"—remobilizing in the face of massive threat—stands out as the principal, but by no means exclusive, rationale for the reserve component (RC) in the restructured, smaller United States Army of the future. If anything, the traditional role of the RC as the reservoir of additional combat power for the active component (AC) is destined to rise with the decline of the active force structure.

The long-nurtured equal partnership of active and reserve forces under the One Army concept continues to apply. It pertains not only to preparedness for major war—in which case the RC, in addition to supplying fighting forces, would also be called upon to operate the national mobilization system and training base. Short of the extreme emergency, elements of the reserve will continue to be routinely needed to support active units in major contingency operations. The call-up of reserve medical and port operations personnel during Operation Desert Shield points a pattern for the future.

In line with the partnership relationship, and the imperative of preparedness for major conflict, the RC must have equal claim on modernized equipment in order for the reserve forces to be truly complementary to the active units. The most modern weaponry, however, is irrelevant if not competently wielded in battle. A strong focus is thus on RC training—on modern-technology simulators for weapons systems crews and small units, and computer-assisted battle staff training for tactical headquarters, from battalion to division.

One way to harness the potential of reserve forces more effectively to the ready combat power of active units is in the operation of certain high-technology weapons systems. As just one example, the Army Forward Area Air Defense System (FAADS) features passive acquisition, active radar, and surface-to-air missiles to protect the maneuver force day and night from enemy aircraft and helicopters. Yet only one (active) crew is assigned to the system, thus limiting its operation. In the German army, a comparable system, Gepard, is operated around the clock by three crews, two of them assigned to the reserves.

With respect to the readiness posture of RC units, the highest priority should go to "roundup" brigade slices for the active divisions. Each of these brigades would be organized with its full support complement, enabling it to join and operate within the given active division as an additional, or fourth, maneuver brigade. Its readiness would be closely monitored by the active division; it would undergo NTC rotations, Battle Command Training Program (BCTP) evaluations, and summer training evaluations with the "host" division. Six brigades would be enough to round up the heavy divisions, and one or two additional light brigades would also be useful, force structure and funding permitting. The roundup brigades would be the first reserve components to be deployed to combat, with the expectation that they would follow the last active force deployments, but by no earlier than 120 days after the initial active deployment.

Following the roundup brigades in readiness priority would be segmented slices of divisional, nondivisional, and service support units. The idea here is to establish two heavy-force segments of three divisions each and a light-force segment of two divisions, for a total of eight divisions in the reserve components. Both light-division segments and one of the heavy-division segments would share a readiness priority of deployability after 150 days, followed by a longer-phased deployment of the remaining heavy-force segments. In addition to these divisional elements, two armored cavalry organizations should be retained in the reserve: one in its armored configuration to support heavy forces, and the other organized around a light-brigade concept for employment with either light or heavy forces. This would provide for ten or more division equivalents in the RC, to reinforce the thirteen division equivalents on active duty, giving the Army a total force equivalent of twenty-two divisions worth of combat power. The

Army Forces for the Future

sustaining base units of the RC would have the mission of operating the national mobilization base, to generate individual replacements from conscription within 180 days and new divisions for deployment within a year.

All the missions outlined could be accomplished with an RC base lower than the current structure of ten divisions and 776,000 soldiers, since many of those now serve as support forces for active divisions. Pending a more detailed calculation of the spaces required, a rough estimate is that those missions could be accomplished with about 640,000 authorizations, or about 100,000 more than the active component. With the cadre concept, for two of those divisions the numbers could be reduced to below 600,000. Meeting the president's 1992–93 budget proposal of 550,000 would require pulling another division or cadre, or reducing three of our roundup brigades.

REQUIREMENTS FOR TACTICAL AND NONTACTICAL FORCES

The ability of the Army to field an active structure of thirteen division equivalents, as outlined above, will depend primarily on two factors; the size of the end-strength force authorized by Congress, and the Army's ability to apportion that end strength between the competing demands of the tactical forces and the nontactical support structure. In the language of the United States Army's force accounting system, the requirements for tactical units are documented in Tables of Organization and Equipment (TO&E). The requirements for nontactical organizations (base operations, recruiting command, schools, etc.) are documented in Tables of Distribution and Allowances (TDA). To retain the 400,000 troops in that projected active force structure, and to do so within the end strength of 535,000 likely to be authorized by Congress, the TDA will have to be modified to make do with 135,000 spaces, which is 40,000 less than the 175,000 assigned in 1992.

Paring down the TDA is no easy task, because no hard ratio can arbitrarily be assigned to the relationship between fighting forces and their needed support. Moreover, the "overhead" (TDA) embraces functions absolutely essential to maintaining a competent fighting force, almost irrespective of its size, e.g. recruitment and retention of qualified personnel, and maintaining the schools and training centers that turn them into soldiers.

As an example of those essential services, the entire Recruiting Command is listed in TDA as a Field Operating Agency (FOA) for the personnel chief on the Army staff. Spread across the nation, it will continue to be needed, perhaps even more than in the past, to attract and process the requisite numbers of volunteers. The Health Services Command, which operates all the hospitals on Army posts, while also tending to Army retirees in their geographical areas, cannot be reduced in size without a change in the relevant law by Congress. The basic training of recruits; the professional education of commissioned and noncommissioned officers in service schools; the codification of Army doctrine, organization, and equipment for the future; the operation of bases and commissaries; the procurement of food for the troops—even the authorizations for Army personnel to serve on the Joint Chiefs of Staff and in the office of the Secretary of Defense—all these and many more are entries in the TDA account. They describe functions and services that will continue to be essential whether the Army commands eighteen divisions or eleven.

A particularly sensitive area is that of training and schooling. Over 30 percent of the military spaces in the TDA are assigned to TRADOC. Major cutbacks in such authorizations will no doubt have to mark TRADOC and its subordinate commands, including Fort Benning, Fort Knox, and Fort Rucker, as well as ROTC attachments in universities, as principal targets. If the TRADOC structure for generating highly trained soldiers is to be preserved, then cuts may have to be made in the part of the command that develops leaders and doctrine and arranges to meet materiel requirements in the future. One might argue that a smaller Army will call for greater skills in preparing for the future, not less. Thus, leaders properly concerned with the nation's lasting security will be understandably hesitant to "eat the seed corn."

Can the Army continue to afford a separate structure for providing basic training to recruits? An alternative pointed out by other nations, including Germany, is for that training to be conducted within the unit of assignment. Yet in the U.S. case, what would be the impact on overall readiness, especially in light of congressionally mandated requirements for minimum time in service, for new recruits prior to deployment overseas?

There are no easy answers. Nor can an attempt be made here to walk through the entire Army TDA structure in search of candidates for radical reductions. Suffice it to say that choices will have to be made, and that the choices will be excruciatingly difficult.

MODERNIZATION REQUIREMENTS

In his earlier-cited August 2, 1990, speech, President Bush made a commitment to the nation's fighting forces.

The men and women in our armed forces deserve the best technology America has to offer.... We have always relied upon [our] technological edge to offset the need to match potential adversaries' strength in numbers.

The president's prescription was amply validated by the Gulf War. As was noted earlier, the victory attested to the fighting caliber and talent of U.S. forces, their high level of organizational competence and readiness, and their superb leadership and sound operational doctrine. It was also achieved by superior arms. Some of the weapons systems relevant to the land campaign were noted in the earlier discussion of the AirLand Battle doctrine. A summary review, however, is useful in illuminating the Army's future modernization needs.

Army Forces for the Future

Overall, superior rocket artillery stands out as having dictated the battle. The vaunted Iraqi artillery, fashioned on the Soviet model, was eliminated from the battlefield by a U.S. counterbattery capability centered on the Firefinder radar, which precisely located any enemy artillery that fired, and the MLRS, which wreaked destruction on the thus located firing batteries, virtually before their rounds landed. With the massive arrays of Iraqi artillery thus essentially removed from the battle, our direct fire forces then destroyed enemy tanks and armored vehicles with accurate cannon fire, frequently at ranges of 3,000 meters, or roughly twice the effective range of the Iraqi tanks. The ability of our thermal sights to penetrate through certain weather conditions frequently allowed our forces to engage the enemy with direct-fire weapons at ranges that made him blind to their presence.

The armor protection of the U.S. M1A1 tanks apparently was never breached by an Iraqi round. The fact that some U.S. forces went into battle in relatively unprotected M60A1 tanks, lacking thermal sights and laser rangefinders, seems unconscionable in retrospect. It was sheer luck that, apparently, none of those obsolescent vehicles sustained damage from enemy fire.

The performance and reliability of other weapons systems belied the gloomy projections of those who had opposed or impeded their procurement in the past. The Apache helicopter, as well as the OH-58D Scout, with its mast-mounted sight, more than lived up to their advance billings. The toll taken by even the limited number of ATACMs that were available makes indisputable the devastating effectiveness of those systems in delivering massive firepower, with precision to ranges beyond 100 kilometers. The list of weapons systems contributing to victory in Desert Storm continues, from the Blackhawk helicopters to the Patriot air defense system.

Even allowing for Iraqi incompetence in the operation and tactical application of their Soviet-supplied arms, the results of Desert Storm vindicate the wisdom of those who designed the Army weapons systems in the 1970s and early 1980s, as well as those who were instrumental in procurement of those systems in the latter part of that decade. Nevertheless, while Desert Storm pronounced some clear technological "winners," it also pointed to key areas requiring modernization. Those requirements can best be categorized in terms of the strategic, operational, and tactical levels.

The Strategic Level

With respect to U.S. land forces, particularly in the context of the evolving posture emphasizing "power projection," the strategic level primarily embraces the projection of those forces to remote battlefields. The emphasis here is on the requisite strategic airlift and sealift, a topic that has already been touched upon in this chapter and will be addressed more fully in Chapter 9. Suffice it to stress here again that the Army's choices in sizing its forces, and their modernization needs, are inextricably tied to the availability of strategic lift.

The Army already has stated the requirement for adequate air- and sealift to deploy a light brigade to a contingency area some 8,000 miles distant within four days, to close a division there within twelve days, and then to bring two heavy divisions to bear within thirty days. The requirement reflects in good part a "negative" lesson drawn from the Gulf War, which is that the entire scenario could have been drastically changed if Saddam Hussein had decided to launch an early attack into Saudi Arabia rather than permitting the five-months' buildup of coalition forces. On a more generic plain, that "negative" lesson also points to the priority of providing light insertion forces with improved capability to survive an early attack by enemy armor, pending the arrival of heavy reinforcing forces.

At the operational level, a clear modernization priority, emphasized by the Gulf War experience, applies to the protection of deployed forces against ballistic and cruise missiles. Active defense against such missiles is a large subject, which ranges beyond a strictly Army modernization purview and is addressed in Chapter 8.

But there is a second dimension to effective antimissile capabilities, one that was sharply highlighted in the only partially successful campaign against Iraqi Scuds during the Gulf War. This is the dimension of seeking out and striking missile launchers. As a notable example of modernization plans, the extended range of the ATACMS Block I, in tandem with airborne sensor systems such as those provided by JSTARS and Guardrail Common Sensor (GRCS), promises a highly accurate capability against targets, including missile launchers, at ranges that have thus far been unattainable.

Priorities of targeting acquisition apply more broadly to Army modernization requirements at the operational level. Although JSTARS proved its value in Desert Storm, it is questionable whether enough of those systems will be procured to satisfy not only battlefield surveillance requirements at the central command levels, but also the need for real-time acquisition of moving targets by maneuver units. The development of the Unmanned Aerial Vehicle (UAV), both as a complement to JSTARS and as a short-range substitute for the latter, will help meet this need, but will require a radar for the detection of moving targets.

More generally, as was emphasized in the discussion of AirLand Battle doctrine, the key to prevailing in modern combat—especially for the smaller U.S. Army of the future—lies in the ability of the forces, at all levels, to "see" the battlefield, to "read" enemy capabilities and intentions well ahead of time, to decide what actions have to be taken, to communicate coordinated instructions across the force, to locate and strike high-value targets with precision, and to constantly monitor the battle. Systems such as JSTARS and UAV are essential components of such a "central nervous system." Also needed are improved means of detecting enemy aircraft and helicopters in the forward area, such as are represented in the Ground Based Sensor (GBS) and Masked Target Sensor (MTS) programs.

Army Forces for the Future

Effective command and control is a function not only of real-time battlefield surveillance, but also of the distillation of a constant and massive inflow of data into actionable intelligence that is quickly and efficiently made available to the appropriate consumers at command and subordinate levels. The Sigma Star program embraces a family of command and control systems that can perform those functions, assuming that these systems can be sustained in the funding levels of the forthcoming budget.

At the tactical level, Army modernization needs fall into two basic categories: new weapons platforms (principally armored vehicles and helicopters) and next-generation weapons systems. The question of needed weapons platforms highlights a more general strategy toward modernization that the Army seems to have adopted of late. Near- and mid-term improvements in fielded systems are being deferred in favor of "leap-ahead" capabilities that are expected to materialize by the end of the century. The strategy has been driven in part by scarcity of investment accounts, but also by trust in the durable competence of existing systems, along with confidence that the "leap-ahead" capabilities will emerge on schedule. The two "leap-ahead" systems typifying that strategy are the light helicopter (Comanche) program and the family of new-generation armored systems in the Armored Systems Modernization (ASM) program.

The leap-ahead strategy has been called into question by several factors. First, ostensibly as a consequence of the embarrassing controversy that led to the cancellation of the Navy A-12 advanced fighter aircraft program, the Department of Defense seems to be intent on hedging future such risks by stretching out all major new procurement programs. Thus the Comanche has been relegated to a 91-month demonstration, validation, and engineering development preparatory to initial, low-rate production. This means that the aging Apache will have to continue to carry the Army's attack helicopter burden well into the next century. Meanwhile, it is not clear what product improvements the Army will be able to afford—with special reference to the revolutionary but expensive Longbow millimeter wave radar fire control system—that can extend the effective life of the Apache.

Second, the Armored Systems Modernization Program has been forced to adapt to Defense Department decisions to eliminate several parallel development efforts in favor of a more "glacial" approach (to borrow terminology used by the Senate Armed Services Committee). In the meantime, the Army has been denied permission to move to a product improvement program for significantly upgrading the M1A1 Abrams tank.

Third, even should the leap-ahead programs materialize anywhere near schedule, Army investment funds may not be available to procure the systems at the expected rates and numbers. The immediate prospects are far from encouraging. It is at least questionable whether the Army will be able to meet its basic modernization requirements from an FY 1993 investment account destined to dip below $14 billion, in comparison with the $36 and $44 billion accounts for the Navy and Air Force, respectively. If the trend prevails, the Army could find itself at the turn of the century fielding tanks and helicopters that will be older than the average age of their crews.

Meanwhile, the primary focus of weapons modernization in the tactical arena must remain on the defense and enhancement of light insertion forces. Top priority in this respect belongs to an emerging family of antitank weapons. One is the Anti-Armor Weapons System–Medium (AASW–M), a light-weight, shoulder-fired missile that could exact a heavy price from enemy armor at close range (2 km). Still, there is the need to engage enemy armor further forward. The Line-of-Sight Anti-Tank (LOSAT) system, to be fielded on a Bradley Fighting Vehicle chassis, promises to perform that mission out to 5 km. LOSAT is the Army's premier rapid-fire, kinetic-energy antitank system of the future.

Finally in the category of antitank weapons, development of the Fiber-Optic Guided Missile (FOG-M) is needed to provide a revolutionary "over the hill" capability for insertion forces and reinforcing formations. With UAVs pinpointing enemy locations, the FOG-M, accompanied by LOSAT, could be deployed to engage enemy armor far forward.

A second priority, applying to both light and heavy forces, concerns antiartillery, or counterbattery, capabilities. The effect of such capabilities was dramatically demonstrated in Desert Storm, but the experience also warned against any tendency to relax our modernization efforts in this critical arena. Advanced Firefinder radar to locate enemy batteries, rapid-fire direction calculations to bring suppressive fire down on those batteries, and appropriate munitions to destroy them with the least tonnage achievable—they are the components of an effective counterbattery system. Search and Destroy Armor Munition (SADARM) is the developmental munition of choice against self-propelled artillery, but it also offers tactical utility against sitting armored forces, such as those defending an objective.

Other high-leverage force enhancements are on the horizon. One is the X-Rod, a kinetic-energy tank round to provide a rocket-assisted smart monition capability to existing 120 mm tank cannon. Although an "evolutionary" development, it promises a revolutionary boost to combat effectiveness, enabling the engagement and destruction of an enemy force literally beyond that force's direct fire capabilities. Another promising weapon in development is the Wide Area Mine (WAM). Designed to sense armored targets and deliver a fly-over, shoot-down smart monition, it offers for the first time an effective mine that can be delivered beyond the observable range of protective fire. It would also reduce exponentially the logistical burden associated with mines.

The above catalogue of Army modernization priorities is representative rather than comprehensive. Meeting those priorities is well within our technological reach. The price is likely to range at $17–$20 billion per year from Army investment accounts over the next decade. That figure, however, has to be seen in perspective; it would represent roughly half as much as the funds projected for the Navy and little over 40 percent as much as for the Air Force. Whether that makes it a "bargain" in relative terms is irrelevant to a more fundamental proposition, namely that the smaller United States Army of the future must be a modern army.

PEOPLE AND TRAINING

Gen. Israel Tal, the legendary leader of Israel's armored forces and designer of the Merkava tank, once was asked by a reporter to name the best tank in the world. Was it Israel's own Merkava, the U.S. Abrams, the German Leopard, or the Soviet T-80? Tal responded that the best tank is the one with the best crew. General Tal and all proven combat leaders understand that the quality of the soldiers, the cohesion of their units, their trust in their leaders, and their confidence in their own tactical excellence are the dominant determinants of victory. That applied to the Gulf War, as it has to countless other engagements in history.

The high-quality soldier of today, who showed his mettle in that war, is a product of the volunteer force. Its detractors notwithstanding, the volunteer concept has worked exceedingly well in attracting highly qualified and motivated young men and women into Army ranks. The share of high school graduates among Army recruits each year has ranged well over 90 percent. In fiscal 1989–90 the Army fully met its goal of almost 90,000 volunteers; over 95 percent of them held high school diplomas. A major attraction for many has been the promise of money for a college education after leaving the service. The Montgomery G.I. Bill has been an excellent investment for all concerned. The Army can look to talented young men and women to fill its ranks, eager to learn and to be given responsibility. The nation as a whole benefits, not only from the assurance of high quality and dedication in its armed services, but more broadly and durably from the resulting infusions of trained, educated, and motivated young talent into its productive mainstream.

In capitalizing on the incoming talent and raising professionalism to maximum levels, the Army has more than lived up to its side of the bargain. The Training and Doctrine Command, created in 1973, broke new ground in fashioning tasks, conditions, and standards for soldiers, leaders, and units. Key elements were the institutionalization of "hands-on" competence, as well as the objective evaluation of training against explicit standards. To those conceptual advances were harnessed over time some of the best and most imaginative applications of state-of-the-art technology that scarce procurement funds could purchase. Prominent among these applications were eye-safe laser adapters on direct-fire weapons, to permit unprecedented levels of tactical gunnery competence; highly instrumented areas for maneuver training against the most demanding representation of enemy forces; and computer-assisted war games, to train battle staffs at battalion to corps levels. These and many other innovations have given the United States Army a level of up-to-date training excellence unmatched by any other modern army.

The principal locus of that excellence is the NTC, the unique characteristics of which are a permanently assigned, highly trained "enemy" force to test units undergoing training, as well as a sensitively instrumented recording system that captures every detail of battalion and brigade "battles." Brigades undergoing training also engage in live-fire exercises against instrumented target arrays. Active Army units, as well as some reserve units, routinely have been subjected to lengthy exercises in the broiling summer of the Mojave Desert. The results of that training were demonstrated on the sands of Desert Storm.

The peacetime Army of the 1990s faces a greater challenge, in maintaining a sharp readiness edge in the absence of a clearly identifiable "enemy." With the exceptions of Fort Hood and Fort Bliss in Texas, local training sites in the United States do not offer adequate maneuver area, especially for a heavy division. Notwithstanding its excellence as a facility, the NTC is now limited to exercises primarily at the battalion and brigade levels. Those deficiencies in maneuver area must be redressed for the smaller Army of the 1990s. Also imperative are training areas away from the lights of civilian communities, to give the air-land teams maximum latitude for exercising with night-vision technology.

More generally, the Army of the 1990s must safeguard against the creeping lethargy that tends to infect readiness across the board in the absence of an identifiable external threat. We must constantly remember the consequences of committing a basically untrained and unprepared United States Army to battle in Korea in 1950. The value of simulation in honing battle skills and capabilities was strikingly demonstrated in Desert Storm. As just one example, some 99 percent of the Apache helicopter crews that fought in the Gulf War had never before fired a live Hellfire missile; they had only engaged targets in a simulator. Nevertheless, there were few reports of missiles failing to strike their targets.

The fuller potential of simulation has yet to be tapped. As one notable example, we have yet to exploit the potential of training entire tactical units in their simulated vehicles on a simulated battlefield, where the "friendly" unit is subjected to air attack, forced to operate in an artillery-delivered mine field and to exercise its battle drills while compensating for "lost" crews and commanders. The same simulation technology offers the capability of identifying future weapons system requirements through experimental exercises at the unit level with conceptual software, before huge procurement funds are invested. Also within our technical grasp is the operational testing of electronic prototypes of new weapons systems under simulated battlefield conditions that cannot be matched by "real" (and inordinately expensive) test conditions. The Army seems to have lost impetus in this important field over the past several years, only partially as a result of inadequate support from the Department of Defense.

This emphasis on training simulation is not intended to detract from the continued importance of live exercises. The combined use of simulation and maneuver exercises is more than complementary, but synergistic. Indeed, the training solution for a smaller but capable Army of the future lies in both expansion of simulation capability and improvement in live maneuver. Moreover, the current emphasis on battalion and brigade in live exercises must be extended to embrace the division and corps levels. If enough skeleton maneuver units are used in the field, realistic training can be provided for the various separate battalions (aviation, artillery, air defense, engineer, resupply, medical, and repair), as well as for the brigades in the division and corps, which cannot be adequately prepared for battle in exercises at merely the battalion and brigade levels.

These requirements will make strong demands on scarcer resources. Preparing Army units for war is never cheap or easy. Always greater, however, is the potential cost of forgoing such preparedness, measurable as it is in human lives.

A DIMLY LIT ROAD AHEAD

Future historians may well view the 1991 war in the Persian Gulf as one of the watershed events in a period of profound global transition that commenced in the last decade of the twentieth century. In the context of U.S. security endeavors, it may mark such a "divider" in a more direct sense.

The victory in Desert Storm was the product of many factors amply described in the preceding pages, above all the quality of the fighting men and the sagacity and courage of their leaders. It was also, in important respects, a legacy from what already is being referred to as the "bygone era" of cold war and military confrontation on a global scale. In human terms, it was the legacy of the visionary stewardship of leaders in the past decades, who brought about the doctrine, weapons, and organizations that exist today—leaders, both military and civilian, who insisted on and provided the resources to mold and train forces ready to withstand the shock of modern battle and able to prevail magnificently.

That legacy was established in a time when a sustained threat of global dimensions kept the need for substantial means of national defense clearly in the consciousness of U.S. citizens and their elected representatives in Congress. The task of extending the legacy into a secure future is likely to be much more challenging. Even with the debris of Desert Storm still on the battlefield, it seems to be the intent of the nation, through its legislature, to reduce precipitously its defense capability.

If our history is any guide, in the absence of a readily recognizable "threat," the cause of farsighted investment in defense will find fewer advocates. Exceptional leadership and persuasion will be required to secure and properly allocate the resources essential for providing the nation with the forces, the technology, and the sharp edge of readiness needed for future conflicts.

4

Naval Forces for the Future

Adm. Harry Train II, USN (Ret.)

Whoever will be serving as Chief of Naval Operations (CNO) of the United States Navy in the mid-1990s will not have to grapple so much with the challenge of acquiring naval forces. Rather, his problem will be one of applying existing forces to evolving tasks, the fuller nature of which will not yet have become clear. The forces under the CNO's command will be the legacy of the farsighted efforts of predecessors many times removed. However, while those predecessors initiated procurement programs in support of a national strategy focused on containment of a rival superpower, the future CNO will preside over the employment of these forces in pursuit of national objectives in a post-containment world.

Will this make a substantial difference in terms of the Navy's overall capabilities? Probably not. At the turn of the century naval forces will be employed in much the same way as they have been throughout the century's second half. Studies and analyses addressing the frequency with which U.S. naval forces have been employed in crisis management since the end of World War II virtually make up a cottage industry. But the reactive forces involved in those many contingencies were procured in response to the requirements generated by the "case one threat"—the threat posed by the Soviet Union. As Sen. Sam Nunn has observed, "If you can skin the cat, you can skin the kitty." In other words, those forces authorized, funded, and procured for the purpose of containing the Soviet Union can also be invoked against challenges to U.S. interests of lesser magnitude, as they were against Iraq in 1990–91.

The problem for the CNO of the mid-1990s thus will be not one of acquiring, but rather of retaining. He will have to find "another cat to be skinned" to enable him to decide what forces to retain and how to justify keeping them.

DESERT STORM: LESSONS AND NONLESSONS

In addressing the problem of defining missions and wherewithal, no doubt the CNO and his fellow chiefs of the military services will draw on the experience of the war in the Persian Gulf. We may assume that the "lessons" of Desert Shield/Desert Storm will still figure prominently in U.S. strategic thought and "military lore" in the mid-1990s—unless, that is, they have had to be displaced in the interim by the lessons of a new conflict involving the United States. However, it is in mankind's nature to be absorbed by the drama of the moment. By very definition, drama lends stark, even exaggerated crags to impressions and conclusions. It obviously takes time and longer perspective for "lessons" to be sorted out and placed in their proper context and durable relevance. This caveat applies no less in the euphoria generated by victory, as in the Gulf War, than it does to exaggerated "lessons of failure," such as those that long distorted our assessment of the Vietnam conflict and its import.

What the prudent U.S. military planner must guard against in the meantime is drawing precipitate conclusions, not only from what did transpire in the Gulf War, but from what did not really take place. This applies, first of all, to lessons adduced from an "air war" that did not occur. A salient fact of the Gulf conflict is that Saddam Hussein did not commit his air forces to battle. Whatever the motive behind it, his objective appeared to be to safeguard ultimate survival of the Iraqi Air Force, in preference to engaging it in a bid for victory.

In a similar vein, we should refrain from drawing elaborate lessons for the future from the ground campaign in Desert Storm, which was not a true testing ground for competing arms and tactics. There were many things Saddam Hussein did not do, a notable example of which is that he did not allow his commanders in the field to communicate with one another. Ostensibly paranoid over operational security, he threatened to execute anyone in his armed forces who communicated by radio. As a consequence, his dug-in soldiers often did not know the enemy was near until a tank rolled upon their bunker, having followed the telephone wire through the sand from the previous bunker.

We should not draw untoward conclusions from the fact that no amphibious operation was launched. The obliging Iraqi army permitted the U.S. amphibious force poised in the Gulf to accomplish its mission without landing. Six Iraqi divisions were crouched in their bunkers, peering out to sea, while the battle flared behind them. In this case, the Iraqis were not inventing new forms of assuring defeat; they were replicating the behavior of Argentinean forces in their defense of Port Stanley during the Falklands War. There, as in Kuwait City, the defenders dug in, with their weapons and defenses pointing out to sea, until they were overrun from the rear.

The Iraqis might have at least profited from the Argentinean example by attacking the naval forces at sea with Exocet missiles. As it was, they did launch some missile-equipped aircraft, but the pilots ejected at first glimpse of approaching coalition planes. In the event, few attacks were experienced by the U.S. fleet, either in the Gulf or in the Red Sea.

The Gulf War did yield useful data regarding specific missions and weapons systems. They will be noted, where applicable, in the discussion that follows. Those specifics, however, pale in the light of an overriding lesson of the conflict—one that hopefully will be built upon rather than squandered in the return by the U.S. military establishment to the comforts of business as usual.

The success story in Desert Storm/Desert Shield was the application of "jointness" to the organization and conduct of operations on the battlefield. Its outstanding manifestation was in the institution of the single air component commander and the single, integrated air tasking order, covering every sortie generated each day. This leap forward in integrated operations (to be taken up in great detail in Chapter 5) seems bound to be a model for future conflict.

This jointness extended beyond the air campaign. The CNO in the mid-1990s no doubt will be aware that his predecessor worked smoothly with the other service chiefs, with a minimum of visibility—that together they solved problems that only several years earlier had appeared insoluble. He will know that the same was true of the unified commanders. But did this signal a new spirit of "jointness" among America's armed forces, or was it, as skeptics contended, simply the function of a fortuitous blend of leadership personalities—of the right people, in the right commands, at the right time—a blend that is now dissolving as the services compete for the dwindling defense dollar?

That is, indeed, a key question regarding the Desert Storm legacy—the word "legacy" being defined as lessons durably absorbed into behavior.

THE CAPITAL SHIP

But let us turn again to the subject of the United States Navy in the future—to the CNO of the mid-1990s and the problems of force structure he will confront. In contemplating those problems, he will be able to look to an element of strong continuity in naval forces stretching over most of a century. Whether the situation in question be post-containment in 1996 or pre–World War I in 1913, the basic force-building block of the Navy remains the capital ship. The naval component of the national military strategy in 1996 will be built around the capital ships that will carry us into the first decade of the twenty-first century. Those capital ships exist today: they are the vessels associated with sea-based tactical air power—the large-deck aircraft carriers.

Historically, at least over the last half-century, aircraft carriers have spearheaded the peacetime response by the United States to threats to its national interests. Again and again, carriers have been deployed, or diverted, on short notice to persuade, to influence, to coerce. In the corridors of power, the first question that tends to be asked at the onset of any crisis is, "Where are the carriers?'' This query is also among the first "what if" questions posed by the National Military Command Center to a unified commander's watch officer—the tipoff to the watch officer that something is brewing, prompting him to think about alerting his commander. The fact that carriers can persuade, can influence, can coerce is quite simply a measure of their ability to fight. And this recognized ability to fight, and to prevail, is an essential component of the panoply of capabilities that constitute deterrence of conflict, and the management of crises that can lead to conflict. The purist reader should not become agitated over the fact that the aircraft carrier is being addressed here in isolation from that which gives it life, the carrier battle group. That aggregation will be addressed later in this chapter, but meanwhile, a few more paragraphs will be devoted to the carrier itself.

A measure of the aircraft carrier's potence is the respect it commanded in the era of containment. U.S. aircraft carriers were the preoccupation of Soviet naval architecture and naval doctrinal planning for decades. The fear of, and intimidation by, the U.S. carrier gave rise to three generations of Soviet ships, aircraft, and weapons. Foremost among them was the antiship missile in all its forms, profiles, launch platforms, and types of midcourse guidance. We saw, in succession, the Soviet Juliet– and Echo II–class guided missile submarines, with long-range (250–300-nautical-mile) antiship missiles incorporating midcourse guidance by Bear Delta long-range reconnaissance aircraft. Later, we witnessed the advent of the Soviet Charlie-class guided-missile submarine, with its short-range (30-nautical-mile) antiship missile, a potent weapon demonstrated in the sinking of the Israeli destroyer *Elat* by a Styx-equipped Egyptian warship. Then along came the much more powerful Soviet Oscar-class guided-missile submarine. While these anticarrier developments were being carried forward in the Soviet submarine force, similar evolutions were taking place in Soviet surface combatants, culminating in the impressive Kirov-class cruiser—and in Soviet naval aviation with the ultimate emergence of Soviet Naval Aviation (SNA) Bear and Backfire bombers, with capable air-to-surface, long-range antiship missiles.

The point here is that the Soviet Union was sufficiently intimidated by the U.S. aircraft carrier to build a modern navy designed to fight it. This Soviet buildup that led to a protracted and often heated debate in the United States over "carrier vulnerability." Theoretically, this debate has been resolved. Since the "case one threat" has evaporated, or at least gone into remission, so also has any palpable threat to the aircraft carrier. The United States has not once experienced an aircraft carrier in jeopardy since World War II—through the long conflicts in Korea and Vietnam, and now through a short war, albeit in a high-intensity conflict environment, in the Persian Gulf. In 1991 the United States still had in commission two aircraft carriers built during World War II to fight Japan. One of those is currently homeported in Japan, with the mission of defending that nation.

Obviously the carrier has given a far better return on its acquisition and operating costs than, for example, the erstwhile Wheelus Air Force Base in Libya or the U.S. airbase left behind at Cam Ranh Bay in Vietnam—such comparisons are more in the line of banter at an officer's club than intellectually supportable analyses. On a more serious note, the British came perilously close to losing one of their small aircraft carriers (actually an aircraft-capable ship rather than carrier) in the Falkland Islands war. Had the Royal Navy still possessed at the time one of its former large-deck carriers, the issue never would have been in doubt, and the British would have been spared the painful loss of ships and lives they suffered in that defense of their national interests in the South Atlantic. The Royal Navy at the time possessed no capital ships, nor does it today. Such ships are the sine qua non of superpower.

The synergy of sea-based tactical airpower of the Navy and Marines, and the land-based tactical airpower of the Air Force (and Marines), is a sharp salient of America's post-containment military and deterrent posture—deterrence not only against a potentially resurgent Soviet threat, but also against adventurism by armed states comparable to Iraq, such as Syria, India, North Korea, Cuba, and other potential seekers of aggrandizement, regional hegemony, and global stature. As the Gulf War heralded, such states, once deemed "third powers" in the shadow of the superpower competition, are assigning to themselves much more primary roles.

SIZING AND DESIGNING THE FORCE

The chairman of the Joint Chiefs of Staff has laid the foundation for a future U.S. force structure, which is to feature (1) an Atlantic Force, which will be a heavy force built around armor and reserves, capable of reintroducing U.S. ground forces onto the European continent; (2) a Pacific Force, a light force built around naval and amphibious forces and tactical air; (3) a Contingency Force for dealing with Third World crises and if necessary interposing in conflict in those regions; and (4) a Strategic Force. The secretary of defense, for his part, has projected a 25 percent reduction in U.S. force levels over the next five years.

Those are the parameters within which the CNO of 1996 will have to develop the naval component. Within these parameters, he must design a balanced force, including:

- Ships and forces that deter but perform only in war, such as the attack submarine, the ballistic missile submarine and tactical nuclear weapons, and
- Ships and forces that persuade in peacetime and also perform in war, such as the carrier battle group and the amphibious battle group with its embarked Marines.

The carrier battle group is what Alfred Thayer Mahan would have called the main battle force—capital ships supported by a balanced force of lesser capable ships of the line, which provide depth, mass, and unique warfare capabilities. This main battle force controls the sea, controls the air space above it, controls the water beneath it, and controls the land mass adjacent to it, out to a radius of 300 to 600 nautical miles. When combined with a second and a third carrier battle group, it can project power and survive in the harshest air, surface, and submarine threat environment that any nation can present.

The CNO of the mid-1990s will not worry a great deal over the air-threat environment, certainly not to the degree that his predecessors a decade or two removed fretted about the northern Norwegian Sea, eastern Mediterranean, and northwest Pacific. However, given the force determinants prescribed by the chairman of the Joint Chiefs of Staff, the contingency of defending Western Europe based on the Atlantic Force, and the evolving character of the potential battleground for the Pacific Force, the CNO would be wise to preserve the capability of the unified commanders to concentrate forces of two and three carrier battle groups if and when needed.

The CNO probably will opt for all nuclear-powered carriers, although he will have to accept several conventionally powered carriers in his force, and all gas-turbine or nuclear-powered surface ships. The reason for this is that the secretary of defense has mandated a 25 percent reduction in naval forces. A steam-propelled carrier such as the Forrestal class has a large machinery box and propulsion fuel storage; because the nuclear-powered carrier does not have to give up so much space and volume, it can carry more ordnance and jet fuel for its aircraft. The volume in this regard is the equivalent of that carried by one ammunition ship and one oiler. Thus, the costs for those vessels can be forgone.

The CNO will opt, to the extent possible, to retain only the gas-turbine surface ships, because they are the most capable. These are the Aegis guided missile cruisers, the Arleigh Burke–class guided-missile destroyers, and the Spruance–class destroyers. Those ships are also minimally manned in comparison with their steam-propelled predecessors, thus saving on manpower, and they are less costly to maintain.

The Main Battle Force

Before he sizes the main battle force, the CNO of the mid–1990s needs to project the uses the national leaders are likely to have for carrier battle groups. His conclusion on that score will be easily reached; his leaders probably will ask for the use of carrier battle groups in almost every contingency. While this is not particularly instructive, knowledge of the past will condition the CNO to avoid saying "never" to his civilian superiors. For instance, some of his predecessors in previous decades took the position that the United States will never put carriers into the Persian Gulf; yet in 1990, in response to Iraq's move into Kuwait, a carrier was promptly dispatched into the Gulf, not necessarily as a tactical move, but as a demonstration measure. And in the course of Desert Storm, several carrier battle groups operated in the Gulf.

The CNO will recall that his predecessors in the late 1970s were disinclined to accept the risks of a Suez Canal transit by aircraft carriers. However, when

Naval Forces for the Future 61

the United States desperately needed a shorter route to the Indian Ocean because of the difficulty in meeting its commitments there, the Navy sent a carrier-commanding officer as an observer aboard a supertanker navigating the Suez Canal. He came back with the finding that a carrier could make it through the waterway without difficulty. Carriers have been using the Suez Canal ever since, in the process effectively increasing the number of carriers available for contingencies east of Suez, by being spared the long voyage around the Horn of Africa.

At least in terms of his own command responsibilities, the CNO will recognize that Desert Shield/Desert Storm marked an upper end of the probable conflict envelope in the late 1990s. Crises like the one that involved Libya in 1983 will fall into the middle of this envelope, while Panama-type actions will comprise the lower end of the contingency scale. Aggregating the projected requirements of these possibilities, with an eye to the remote likelihood of having to support a forced reentry of U.S. forces into Europe, the CNO can be expected to conclude that the Navy needs seven surface warfare combatants per carrier battle group.

The major question he will have to address is: How many carrier battle groups are enough? He will have to base his answer on the parameters laid down by the chairman of the JCS in 1991: There must be enough carrier groups to support the Atlantic Force and the Pacific Force. He will have to subsume the requirements of the Contingency Force within those of the other two forces. The logic goes as follows:

- Return to European shores would involve fighting the Russian navy and air force at sea in the Atlantic and Pacific.
- Sealift would be a major element in reentry into Europe.
- Sealift protection would entail denying Russian submarines access to the North Atlantic.
- Denying access to the North Atlantic would require control of the Norwegian Sea.
- Control of the Norwegian Sea would require control of the Norwegian littoral.
- Control of the Norwegian littoral and the Norwegian Sea would require sea-based tactical air in a concentration of force equal to three carrier battle groups.
- Forced reentry into Europe would also require control of the Mediterranean Sea.
- Because of the geography of the Mediterranean Sea, and assuming French support of naval operations in the Mediterranean, a force of two carrier battle groups, either concentrated or spread out across the Mediterranean, would be required.
- A war at sea with Russia in the Atlantic could not be confined to the Atlantic, but would also involve conflict at sea in the Pacific and Indian oceans.
- Three carrier battle groups would be required to defend vital lines of communication in the western and central Pacific.
- One carrier battle group would be required for defending the Indian Ocean lines of communication.
- One carrier battle group in the eastern Pacific and one in the western Atlantic would be required as swing forces, contingency forces, reserve forces, and attrition forces.

This adds up to the total of eleven carrier battle groups for which the CNO can be expected to opt, noting that carriers in overhaul must not be included in it. There was a time when it was to the U.S. advantage to count every carrier and flaunt the largest force possible vis-à-vis the world (and the Soviets)—it was called "Cold War posturing." We can now afford to be more realistic. The carrier being overhauled is no more in commission, and no more employable, than the carrier at the Newport News Shipbuilding and Drydock Corporation. If we count either the carrier in a two-year overhaul or the carrier under construction, we may be deceiving not only our potential adversaries but also ourselves.

The Aegis guided-missile cruisers and the Arleigh Burke–class guided-missile destroyers that support the U.S. main battle forces are the most capable antiair weapons systems the world has witnessed. They are also exceptionally capable antisubmarine warfare systems. The Spruance–class general-purpose destroyer and the older nuclear-powered guided-missile cruisers round out the surface warfare component of the main battle force. That component will total eighty ships.

The CNO will fret over the main battery of his main battle force. His concern will be about the age of the F-14 fighter, the range of the F/A-18 fighter/attack aircraft, and the speed and range of the A-6 medium attack aircraft. That concern will no doubt have been heightened as a consequence of Desert Storm, when the ranges from carrier decks to targets proved somewhat extreme.

Given the cancellation of the A-12 program in 1991, however, the choices for the CNO will be somewhat limited. Especially since he will have to make do with the aging A-6 aircraft for a number of years to come, he can accept range limitation as a built-in geographical constraint on carrier air, just as for years his Air Force counterparts have accepted geographical limitations on land-based tactical air. Alternatively, he might mount a new campaign, pending the "A-X" of the future, to replace the A-6 with an aircraft capable of carrying a large payload over a greater distance at relatively high speed. The F/A-18E and F/A-18F may well be that aircraft, although Congress probably will suggest the F-14D as a preferable candidate. Whatever may be the ultimate choice of a "gap-filling" aircraft, the prospect of the A-6 staggering through the skies for another decade is not likely to be inspiring for anyone concerned.

In any event, a force of 420 fighters and 400 attack aircraft will be required to give the carrier battle groups and fleet commanders the punch they need. The array of airborne early warning aircraft, electronic warfare aircraft, tankers, and sea-based antisubmarine warfare aircraft to round out the air wings is important. The CNO would be prudent to press, however, for one additional air wing, over and above the number of active carrier battle groups.

Submarines and Antisubmarine Warfare Forces

In addressing numbers of submarines required by the Navy of the mid-1990s, the CNO will need first to reexamine the complex subject of antisubmarine warfare (ASW), which has, at a minimum, three components:

Naval Forces for the Future

- Area or theater ASW. This is antisubmarine activity performed over wide ocean areas by submarines, maritime patrol aircraft, fixed sonar surveillance systems, and towed-array surveillance (T-AGOS) systems.
- Barrier ASW. This is the ASW campaign performed at choke points such as the Greenland-Iceland-UK gap, the Strait of Gibraltar, the La Perouse Strait, and the Korea Strait by submarines, maritime patrol aircraft, fixed sonar surveillance systems, and T-AGOS systems.
- Protection ASW. This is the classic World War II convoy escort or battle group screen-formation ASW, performed by surface ships, carrier-based ASW fixed-wing aircraft, surface ships, carrier-based ASW helicopters, surface-ship-based ASW helicopters, and tactical towed-array sonar.

Most of the weapons systems involved in ASW are multimission. There will be some difficulty in quantifying this ASW requirement in the post-containment world. In the past, we were accustomed to gauging our submarine order-of-battle requirements in accordance with the Soviet threat. For the sake of prudence—and our security as a nation demands no less—we must continue to keep an alert eye on the Russian potential. For that reason the Seawolf SSN-21 must be procured to ensure our naval edge—with the goal of never having to use this force. We should recall that in the Falklands conflict, several Royal Navy nuclear attack submarines held the entire Argentine Navy at bay and sank the Argentine cruiser *Belgrano*. Conversely, however, several Argentine diesel submarines caused such apprehension among the British commanders that virtually every ASW weapon in the British task force was expended in the course of the conflict. Our CNO will probably opt for seventy-five attack submarines, of which several will be Seawolf class and three will be dry-deck shelter capable, to support the U.S. Special Operations Command.

The surface ships involved in the ASW are multimission, and the numbers are not affected by the ASW mission as such. The surface ships required for amphibious task group protection, combat logistics force protection, and convoy protection will be discussed later. The T-AGOS ships are dedicated solely to ASW. They are new, effective, and manned by civilian crews. The CNO will probably elect to keep all twenty-three of those vessels.

The maritime patrol air force will be a problem for the CNO. He will know, intuitively, that this force can contribute more than ASW against Russian submarines. Additional missions will have to be developed and institutionalized. We may find, to our distress, that we did too effective a job in designing and training this force to detect and kill Russian submarines, while ignoring its ability to detect and identify surface ships (with precision) and engage those surface ships with Harpoon missiles. We certainly have not touted its capability to contribute, for example, to interdiction of narcotics trafficking. While the CNO will probably be successful in keeping eighteen squadrons of P-3Cs in the active order of battle, the very effectiveness of the aircraft will tend to militate against acquisition of the P-7 follow-on maritime patrol aircraft.

The Amphibious Force

The amphibious force is the CNO's true "switch hitter." The force has been an exceedingly effective tool in crisis management and has been a daunting warfighting force in the eyes of potential adversaries. As was noted earlier, that value was by no means negated by Operation Desert Storm.

When the amphibious force is combined with the Marine expeditionary brigades supported by prepositioned equipment, the Marines' ability to project fighting force rapidly over distance is impressive. The Marine Corps is the subject of another chapter in this volume, but it is difficult to discuss in complete separation two integral parts of a category of warfare. Our CNO of the mid-1990s and his counterpart commandant of the Marine Corps will be working this warfare area together.

Today's amphibious ships are truly effective weapons systems. They are modern, fast, and capable of landing potent Marine contingents in rapid and effective deployment. Navy and Marine commanders will probably agree on keeping twenty-four air-cushion landing crafts (LCACs) in the force.

The Marines today are on the cutting edge of evolving strategy. They performed superbly, and precisely in accordance with design, in Desert Shield and Desert Storm. Because of their success, amphibious ships will be under less pressure for force reductions than many other Navy components. The Navy and Marine commanders of the mid-1990s probably will be able to sustain a force of fifty amphibious ships and the full Maritime Prepositioning Ship order of battle of thirteen vessels. The CNO will be able to plan an escort force of forty surface combatants to round out the amphibious force in its combatant configuration.

Anti-Surface and Strike Forces

The turn from amphibious to anti-surface warfare is a good place to discuss the battleship. The extended life of that trusty old warhorse of naval combat and power projection is approaching its conclusive end.

Much though it will trouble him, the CNO will have to bow to political realities and decree a final resting place for the battleship. Save for the aircraft carrier, since World War II the battleship has been one of the most effective platforms of firepower and intimidation afloat. It is huge; it is visible; it can absorb the impact of 2,000-pound projectiles flying through the air at three times the speed of sound; it can fire swarms of Harpoon and Tomahawk missiles—and more generally, it can perform tasks that otherwise must be accomplished by the aircraft carrier, because there is no other "impressive presence" in our naval order of battle.

The battleship once again proved its versatility as a platform for both anti-surface and strike warfare in Desert Storm, where in addition it provided the needed standoff capability for naval fire that enabled the forces to avoid dangerously mined waters closer to shore. Informed reasoning based on track record does not necessarily drive political decisions, let alone the budget debate, however, and the CNO will have other priorities on his agenda.

With the likely loss of the battleship as a platform, the full dimension of antisurface warfare will remain vested in the Harpoon and Tomahawk antiship missiles. They are carried in the vertical launch systems of surface ships, the torpedo tubes of attack submarines, and (in the case of the Harpoon) in the wing mounts of the P-3 force and the attack aircraft of the carrier battle group. The CNO will thus not be able to count them separately.

Strike warfare—the employment of naval power against targets on land—entails the same ships, vertical launch systems, and carrier aircraft as antiship warfare, but different ordnance. The Tomahawk land-attack missile (TLAM), in all three of its variations, has captured increasing attention since its performance in Desert Storm. Not only did that represent the first test in combat for this missile, but it was employed under the most demanding conditions in which the missile is capable of performing. Despite the flat topography and paucity of the terrain features upon which the missile depends for accurate guidance, its success rate, particularly in the critical early days of the air campaign, far exceeded expectations.

As in the case of the battleship, memories of success related to specific weapons systems have a way of fading quickly in myopic deference to the concerns of the moment. The CNO in the mid-1990s probably will still be expending considerable time and energy in touting the effectiveness and utility of this weapon to political leaders, who might be prone to trade it away on the arms control bargaining table. In the process, he will be acutely aware of the dilemma this weapon imposes upon his submarine fleet.

Picture yourself as the submarine force commander charged with conducting an antisubmarine campaign in the Norwegian Sea with Los Angeles–class submarines, the finest ASW platform available today. You would like to station your submarines where the adversary's submarines are, but instead you are directed to position your submarines in locations from which they can launch Tomahawk missiles against land targets. The submarine cannot be in both places and perform both missions at the same time.

The dilemma was spotlighted in a somewhat different way during Desert Storm, when members of the U.S. media raised the question of why submarines were brought into play in the conflict. They had to be told, "Because Tomahawks are launched from submarines." This experience suggests another reason why the CNO of the mid-1990s will be all the more apprehensive about diverting submarines from their primary mission in order to launch cruise missile attacks. He may seek, therefore, to install some basic Tomahawk launch capability on virtually every surface combatant in the U.S. Navy. And again he will agonize over losing the battleship as a platform capable of carrying and launching more Tomahawk missiles than U.S. industry could manufacture in a decade.

The Mine Force

Desert Shield/Desert Storm documented deficiencies in U.S. shallow-water minesweeping capabilities. Nevertheless, when addressing mine warfare, our CNO probably will be reluctant, like all his predecessors, to invest much capital in preserving a mine-countermeasures force. He will perhaps retain the fourteen new mine-countermeasures ships and the five new mine hunters, but at the same time, he will be exhorting his mine-warfare commander and planners to look for innovative ways in which the Navy can exploit modern commercial technology and enlist the commercial trawler fleet for minesweeping.

During the Vietnam war, the United States was able to shut down Haiphong for two years with a mine blockade. The sparsely mined waters of the Persian Gulf offered a mild preview of the possibility that the United States will be presented with a challenge of much greater magnitude in a future contingency. There are solutions. Commercial trawlers can tow trawls precise inches over the ocean bottom and have the basic hardware available to perform mine-countermeasure work, and thus they represent an untapped resource. Meanwhile, with respect to the other side of mine warfare, the CAPTOR encapsulated torpedo mine is a capable weapon for employment in very specialized situations. Other mines can be laid by a variety of platforms, ranging from Air Force B-52s to Navy P-3s and A-6s, as well as submarines.

The Combat Logistics Force

The CNO will be acutely aware that it is in the logistical arena that a campaign, an engagement, or a crisis halfway around the world can be lost if the necessary support is not forthcoming. The Navy has consistently, since World War II, adhered to the concept of supporting every combatant force or group with its own combat logistics force. It has mustered an effective array of fast combat support ships, replenishment oilers, ammunition ships, combat-stores ships, and oilers. When we had difficulty maintaining the stores ships, we procured some from the British.

If we are to sustain the Atlantic, Pacific, and Contingency forces mandated by the chairman of the Joint Chiefs of Staff, we cannot take too many cuts in the combat logistics force. The CNO of the mid–1990s is likely to conclude that sixty of these ships are needed. Thus, in the challenge of meeting his force reduction goals, he will probably also opt for some fallback, such as the British concept of Ships Taken Up From Trade (STUFT) employed by the Royal Navy in the Falkland Islands. The CNO is likely to plan for some forty surface combatants to defend the combat logistics force.

Obviously affecting the sizing of a combat logistics force of the future will be the outcome of interim negotiations on U.S. naval bases and facilities. Some historical background is needed at this juncture. The structure of U.S. naval bases in the Atlantic/Mediterranean region and in the Pacific evolved along separate tracks. Prior to World War II, U.S. fleet activity in the Atlantic was limited. The Atlantic and Mediterranean were the domain of Britain's Royal Navy, and the fundamental compatibility of British and American national interests obviated the need for any large-scale U.S. naval investments in general, let alone for any large-scale logistic structure to support them. The story, of course, was different in the Pacific Basin, which emerged in the first half of the twentieth century as the focal arena of U.S. commercial and foreign-policy interests and the supporting U.S. naval power.

If anything, World War II accentuated the contrast in relative naval theater investments, particularly on the logistics side. Underlying the contrast were, first of all, fundamental facts of geography. Sailing distances in the Atlantic and Mediterranean are, relatively speaking, modest. As the war progressed, the United States Navy needed island bases in the Atlantic to support operationally the campaign against German U-boats, but it was not dependent on overseas bases for logistic support. In the Pacific, meanwhile, the vast distances, combined with a U.S. wartime strategy centered on naval, air, and amphibious forces, entailed the creation of a complex and extended islands-infrastructure of supply depots, ammunition depots, ship repair facilities, and large, fixed drydocks.

Those patterns extended into the buildup of U.S. naval power during the containment era. Irrespective of the convenience of such U.S. naval facilities as those in Spain and Greece, the Atlantic and Mediterranean naval posture of the United States was built upon the combat logistic support and ship repair provided either by deployed tenders and floating drydocks or by foreign shipyards. Indeed, U.S. fleets in the Atlantic and Mediterranean became almost totally dependent upon fast combat stores ships (AFSs), fast combat support ships (AOFs), fleet oilers (AOs) and ammunition ships (AFs), and aircraft of the Military Airlift Command. When in 1981 a fire laid up one of the AFSs for a considerable period of time, and a second AFS was in the midst of an extended overhaul, the Navy was forced to resort to the following measures: (1) convert an aged refrigerator ship, an AF, to an AFS; (2) purchase several AFSs from the British; (3) charter a large, fast container ship to shuttle between the Navy's depot at Bayonne, New Jersey, and the Mediterranean Sea; and (4) invent a phased maintenance system for the AFSs that eliminated the requirement for extended overhauls of these rarest of vessels. Every bit of support for the U.S. Sixth Fleet moves to its combatant ships through the Strait of Gibraltar and is delivered via underway replenishment, or arrives in the Mediterranean on MAC aircraft and is delivered by similar means.

In the Pacific, meanwhile, the legacy of the wartime base structure was emphasized and expanded by the demands of new conflicts, first in Korea and then in Vietnam. Moreover, in the 1960s the decision by the United States to move into the power vacuum left by the departure of residual British forces "east of Suez" substantially enhanced the effects of the distances involved. The briefings given to visitors to the U.S. Pacific Command have never failed to stress that the command's area of responsibility, embracing the Pacific and Indian oceans, spans more than 70 percent of the world's ocean waters. It takes a carrier task force eleven days to sail from San Diego to the former Subic Bay base in the Philippines, and another six days to reach an operating location in the Indian Ocean.

In short, in the Pacific, ships go into port in order to replenish. In the Eastern Atlantic and the Mediterranean, ships get underway in order to replenish. This is somewhat of an oversimplification, in that the United States does operate combat logistics support forces in the Pacific as well. Yet it makes the point of relative dependence, in one theater upon overseas bases and in the other upon a mobile support force.

How, then, will the CNO of the mid–1990s cope with a loss of U.S. bases in the Western Pacific? He may well be forced to the recognition that the United States can dispense with supply docks, ammunition depots, ship repair facilities, and graving docks overseas by introducing into its naval order of battle the following additional vessels: three AFSs, two AOs, two AFs, and four tenders or repair ships. Needed as well would be several shuttle ships: large, fast merchant vessels to haul "fill" materiel from Hawaii and the U.S. West Coast and deliver it to AFSs in the Western Pacific and Indian Ocean.

The CNO may not be able to obtain those compensating resources from the constrained and fought-over defense budget. Even should he be successful, he will still face a related problem, which is that part of the Pacific Fleet support will have to move by air. The airfields of destination may well have to be commercial ones, which could be denied to fleet commanders in a given crisis. Another problem will be the loss of training and maneuver areas, which will have to be found elsewhere, lest a price be paid in readiness. Those, of course, are problems that will be shared, in one measure or another, by all the U.S. military services in the retrenchment from forward positions.

Reserve Forces

Reserves are a complex subject for the Navy. It is difficult to man reserve ships. Each such vessel requires a large active-duty crew, and it is problematic to deploy reserve ships away from their homeports for more than two weeks without a reserve call-up, because of the obvious limitations on reserves on active duty. A similar problem does not apply to naval aviation units. For years the Navy has used reserve crews on P-3s and in airlift squadrons, and has done so with great success.

The CNO will have to decide how he will effectively incorporate the twenty-eight to thirty-four FF1052-class frigates into the reserve force. This component of the reserve program will absorb substantial numbers of active-duty personnel. It may be difficult to keep these ships employed in a useful way while not further burdening the already overworked active-duty force.

THE LIKELY NAVAL POSTURE IN THE MID–1990s

The United States Navy forces of 1996, based on the preceding projections, are shown in Table 4.1. It is a 450-ship navy manned by 490,000 personnel. There will need to be trade-offs if the United States loses overseas bases; in that case, the additional combat logistics force ships required, if they cannot be supported within the extant operations and maintenance budget, will have to be procured at the expense of other functional categories. In other words, this naval force will be an exercise in the art of the possible.

Table 4.1
The United States Navy of the Mid-1990s

Aircraft carriers (deployable)	11
Surface combatants	160
Attack submarines	75
T-AGOS ships	23
Amphibious ships	50
Maritime pre-positioning ships	13
Combat logistics force ships	60
Mine warfare ships	19
Other	15
Ballistic missile submarines	18
Strategic support ships	6
Total Ships	**450**
Maritime patrol air squadrons	18
Carrier-based fighter aircraft	420
Carrier-based attack aircraft	400
Personnel end strength	490,000

In general, this projected naval force would seem to fit within the envelope prescribed by the chairman of the Joint Chiefs of Staff and the secretary of defense. It should be capable of performing the roles and missions assigned to it. Should it be pared down below these levels, however, the United States may be placed into a position of relearning some of the lessons absorbed by the British in the Falklands conflict, about the penalties of self-denial for a maritime power.

Those lessons are both clear and instructive. While the Royal Navy's decline into quasi-obscurity had been the consequence not only of economic decisions, but also of the British equivalent of savage struggle among the military services, the effect of the conflict was to aggravate the economic conditions that prompted the decline. Without question, the decision by the Argentine government to invade the Falklands was motivated in large part by the perception that British naval capabilities had sagged to the point where the government would hesitate to mount a defense of interests some 8,000 miles remote from the United Kingdom. The junta in Buenos Aires miscalculated. The cost of that miscalculation for the British was great; it exceeded all the treasure London had saved by withdrawing forces from east of Suez and from Malta, and from decommissioning British aircraft carriers and withdrawing the Royal Navy from the Mediterranean.

In Britain's case the expensive lesson in lives and treasure was learned after the fact of retrenchment in the interest of economy. In the U.S. context, perhaps Saddam Hussein will be remembered, if not commemorated, in future history books as the leader whose miscalculated challenge served as a warning. The Gulf War may have arrested a precipitous decline, prodded by economics and a comfortable view of the global future, in the nation's wherewithal to safeguard its interests—particularly its vital interests as a maritime trading nation, ever more reliant on an interdependent world economy.

If this warning is heard, hard factors of economy and budget will nonetheless obtrude. They impose on the nation's civilian and military leadership the task of constructing a truly balanced force posture within constrained resources—a posture that preserves and hones the means of needed defense, while sacrificing those forces, systems, and concepts that no longer are vital, relevant, and affordable. From the military side of the U.S. defense establishment, that task demands a spirit of "jointness" even stronger than displayed in Desert Storm.

5

Tactical Air Forces for the Future

Gen. John L. Piotrowski, USAF (Ret.)

The Gulf War showed yet again that in the modern era tactical air power is virtually synonymous with the projection of military power. By design, shaped and honed by a half-century of experience, tactical aircraft make up the spearhead of rapid deployment, with the inherent capability of immediate engagement upon arrival at the target destination. That capability has been dramatically boosted by technological advances in weaponry and in the electronic "eyes and ears of the battlefield" that played such a key role in Operation Desert Storm.

Tactical air forces are embedded in three U.S. military services: the Air Force, the Navy and the Marine Corps. The United States Army commands an aerial capability of its own in a formidable force of attack helicopters, effective in the close air support of ground warfare and other missions, as will be brought out below. Still, attack helicopters have yet to achieve the needed speed, range, firepower, and survivability for coping with the fuller spectrum of tactical missions.

The United States Navy's tactical air arm is an important factor in power projection. Aircraft launched from the decks of carriers have the advantage of flexible deployment from operating platforms not dependent on access to facilities on land. The speed and effectiveness of their deployment, however, are a function of the proximity of the given carrier task force or battle group to the target area, along with the distance of the military targets to be struck inland. The experience of past contingencies, Desert Storm included, has pointed to the synergistic combination of land- and sea-based tactical air power.

This synergism had already been graphically demonstrated in an earlier contingency, the punitive action by the United States against Libya in 1986.

When the decision was made to stage the attack, two U.S. carrier battle groups were in the Mediterranean, ready to be brought into action against Libyan terrorist-supporting installations in and around Tripoli and Bengazi. The National Command Authority determined that five targets, three in Tripoli and two in Bengazi, were to be assaulted. Attacking all those targets in a single, coordinated strike, with sufficient probability of the desired damage infliction, called for aircraft from a third carrier. The time needed to deploy such a carrier to the Mediterranean, however, meant complicating delays in the execution of the attack. Moreover, unscheduled departure of the carrier from Norfolk, Virginia, risked confirmation of ongoing rumors that a punitive U.S. strike was in the offing, thus giving Libya's strongman, Col. Muammar al-Qadaffy, time to alert and better employ his defensive forces. A second option was to conduct strikes against Libyan targets on successive evenings. This was rejected on the grounds of the high losses that might be suffered against an aroused and prepared adversary in the second night's attack. The optimal, and decided-upon, solution was to deploy F-111s from their bases in the United Kingdom to strike the three targets in and around Tripoli.

CONSTITUTION OF A SINGLE TACTICAL AIR FORCES COMMAND

The Libyan experience is directly relevant to the outcome of Desert Storm, because it helped set the stage for a historic step toward institutionalizing the synergism of U.S. tactical airpower. In 1986 the Joint Chiefs of Staff, under its chairman, Adm. William Crowe, decided that in any contingency operation, all of the air forces assigned to the commander-in-chief of a particular theater would be placed under the direction of a single Air Forces component commander. In Desert Storm this task was assigned by Gen. Norman Schwarzkopf, as Commander-in-Chief of the Central Command (CINCENT), to the Commander of the Central Air Forces (COMCENTAF), Lt. Gen. Charles A. "Chuck" Horner of the Air Force. As the Joint Force Air Component Command (JFACC), General Horner was responsible for melding and orchestrating the available tactical, strategic, and maritime air resources in support of the operational strategy set by the CINCENT in the close air-support, counter-air, interdiction, and airlift roles. The Gulf War thus represented the first major conflict in which all elements of U.S. airpower were directed by a single air forces commander acting under a theater commander-in-chief. This unprecedented arrangement in joint command, implemented with superb professionalism by those concerned, was a key element in the all-arms offensive so devastatingly carried forward in Desert Storm.

There were striking examples of the efficacy of the single air-tasking authority. The first blows in the air campaign of Desert Storm were struck by Army AH-64 Apache helicopters, led to their targets by Air Force HH-53 Pave Low special operations helicopters. Those targets were three forward-deployed Iraqi early-warning radars. Helicopters were the weapons of choice for this mission because they could approach undetected beneath the beams of the radars by exercising "map of the earth" tactics until within firing range, whereupon the Apaches opened lethal fire with highly accurate Hellfire missiles and 30 mm cannon. Once the radars were taken out, large numbers of fixed-wing, "non-stealthy" U.S. and coalition aircraft could pass undetected through the gap in the Iraqi air defenses.

Offhand, the selection of Army helicopters to open an air campaign may seem unusual, especially coming from General Horner, a career fighter pilot. Yet it was a sound gambit, and typified the all-assets approach and absence of service parochialism that made the air campaign in Desert Storm such an astounding success. The efficacy of the "single tasking authority" was also reflected in the fact that not a single midair collision marred the campaign, notwithstanding the staggering density and diversity of aircraft over the battlefield, in constant day and night operations. The success of the single air command thus towers among the lessons of Desert Storm. Perhaps in the future that lesson should be applied to ground operations as well.

THE LEGACY OF CENTRAL COMMAND

Special note should be made of another background factor that bore directly on the outcome of Desert Storm. The air campaign was a study in excellence of preparation, planning, and execution. In that preparation and planning, however, General Schwarzkopf and his command were able to draw upon organization, resources, and a general body of knowledge relevant to the contingency that had been built up over the course of the previous decade.

The storming of the U.S. embassy in Teheran in 1978 and the agonies of the subsequent protracted hostage crisis, along with the more broadly perceived need for U.S. military capabilities in the face of continuing turmoil in the Middle East, led the Carter Administration to establish a Rapid Deployment Joint Task Force (RDJTF), under the initial command of Lt. Gen. P. X. Kelley of the Marine Corps. The forces assigned to the RDJTF were the XVIII Airborne Corps, the 9th Air Force, and an unspecified Navy component. The area of responsibility of this joint force encompassed nineteen nations, including Egypt, the East African states down to Kenya; Saudi Arabia and the neighboring states on the Arabian Peninsula; and Iraq, Iran, Pakistan, and Afghanistan. The focal points of concern, however, quickly became the confronting states of Iran and Iraq.

In 1983 the RDJTF was elevated to unified command status as the Central Command (CENTCOM). The 9th Air Force became Central Air Forces (CENTAF), with additional units assigned. The Third Army was reborn as the Army Central Command (ARCENT) as the land component disposing over XVIII Corps and the Central Marines (MARCENT), and the Navy "dual-hatted" an admiral in the Pacific Command in Hawaii as the commander of the Central Navy (NAVCENT), but assigned him no specific forces. Those changes came shortly after the start of the Iraq-Iran war, which sharpened the focus on that part of the theater and its potential contingency demands. Gen. Charles A. Gabriel, then Air Force chief of staff, called for an Air Force-wide, high-level review of the Central Air Force (CENTAF) air campaign plans, and Army Chief of Staff Edward C. "Shy" Meyer summoned Army corps commanders to Fort Leavenworth for a similar review of ground campaign plans.

As the 9th Air Force/CENTAF commander from 1982 to 1985, I directed the establishment of a war room and the amassing of comprehensive data relating to potential adversary aircraft and interdiction targets, with the available target photographs. Huge stocks of Air Force vehicles, medical supplies, jet fuel, air munitions, and water were pre-positioned in and around the Arabian Peninsula to reduce the time needed for deployment of forces and their equipment to the area. Fragmentary orders for the first several days of an air campaign were prepared and exercised, with the recognition that although no prepared plan might precisely fit an arising contingency, nevertheless a well-conceived plan would encompass a majority of the critical targets to be struck in the initial forty-eight to ninety-six hours of conflict. CENTAF headquarters and the assigned forces were directed to be prepared to deploy rapidly, engage immediately upon arrival, prevail quickly in the air war, interdict enemy ground forces until the 3rd Army could get into position, and then wage the AirLand campaign forged by the Central Command.

Such planning was continually upgraded and refined in subsequent years. Meanwhile, the deployment of AWACS aircraft to Saudi Arabia against the backdrop of the Iraq-Iran war, and the later U.S. naval involvement in the Persian Gulf in 1988–89, gave the commanders of CINCENT and COMCENTAF, and their staffs, ample opportunity for regular visits to the regional states. Surveys were undertaken of military bases in Oman, Bahrain, Saudi Arabia, Qatar, and the United Arab Emirates.

Moreover, contrary to early dire predictions in the U.S. press about the extreme difficulties awaiting U.S. forces and their equipment in desert warfare, those forces were well prepared. As generals Donn Starry and John Woodmansee brought out in Chapters 2 and 3, the United States Army armored units had been well trained in desert warfare at the NTC. In virtually every summer after 1981, elements of the Central Command's air and land forces were deployed to and conducted exercises in Jordan, Egypt, Oman, Somalia, and other regional states. Those deployments were timed for the months of July and August to ensure that personnel and equipment were "checked out" in the most demanding climatic conditions. For several years before Desert Shield, the Royal Saudi Air Force (RSAF) operated F-15 aircraft under the supervision of the U.S. Military Training Mission, and Egyptian pilots were flying F-16s. Furthermore, the U.S. Middle East Force, operating from Bahrain, had sailed the Persian Gulf for decades. Elements of CENTAF flew Airborne Warning and Control System aircraft (AWACS) from Riyadh and Dhahran continuously after October 1980.

Thus, when Desert Storm was launched on January 16, 1991, the campaign benefited not only from some five prior months of buildup and operational planning, but more meaningfully from almost a decade of relevant military organization, accumulated knowledge of the region, its military forces and targets, prepositioning of equipment, and training of U.S. forces. Above all, Desert Storm profited from detailed and continuously updated contingency planning that basically needed only the refinements of the final operations plan. However, the last statement is not intended to detract in the least from the brilliance of that plan and the manner in which it was executed.

A second and related point is that Desert Storm speaks directly to the success of a regional command: CENTCOM. That relationship of success is worth pondering, at a time when proposals are being discussed, in the context of the Base Force concept, for "simplifying" the present structure of twelve unified and specified commands to essentially four combatant commands. These would cover the (extended) Atlantic and Pacific theaters, strategic forces, and "contingency forces," plus two supporting commands involving transportation and space activities. The scheme symptomizes the old, facile notion—call it "organizational disease"—that equates centralization with cost savings and greater efficiency. The only "savings" to be effected by the proposed scheme would be in the billets for several flag officers and their personal staffs. The penalties would be a vast broadening of command areas of responsibility, and thereby an inevitable diffusion of the kind of focused attention, surveillance, and planning that a command such as CENTCOM has been able to devote to a more circumscribed but critical geographical region.

The more general lesson to be learned is that success was the consequence of preparedness. The Gulf War featured the first clear-cut military victory for the United States in a major regional conflict since World War II, because it was the first such conflict that the nation was prepared not only to wage but also to press to a military conclusion. I will return to this point later in this chapter.

"CAUTIONING" LESSONS OF THE GULF WAR

The air campaign in Desert Storm has been the subject of intense study, with undoubtedly more still to come. In assessing its implications for future contingencies, however, care must be exercised in identifying some of the unique circumstances—call them "fortuitous factors"—that facilitated the U.S. military action in this case, but may not apply in future contexts.

First there is the Soviet factor. Throughout the crisis triggered by the Iraqi invasion of Kuwait, the Gorbachev regime, from its initial agreement to UN economic sanctions against Iraq to its last-ditch effort to avert the implementation of military sanctions, displayed an ambiguous posture, albeit one generally favorable to the objectives of the United States. The reasons and motives behind the Soviet position can only be speculated about. In the main, however, they seemed related to the Soviet internal crisis and power struggle. President Gorbachev obviously did not want to jeopardize his ongoing policy of accommodation with the West, which was needed to attract Western capital and other assistance for relieving the Soviet Union's economic plight. At the same time, however, Gorbachev needed to placate the Soviet military, which had been the main source of arms, supplies, training, and advice for Saddam Hussein's military forces during the lengthy Soviet-Iraqi alliance relationship.

Whatever the motivations behind the Soviet stance, it afforded important leeway for U.S. military assets to be brought to bear in the Persian Gulf, particularly assets from the European theater tied to the NATO commitment. A question for any future contingency is whether the same leeway will be available. But another question arises: Given the deep reductions projected in the U.S. force presence in Europe, what will be the extent of those transferable assets in the future?

The decision by the Saudi government to open its territory to U.S. and coalition forces enabled the largest military buildup since World War II. Even then, the buildup was agonizingly slow. Moreover, Saddam Hussein was an obliging adversary, at least in permitting time for the buildup. Had the Iraqi forces continued their armored thrust beyond Kuwait and down toward the Strait of Hormuz, the U.S. land-based aircraft would have had to operate at best from one (woefully inadequate) airfield in Egypt, three airbases in Oman, and perhaps a base in Turkey. Such a dispersal over bare-boned facilities would have substantially handicapped the U.S. military response. Furthermore, aircraft carriers and other naval vessels would have been forced, at least at the outset, to wage battle from a greater distance, beyond the Strait of Hormuz. As it was, even from proximate and reasonably secured Persian Gulf waters, carrier-based air contributed less than 15 percent of the sorties over Iraq and Kuwait.

In short, Desert Storm provides a modern textbook on the optimal conduct of an air campaign as the spearhead of an all-arms offensive—in strategy, tactics, command and control, high-tech weapons, logistical support, and surgical application of airpower. While studying that textbook, however, military planners will have to question whether similarly optimal conditions for waging such a campaign will be available in future contingencies.

PROJECTED TACTICAL AIR FORCES

The future structure and size of the United States Air Force tactical forces have been projected by the Department of Defense in its Base Force concept, first made public on the very eve of the Persian Gulf crisis in early August 1990 and then elaborated upon more explicitly in the Defense Department's submission to Congress of its fiscal year 1992–93 budget. In essence, the projection, as summarized in Table 5.1, calls for a paring-down of USAF tactical forces to between 24 and 27 air wings by 1995.

Even the figures reflected in Table 5.1 are not a reliable guide to the future, because more drastic cuts are being bandied about in the continuing budget

Tactical Air Forces for the Future

Table 5.1
Projected United States Air Force Tactical Air Forces under the Base Force Concept

Types of Forces	Requirements
Atlantic Forces Forward Deployed	3-5 tactical fighter wings
Atlantic Forces Conus based	2 tactical fighter wings (active) 9 tactical fighter wings
Pacific Forces Forward Deployed	3-4 tactical fighter wings
Contingency Forces Conus based	7 tactical fighter wings plus SOF/counter-terrorist capabilities

debate. In general there is profound danger that the wrong questions are being addressed in that debate.

The real issue at hand is not reductions in force, which have been a fact of life since 1986, but rather what essential force levels are needed to underwrite long-range U.S. global interests and the national security. Historically, the twentieth century has witnessed deep, unbridled U.S. force reductions after each conflict in which the nation was embroiled—a trend that would be reversed only in stark contemplation of the next military involvement. The penalty in each case was expensive crash development, modernization, and production, as well as loss in lives of poorly trained forces. This quasi-cyclical pattern of defense cuts and buildups occurred after World War I, World War II, Korea, and Vietnam.

Desert Storm proved an exception to the pattern, but for unusual reasons. Somewhat out of character, the U.S. defense build-up in the early 1980s came in response to a number of stimuli rather than a single threat: the Iran hostage crisis, amid increasing turbulence in Southwest Asia; the Soviet invasion of Afghanistan; the military embarrassment suffered by the United States in Lebanon; and rapid advances in Soviet strategic, tactical, and naval weapons systems. Without the vision of President Carter to develop the F-117 and create the Rapid Deployment Force, and the vision of President Reagan to rebuild and rearm the U.S. forces, Desert Storm would have had a far more sobering result.

Yet in the aftermath of the victory in the Gulf War, perhaps to a large extent in the comforting afterglow of that victory, the pattern is being repeated. Again the issue before the nation is not, or should not be, framed in the question: How deeply and/or by what percentages should we cut our military wherewithal? Rather the question is: Is there an objective force level based on national security interests? Or should the nation's defense again be consigned to a fiscal free-fall, until the next threat emerges on the horizon?

From the vantage point of an Air Force planner, the projected cuts penetrate beyond needed muscle into the bone and marrow of required resources. It is useful, first of all, to make some correlations between the numbers of land-based tactical aircraft that were employed in Desert Storm and the projections under the Base Force concept. As of this writing, the precise numbers have not been publicly released, but some approximations can be made. According to unofficial reports, some 2,600 aircraft of the United States and its coalition partners participated in the Desert Storm campaign. Of this total, between 250 and 300 were allied aircraft and another 570 or so represented naval aviation, operating from carriers in the Persian Gulf, North Arabian Sea, and Red Sea. In addition, the Marine Corps had roughly 230 fixed-wing aircraft ashore. Those (admittedly broad) estimates suggest that between 1,500 and 1,550 land-based Air Force aircraft were deployed. Subtracting from this number 250 airlift, AWACS, JSTARS, and other highly specialized aircraft, we arrive at an estimate of 1,250 to 1,300 USAF tactical fighters and reconnaissance planes operating under the command of CENTAF during all phases of the air battle.

That estimate is not surprising in light of the fact that major elements of nineteen active tactical fighter/reconnaissance wings, and of thirty-four Air National Guard and Reserve fighter/reconnaissance squadrons, were deployed to the Persian Gulf. "Major elements" connote at least two squadrons of a tactical fighter wing, or approximately 75 percent of squadron strength in the case of an Air National Guard or Reserve squadron. There are several reasons why full wings tend not to be deployed in a contingency. For one, aircraft undergoing modification or repair at deployment time may take weeks to be returned to operating status. Also, in the normal pattern of personnel turnover as a consequence of attrition and reassignment, the required number of combat-ready crews may not be available. It generally takes up to three months to raise a pilot just arrived from an F-16 basic course to the level of combat proficiency demanded by an operation like Desert Storm. "Red Flag," or realistic, combat training, to which General Horner credited the exceptional performance of the CENTAF aircrews, takes an additional six to nine months. Lastly, the shortfalls in funding for spare parts over the previous six years imposed limits on combat sortie rates.

In all, the number of land-based tactical aircraft that were deployed in Desert Storm would seem to exceed the levels that would be available, under the projections of the Base Force concept, for commitment to future contingencies comparable in intensity to the Gulf War. On the assumption that a minimum of five wings would be required for basic fighter entry-training, and that at least two wings assigned to the European and Pacific theaters would have to remain in place, only seventeen wings envisioned under the base force—amounting to some 83 percent of the size of the force used in Desert Storm—would be available for contingency commitment.

One can only speculate about what this implies for the conduct of future

Tactical Air Forces for the Future

contingency operations. Clearly, however, it means that a theater commander would not only have fewer capabilities with which to plan and execute, but also commensurately more limited options. Proper allocation of air power is one of the more difficult tasks confronting a theater command. The task is not so demanding when enough air assets are available, as in Desert Storm, to cover all important missions and targets—especially against an enemy who chooses, for the most part, to keep his aircraft on the ground. With less air power available, more difficult allocation choices are imposed. More than likely, this would place an even higher priority on achievement of air superiority, to ensure that enemy aircraft are not able to strike at rear areas or forward-deployed forces. By the same token, interdiction and close support missions would have less claim on the available sorties. This would inevitably translate into higher casualties for ground forces once they were engaged.

Lastly, future conflicts more than likely will involve, as in Desert Storm, ballistic missile attacks against allied population and industrial centers. Hence, again as in Desert Storm, the combatant commander-in-chief will have to dedicate a significant percentage of his interdiction sorties against mobile ballistic missile targets.

DESERT STORM LESSONS FOR TACTICAL AIR SYSTEMS

Beyond force structure issues, Desert Storm illuminated requirements for weapons systems improvements and future systems. For example, the F-117 stealth fighter performed as expected in nighttime missions. Reportedly, in the critical first two days of the air campaign, the F-117 accounted for slightly more than 2 percent of the total sorties flown, but some 30 percent of the targets struck. It was the only aircraft that attacked heavily defended targets in Baghdad. Its use was limited to nighttime, however, because while the F-117 has excellent stealth characteristics, its performance and agility are at the low end of the tactical fighter scale, making it extremely vulnerable to optically guided air defenses. The issue of stealth versus performance criteria will be taken up again later in this chapter.

Such operational limitations notwithstanding, the suppression of enemy air defenses was brilliantly executed at the outset of battle through the combined effect of F-117s, of the initial strike by an all-helicopter force already described, and of the Tomahawk cruise missiles fired from naval vessels. Those opening sorties were immediately followed up by attacks with more conventional aircraft, supported by F-4G Wild Weasel and EF-111 Electronic Counter-Measure (ECM) planes to disrupt and destroy Iraqi defensive systems.

Precision-guided weapons clearly were the stars of the air interdiction campaign. Still, the celebration of their success should be tempered by recognition of the favorable operational conditions for their use, notably complete air superiority and early defense suppression. The drawback of precision-guided weapons is that they require the delivering aircraft to fly almost directly over the target and thus into heavily defended airspace. Stealth may be part of the answer to that problem, but in the longer term the U.S. inventory of stealth capabilities will continue to be relatively modest, largely limited to nighttime operations, and subject to countermeasures. Needed as well are air-delivered standoff weapons with precision comparable to that of laser-guided bombs.

Development of such standoff weapons, long desired, has been blocked in the past by their complexity and expense. That is now changed with the fielding of the space-based Global Positioning System (GPS), which provides positional accuracies of 15 m (49 ft.) in three axes, thus offering precision all the way to the target. For example, with GPS guidance as their sole navigational capability, standoff weapons, irrespective of the range over which they are delivered, can impact within 15 m of their designated impact point. This opens up targets such as airfield ramps, military headquarters, aircraft shelters, bridges, large buildings, port facilities, and storage areas. Moreover, GPS does not require such support systems as terrain contour-mapping or digital scene-matching techniques in the terminal guidance phase. Stand-off ranges of 100–200 nautical miles are desirable; shorter ranges of 50–75 nautical miles would enable a "package" of tactical aircraft to "walk their way" through heavily defended areas to a priority target, day or night. The adaptation of cluster munition warheads to stand-off weapons would enlarge their target set to include smaller and "soft" targets such as radars, surface-to-air missiles, and troop encampments. Such standoff weapons would prove far less costly than cruise missiles.

It can safely be assumed that all aspects of the Gulf War have been assiduously studied in Moscow and in the capitals of other military-industrial powers. Especially given the rapid spread of technology, it can be further stated that stealth will not remain a U.S. monopoly for long. On the defense side of the equation, current U.S. radar systems are woefully inadequate in their ability to detect, track, and support the engagement of aircraft that are "stealthy" in radar and infrared profile. A possible near-term "fix" is to improve the radar sensitivity of AWACS to the point where it can easily detect low Radar Cross-Section (RCS) targets at sufficient distance to support an AWACS-controlled intercept. In the longer term, however, a major radar/sensor development program is needed in order to detect, track, and support the engagement of stealthy air vehicles, in the defense of both the United States itself and U.S. forces deployed overseas. A space system with global coverage may provide the best answer.

Also in the context of space, it is noteworthy that the Soviet Union and later Russia launched several satellites after Desert Shield was put in motion on August 7, 1991, and that the orbits of those apparent surveillance satellites were adjusted periodically to permit maximum coverage of the Middle East area. It must be assumed that not only did the Russians thereby gain incisive insights into all aspects of the U.S. combined arms operations, but that they also detected the preparations for General Schwarzkopf's "Hail Mary" maneuver to kick off the ground campaign. The Soviets either did not share that intelligence with the Iraqis or failed to do so in time; otherwise the flanking thrust, which depended on surprise, might have proven far more difficult, certainly at a higher price in casualties.

There are broader implications to be pondered with respect to the significance of space capabilities for terrestrial combat. The Soviets demonstrated once again their ability to augment their space surveillance assets rapidly in response to crisis demand. The United States could thus find itself at a decisive disadvantage in future contingencies involving clients of the Russian Federation, let alone in any direct confrontation with Russian forces. The prospect calls for a concerted effort by the United States to field operational space surveillance systems that are directly taskable by, and report to, the theater commander.

STEALTH VERSUS PERFORMANCE IN U.S. AIRCRAFT

The issue of stealth, touched upon in the context of the F-117's performance in Desert Storm, reflects significantly on the question of optimal aircraft design for the future. Incorporation of stealth characteristics clearly enhances the survivability of an aircraft. Still, notwithstanding its dramatic advances, stealth is not the only prop of survivability. A sensitive balance needs to be maintained in aircraft design between stealth characteristics, on the one hand, and the high-performance criteria of agility, speed, range, and firepower, on the other.

Such a balance bears not only on the makeup of tactical airpower and the optimal distribution of mission coverage in the near term, but also on hedging against the future. Generally speaking, the overall performance of an aircraft tends to be degraded only gradually by time and adversary aircraft advances. By contrast, stealth typifies a stride in technology that, however significant, can be negated quickly and dramatically by breakthroughs in counter-capabilities. History documents that no technological advance has gone unchallenged for long.

Therefore, while stealth is an important consideration in new aircraft design, it should not be allowed to dominate. The emphasis must continue to be on high-performance criteria; otherwise the United States may find itself dependent on an inventory of aircraft that, while impressive in their own right, would only be able to cover limited parts of the missions spectrum and would face an uncertain future, such as the F-117 fighter and B-2 bomber. Perhaps, with the advent of the F-22, a fighter design is on the verge of maximizing both performance and stealth without compromising either. However, this optimal blend has yet to be demonstrably made applicable to aircraft assigned to the ground-attack role, where payload (i.e., external carriage) remains a major performance factor.

However, the perceived equation of effective payload for ground attack with external carriage may have to be modified once the lessons of Desert Storm are fully digested. It may turn out, for example, that two precision-guided 2,000-pound bombs carried in the interior of an aircraft provide greater effectiveness than twelve 500-pound "dumb" bombs carried externally. However, such exceptions as area denial weapons and sensor-fused anti-tank cluster munitions do yield greater sortie effectiveness when carried in large numbers externally. Moreover, some specialized munitions, such as the 12.5-foot-deep penetrating bomb used late in the campaign to take out a buried command center, are not compatible with internal carriage by aircraft.

FUTURE MAKE-UP OF TACTICAL AIR FORCES

Even casual considerations of the projection forces that will make up the heart of America's future military posture suggest that tactical air power is expected to provide the heavy firepower needed to limit the enemy's force deployments to the forward edge of battle and to halt and destroy his armored formations—as tactical air did in Desert Storm. While striking armor and attacking second-echelon forces, tactical air power must also maintain air superiority, provide close support to engaged land forces, and furnish reconnaissance to the various elements of command.

Those roles and missions call for at least two types of tactical aircraft for the forces forward-deployed in each theater: first, a high-performance air-superiority fighter, incorporating as much stealth as possible, and second, a high-performance, day-night, all-weather ground attack aircraft to perform both battlefield interdiction and close air support missions.

Ideally two additional aircraft types should be theater based as well: deep interdiction aircraft (such as the F-15E) and a very stealthy fighter-bomber (such as the F-117) to add penetrating striking power at the outset of battle, concentrating on such targets as command, control, and communications systems; surface-to-air missile systems; airfields; and ballistic missile launchers. Given their relatively high cost, however, such aircraft are likely to be procured in modest numbers at best. They therefore seem destined to be based in the continental United States, ready to be deployed rapidly to contingency areas as the need arises. In addition, as the EF-111s and F-4G Wild Weasels demonstrated in Desert Storm, a force of ECM and hunter-killer aircraft would greatly reduce attrition from penetrating aircraft. Yet such special-purpose planes are not likely to survive the budget axe. Their loss will have to be compensated by the provision of high-performance ECM systems to tactical fighter/reconnaissance aircraft.

On the subject of aircraft types, design, and "special purpose," a word of warning is in order concerning the configuration of aircraft for the mission of close air support to ground forces. The mission is critical, even indispensable; the question is whether it can best be served by an aircraft specifically (let alone exclusively) addressed to it. That question is underscored by the A-10 interdiction fighter.

The A-10 was specifically designed for close air support of ground operations. Arguably, that design was inspired not only by operational purpose, but also by the "political" (interservice) motive of reassuring Army commanders that the Air Force would not place its own, putatively "glamorous" missions of air-to-air battle above the interests of the combined-arms campaign. The notion that

Tactical Air Forces for the Future 83

such reassurance is needed rests on sheer fiction. Moreover, it loses all credibility in the all-arms, joint command structure described earlier, in which the theater commander, through his air component commander, decides how all available air assets may best be allocated over the full spectrum of missions.

In any event, whatever the intent behind it, the A-10, although a fine aircraft within the limits of its mission (and the emphasis is on "limits"), is of little avail even in the interdiction role because of its lack of penetration capability in the face of viable enemy air defenses. In a high-intensity threat environment, the aircraft cannot hope to survive beyond the Forward Line of Troops (FLOT). Specifically designed for close air support, in practice it has actually proven to be counter-productive (and also expensive) in support of ground operations.

The shortcomings of the A-10 became well recognized in the context of the AirLand Battle Doctrine embraced over the past decade. The shortcomings were largely obscured in the "permissive environment" of Desert Storm—specifically the tens of kilometers of air space beyond the Kuwait-Saudi border that were carved out once the forward-deployed Iraqi radars and SAMs were destroyed and the Iraq forward echelons had been pounded for several days by B-52s and high-performance fighter aircraft. In this environment, the Wart Hogs, as the A-10s are affectionately dubbed by their pilots, performed superbly, destroying large numbers of Iraqi tanks, armored vehicles, trucks, and artillery pieces with their 30 mm Gatling guns and Infrared Imaging Maverick missiles. They were aided by the tactic of not flying below 8,000 feet while engaging targets, thus minimizing the risk from antiair artillery fire.

The early performance of the A-10s was so impressive, in fact, that the aircraft were subsequently tasked to go after some of the same targets among the Iraqi Republican Guards divisions dug in beyond the Iraq-Kuwait border. Almost immediately, however, the A-10s ran into difficulty in the face of stronger antiaircraft fire. Two A-10s were shot down; one bullet-riddled aircraft made it back to the base. Thereupon, the A-10s were shifted back to safer missions, while high-performance fighters and high-flying B-52s were pitted against the Republican Guards.

In essence, the Desert Storm experience confirmed that A-10s can only be employed in a close air support role over engaged forces, darting across the line to take out targets before quickly returning to safer skies, or in a permissive interdiction environment, which is rarely obtained in modern combat. Those inherent shortcomings are likely to become ever more conspicuous in the ongoing shift toward light, mobile ground forces, in which airpower must make up for reductions in artillery and armor.

In terms of cost and combat effectiveness, a better alternative to the A-10 is the F-16/A-16 swing fighter. That aircraft is unparalleled in the air-to-ground role, as well as flexibly adaptable to a broader spread of missions. Quick and agile, and equipped with Low Altitude Navigation and Targeting Infra-Red Night system (LANTIRN), the F-16 is a day-night penetrator capable of near-perfect precision with a variety of weapons. If provided with a reconnaissance pod, or "recce pod," it can function as a creditable in-theater, low-altitude, under-weather reconnaissance platform. Devastatingly capable in close air support, it also excels in the air-to-air role, in point defense if needed, and in defending itself while penetrating hostile air space.

True, the F-16 is slated to be phased out of production in fiscal 1993. Still, there is a sufficient inventory of F-16s extant, or being produced for modification to the A-16 or F/A-16 configuration, to replace all A-10s now committed to the close air support role. Moreover, foreign sales are likely to keep the F-16 production line open for some time, holding out the chance for additional procurement of the aircraft if fiscal constraints ease.

INADEQUACY OF PROJECTED TACTICAL AIR FORCES

Against the background of the "generic" mission and the aircraft requirements outlined above, let us now turn again to the tactical air forces structure proposed under the base force concept.

Over the past decades, projections of force requirements were rationalized in terms of "the threat," as well as in terms of what theater commanders-in-chief would want in order to ensure a reasonable chance of victory—a projection basis referred to as "minimum risk or unconstrained force." Projections thus made yielded a requirement for approximately a hundred land-based operational tactical fighter wings. It was recognized that such force levels, while desirable, were unrealistic. They were then pared down to what was euphemistically termed the "prudent force level"—a number approaching sixty tactical fighter wings. Finally, constraints of budget were applied, reducing the number of land-based tactical fighter forces, both active and reserve, to a still-respectable forty wings. That number never has been attained; over the course of the past twenty years, the maximum number of operational tactical fighter wings was slightly over thirty-five, with a third of them obsolescent.

Even at the height of the U.S.-Soviet confrontation, any calculation of "the threat," no matter how carefully and objectively it was drawn up, was always subject to varying interpretations and controversy. In practical terms, therefore, it proved to be a useful basis for developing force levels and defending them through the programming and budgetary process. At the present juncture of confusion about the true state of "threatening" Russian military capabilities, a generally more relaxed view—whether warranted or not in a longer-range strategic perspective—is taken regarding Russian military intentions. This makes calculation of "the threat" even less persuasive as a force-sizing tool. At the same time, the composite picture of "new" threats, heralded by the Iraqi challenge in the Gulf War, is indistinct at best.

An alternative way of projecting and justifying tactical air force requirements is by means of "level of effort." The question addressed, for example, is: What level of effort—measured in numbers of sorties, which translate into numbers of aircraft—is required to support an engaged division of ground forces by providing close support at the Forward Edge of the Battle Area (FEBA), interdicting to slow and cripple reinforcements en route to the battle and achieving air superiority to protect our troops from enemy air strikes? While such "level-of-effort" calculations can only be generalized, nonetheless they yield a useful means of projecting future force-level requirements for U.S. tactical air power.

Let us take the European theater first. One can calculate that in the initial phase of a conflict in Europe, at least a full wing of air-superiority fighters will be needed to protect from air attack a corps front and its supporting air bases, rear areas, and so on. Close support and battlefield air interdiction for the same corps will take all the sorties that can be generated from two wings of F-16s. This assumes that eighteen battalions are on the line, with nine held in reserve. Those two wings will generate approximately 576 sorties per day in the early days of a conflict, or four sorties per fighter—a high but not unrealistic expectation. This equates to 32 sorties engaged per battalion per day, or just over one sortie per hour; this would not be much air support in the European theater environment. Lastly, deep interdiction will take the full effort of an F-15E or F-111 wing. While there may be few U.S. ground forces deployed on NATO's Southern Flank, U.S. tactical air power nevertheless will continue to be needed for presence, stability, and reinforcement of the limited air resources of NATO allies in that region—perhaps increasingly so, considering the growing "southward" orientation of the NATO alliance.

There are, admittedly, many imponderables in the ongoing evolution of the European theater. They relate, on the one hand, to the residual Russian threat, as well as to the rumblings of new instabilities to the south of the continent and in Eastern Europe, already expressed in the bloody military conflict in Yugoslavia. They apply, on the other hand, to the willingness and ability of the NATO allies, particularly reunified Germany, to take up the slack of the withdrawing U.S. military power, especially air power, within a general "reconstitution strategy." Decisionmakers and defense planners in the alliance need to concern themselves not only with possible future contingencies, but also with the requirements of stability in transition, with emphasis on crisis management. A continued viable and visible U.S. military presence in Europe is essential to the maintenance of a modicum of stability on the continent, particularly in the face of virulent and unpredictable forces unleashed in the crumbling of the Soviet empire.

In light of those requirements, a reduction of the U.S. land-based tactical air forces in Europe to four wings, entailing a cut of more than 60 percent in current such force levels, looms as drastic and destabilizing. Five wings are believed by this writer to be the minimum needed to provide a viable force and ensure stability in the transition. Those five tactical wings should consist of one F-15C/D wing and one F-16 LANTIRN-equipped wing in Germany; one F-16 wing, along with a wing of F-111s or F-15Es, in Great Britain; and one wing of F-16s (partially LANTIRN-equipped) along the Southern Flank. Turkey would be the preferred location for this latter wing, but an acceptable alternative could be a main operating base in Italy, with rotational deployments to Turkey. Such a forward-deployed U.S. tactical air presence, in support of residual NATO land forces, would offer a modicum of stability/ensurance, especially for contingencies in which tactical air strike capabilities would have to play a leading role, and a safe "air envelope" for any NATO reconstitution strategy against a resurgent threat from the east.

Similar considerations apply to the Pacific theater. The vastness of this theater, and in the case of land-based tactical air forces, the remoteness of potential target areas from permanent or contingency U.S. bases in the region, makes distance a dominant criterion for U.S. power projection. A second, significant gauge for U.S. force sizing in the region relates to the prevalence of large, standing military forces, notably those of the Soviet Union, China, North Korea, Vietnam, India, and Pakistan.

Here again, the size of the residual U.S. military presence, combined with the relative U.S. ability to respond rapidly over long distances, dictates the framework for any viable U.S. posture and strategy intended to sustain stability and safeguard U.S. interests in the region. In terms of tactical air forces, the task calls for four wings: two F/A-16 wings based in Korea, and third F-16 wing in Northern Japan, plus one wing of F-15Es or F-111s in Okinawa.

It may be argued that some of the tactical fighter squadrons allocated to the Pacific theater could be based in Alaska, whence they might be deployed into the depths of the Pacific theater on receipt of strategic warning. While this may seem cost-effective, however, the Alaskan basing option suffers on several counts. First, from the vantage point of regional actors, it obviously lacks the stability-enhancing credibility of forward-deployed tokens of U.S. air power. Second, the option does not seem to be cost-effective at all, but rather expensive—at least so long as the United States can continue to persuade the Japanese and South Korean governments to host U.S. forward bases and share in their upkeep. Third, it would impose additional demands of "detouring" on U.S. airlift capabilities. Fourth, it would have an undesirable effect on training and conditioning. Alaskan winters may be comparable to climatic conditions that air crews could encounter, at times, in Korea or the northern Japanese islands, but they are hardly suitable for conditioning them to operate in and over the tropical rain forests of Southeast Asia.

BROADER QUESTIONS REGARDING OVERSEAS BASING

The issue of residual U.S. base rights in the Philippines leads to the larger question of U.S. access to overseas airbases. It is one thing to postulate the level of tactical air forces in a given theater, but quite another to project with any confidence that these forces will continue to be welcomed by our current allies in Europe and the Pacific. Moreover, even if they are accepted, the U.S. forces may not be able to train realistically, in the face of growing operational restrictions applying to usable airspace, noise abatement, and so on.

The political context of U.S. force presence, and bases, abroad has changed in line with shifts in overall threat perception. In the past decades of the Cold War there was little question about the long-range stability of forward basing, occasional disputes over "offset" arrangements and jurisdictional issues notwithstanding. In fact, in the past, contemplated withdrawals by the United States of forward-deployed forces and/or relinquishment of bases or facilities would send sharp tremors through alliances in both Europe and in Asia. Today, not only is the prospect of such withdrawals generally taken for granted, but the infrastructure for supporting even the residual U.S. forward deployments—that is, those bases and facilities that the United States needs and wants to maintain— is becoming ever more hostage to local politics. For example, a return to power by the Labour party in Great Britain could place into jeopardy, or at least seriously constrain, access by U.S. military aircraft to current bases in the United Kingdom. A comparable shift in political power in Germany could similarly put into question the future of the remaining bases in that nation from which the U.S. Air Force is operating.

Inasmuch as such political variables are in one measure or another beyond U.S. control, there is no confident answer to the question of future availability of forward bases, whether in Europe or in Asia. Clearly, however, those political uncertainties argue for a gradual, rather than precipitous, retrenchment of the U.S. military forces and supporting infrastructure from their present, forward-deployed positions. Sweeping unilateral withdrawals send all the wrong political signals. They tend to dishearten, and disadvantage, those political forces that continue to see reinsurance value in the remaining tokens of the U.S. military commitment, while encouraging the radical-pacifist forces, which envision a new world order in which military power has lost all relevance to security. A more gradual shift from forward-deployed power to a posture more reliant on projection of power from the United States also accords with military wisdom and allows some insurance against the uncertainties ahead.

THE NEEDS OF A "ROTATIONAL BASE"

The allocation of end-strengths to USAF tactical air forces under the proposed Base Force concept has been faulted above on the grounds of the likely military requirements. It is also flawed, perhaps even more fundamentally so, in terms of manpower requisites.

Intrinsically involved are the incentives and career prospects that draw a potential recruit, within the competitive American marketplace of job opportunities, to a career in his or her country's military service. A large number of considerations bear upon that choice, and they vary from individual to individual. One clear common denominator, however, with particular relevance to the overwhelming majority of recruits who have wives or husbands and children or who look forward to family life, is the prospect of reasonable stability of working location—or expressed in negative terms, the prospect of "tolerable" disruption to family life from separation or reassignment. This prospect tends to be identified primarily in terms of likely "rotation" of assignment between the continental United States and overseas. A minimally tolerable "rotational base" in this respect reflects a two-to-one ratio of expected service within the United States, as against service overseas. That "rotational base" of U.S. versus overseas service, in turn, tends to correlate almost directly with the ratio of the number of U.S. forces stationed in the United States to the number stationed abroad.

Keeping this in mind, and looking at the proposed end-strengths and their allocations under the Base Force concept, we find some disturbing differences affecting the military services. For example, of the twelve United States Army divisions projected for 1995, eight will be based in the United States and four abroad. What this means to potential Army enlistees and their families is that they can expect to spend two-thirds of their projected military careers in the relative stability of U.S.-based assignments and only one-third abroad (not counting possible war or contingencies). Potential enlistees in USAF tactical air forces would face a far more difficult prospect, however. The ratio of U.S. and foreign-based forces under the Base Force concept would be 1.125:1, or virtually one to one. Fighter pilots, maintenance personnel, munitions maintenance personnel, and so on, along with their families, thus would have to contemplate spending almost half of their careers in overseas assignments—again not counting possible contingency operations—with all the potential disruptions and hardships likely to be entailed in the process.

The point may seem trivial to the casual reader, especially one who tends to equate overseas assignment with glamor and adventure. Nevertheless, the importance of the "rotational base" has been verified by long experience, backed by recruitment and retention statistics. And in the final analysis, the efficiency and effectiveness of any military force are a function not so much of the quality of its equipment as of the human factor—of requisite numbers of competent and dedicated professionals who handle the equipment. To be sure, the "rotational base" problem for the Air Force may be mitigated, at least somewhat, by the imperative of training base.

A MORE VIABLE TACTICAL AIR FORCES STRUCTURE

The foregoing projection of realistic tactical air requirements would add up to an overseas force of nine wings, five in Europe and four in the Pacific, as reflected in Table 5.1. For the purpose of gauging rotational bases, Alaskan-based squadrons must also be counted in the overseas total. As has been pointed out, generally speaking the rotational base should be twice the size of overseas forces. The training base may be considered by some to be part of the rotational base, yet training units tend to lack full complements of crew members and maintenance disciplines. For example, a fighter training squadron has fewer combat-skilled pilots per assigned aircraft and fewer weapon system operators

Tactical Air Forces for the Future 89

for two-seated fighters like the F-111, F-111E and F-15E. Training units also lack the requisite numbers of qualified munitions technicians.

In accordance with the two-to-one rotational base ratio, and injecting a 20 percent factor for training, the tactical fighter force based in the Continental United States (CONUS) should consist of at least twenty wings, making up a total force of thirty tactical fighter wings. Those twenty CONUS-based wings, while justified on the grounds of rotation base, may exceed anticipated requirements for theater reinforcements and contingency deployments. In order to meet budgetary constraints, some shifts may have to be considered in the relationship between active and reserve forces.

Combat Crew Training (CCT) to support a force of this size calls for a minimum of five wings, or approximately fifteen Combat Crew Training Squadrons (CCTS), as part of, rather than in addition to, the thirty-wing force. A caveat is in order here. In times of declining defense budgets, the notion sometimes gains currency that one way to effect savings is to shift some of the training burden from CCTS to operational units, thereby reducing the number of training squadrons. This is a facile concept, fraught with risk for the fighting potential of the force that is brought into actual battle. True, the pilots transferred early to combat-ready squadrons under this concept may fly their aircraft safely and perform fundamental combat tasks. By no acceptable measure, however, can they be adjudged combat ready. In the process of on-the-job training under the stressful conditions of combat, they pose a high risk to themselves and their fellow pilots, also leading to higher attrition rates for the scarce aircraft.

To summarize, it has been argued here that projected theater requirements, particularly for the Atlantic forces, as well as the requirements of rotational base (a prerequisite for needed recruitment and retention), urge an expansion of tactical air forces under the Base Force Concept. A more viable force would consist of ten forward-based wings (including one in Alaska) and twenty wings based in CONUS. Of the latter, forty-two squadrons (fourteen wings) would be assigned to the contingency force and a minimum of fifteen squadrons to combat crew training. The thirty-wing force must be an all-active force, because only active duty personnel are rotated overseas, except for contingencies such as Desert Storm, when reserve and Air National Guard units are deployed in support of active forces. Some cost cutters will seek to categorize units based in Alaska as part of the core rotational base. This, however, distorts the true picture, because personnel stationed in Alaska are on fixed-length tours requiring an annual replacement rate of some 30 percent.

In general, the axioms of a rotational base put into sharper perspective the painful choices involved in force reductions that bear significantly on the fundamental issue of the prospective U.S. presence, and role, on the world stage, as well as on domestic politics. On the one hand, cutbacks in tactical airpower, to be meaningful while sustaining anything resembling a viable force posture, must begin with reductions in deployments abroad, according to the basic two-to-one ratio of home-based versus overseas assignments. That entails not only pullbacks of forces, but abandonment of overseas facilities that are not likely to be easily recoverable (or viable) in the event of new contingency needs. The ratio also dictates, on the other hand, that the major part of the reductions occur in the CONUS part of the posture, much to the distress of congressional representatives of districts economically affected by closures of air bases in the United States.

The result is multiplied burdens, in terms of reach and effectiveness, imposed on tactical air forces that must rely increasingly on "projectable power" from the continental United States. This presents an excruciating dilemma; there are no easy ways around it.

A LARGER HISTORICAL LESSON

Earlier in this chapter the Gulf War was referred to as the first major conflict since World War II from which the United States has emerged with clear-cut victory. The Gulf War can also be characterized, and not coincidentally, as the first such major conflict for which the United States was reasonably prepared—in forces, military organization, weaponry, and tactical and operational doctrine. The qualifier "reasonably prepared" reflects certain shortcomings, for example with respect to military lift capabilities, which will be probed in greater detail in Chapter 9 of this book.

Preparedness for conflict is a composite of complex objective and subjective factors and variables. The objective factors embrace the quantity and quality of military forces and their equipment, training, doctrine, sustainability, and so on. Subjective variables relate to such intangible elements as the morale of the fighting forces, the quality of their leadership, and the degree of popular support of the war effort. Another significant subjective factor—significant at least in recent American experience—is the political goals for which the war is waged and the constraints that these impose on its conduct.

After World War II, the United States entered two more major conflicts ill prepared, by both objective and subjective criteria. Thus in 1950 the Korean War, following the demobilization of U.S. military forces after victory in World War II, caught the nation almost totally unprepared. For example, the then fledgling U.S. Air Force had jet aircraft in development and some in flight testing, but virtually none in the field. Large formations of propeller-driven P-51 fighter aircraft were thrown into combat against vastly superior YAK-9s and MiG-15s. Nor was long-range, high-capacity airlift available to carry what remained of the Army combat units halfway around the globe. Army, Navy, Marine Corps, and Air Force training camps were expanded into tent cities to meet the urgent manpower needs.

Once the training and industrial bases were raised to surge productivity, U.S. forces, with their UN allies, pushed the North Korean and Chinese forces to the Yalu River. They fought fiercely, even brilliantly, but they also fought in pursuit of limited and indistinct territorial and political objectives. Chinese territory beyond the Yalu was permitted to serve as a sanctuary for the Communist forces; the lines of communication supplying those forces were never put at risk. Because the United States was ill prepared and ill armed for the conflict, and self-constricted in its conduct, the price paid in casualties was staggering, as were the economic costs. And the return for those sacrifices was an uneasy armistice that continues on the Korean Peninsula even today.

The Vietnam War was a repetition in ultimately harsher form and with even more traumatic consequences. Again the nation was ill prepared, at least in conventional forces. The major portion of its military investments after Korea had gone into the build-up of strategic and tactical nuclear forces. In October 1961, the first elements of U.S. tactical air power—a composite force of obsolete AT-28Bs, B-26s, and C-47s—were deployed to Bien Hoa, South Vietnam. Yet lack of conventional forces did not faze the pundits of "counterinsurgency" warfare in the Kennedy Administration, who believed that the "dirty little war" could be handled by an expansion of the Green Berets, Seal Teams, and Air Commandos. The "dirty little war" would last the better part of twelve years, leaving more than 50,000 Americans killed and another 125,000 wounded.

It is not the intent here to chronicle the painful history of the Vietnam conflict, but simply to point out that the waging of that conflict violated practically every canon of successful conduct of war in the modern era. Not only was the United States ill prepared, but it "groped" into the conflict with mistaken notions regarding its fundamental nature. We waged essentially defensive warfare, relinquishing the initiative to the enemy. Worse than that, even after substantial U.S. forces had been amassed, they were stymied in the use of available force by territorial and political restrictions even more onerous than those that had obtained in Korea. Strategy and tactics were not entrusted to professional military commanders; instead they were pronounced and micromanaged from afar by civilians in the Pentagon and the White House, in a constant and debilitating process of "fine-tuned" escalation and de-escalation.

The bombing of Hanoi in late 1972 finally brought the North Vietnamese to the bargaining table. Had Hanoi been struck with the same intensity a decade earlier, arguably a free and independent Republic of Vietnam would continue to exist today.

The tragic mistakes and foibles of the past apparently were finally recognized, and redressed, in the decisions, planning, and execution of Desert Storm—explicitly so by President Bush in his iterated pledge that the United States would not repeat the Vietnam experience, and that U.S. forces would not be called upon once again to "fight with one hand tied behind their back." Although political decisions properly governed the objectives of the campaign, its planning and implementation were left to the professional acumen of the military commanders. The initiative was grasped, with a massive assertion of the available military power from the outset, and maintained until the objectives had been achieved and the conflict terminated.

Has America overcome its past and, as it were, "jumped over the (long) shadow of Vietnam?'' Will the lessons of Desert Storm be absorbed, by the American public and their elected representatives, in their proper import of what it takes to be prepared for modern conflict and for success in its prosecution? Or will the afterglow of stunning victory sponsor a new relaxation in national preparedness to meet future challenges—a relaxation that may prove comparable, in basic consequences, to the sense of national fatigue that followed the stalemate in Korea and the sense of frustration from Vietnam? It may be unusual for a projection of the future to conclude with self-questioning. Nevertheless, those are the key questions.

6

Marine Forces for the Future

Gen. George Crist, USMC (Ret.)

The Marine Corps has always lived on the margin beside the larger U.S. military services. Historically the strength and capabilities of the Corps have followed a sine curve, rising and falling in direct relation with the extent of America's military commitments and involvements. The era of U.S.-Soviet confrontation, and related conflicts in Korea and Vietnam, marked nearly forty years of historically unprecedented stability for the Corps.

The fading of the confrontation era is stripping away the commitment by the United States to a global war posture, and with it the cushion against descending military manpower levels and reduced resources. Now the Marine Corps again faces fierce competition for a share of defense allocations and for the visibility of its role in the post-containment strategy.

A DIFFICULT ROAD AHEAD

The fortunes of the Marine Corps have traditionally been founded in four potential missions: large wars, limited or regional wars, small wars, and demonstrations of force. By public law the roles and missions of the Marine Corps are primarily naval and amphibious: they focus on the seizure and defense of advanced naval bases and the conduct of land operations essential to the prosecution of naval campaigns. In reality, however, what the Corps is called upon to undertake often has little relevance to the words of the law. The Marine Corps is proscribed from being a "second land army." Yet in World Wars I and II, in Korea, in Vietnam, and more recently in the Persian Gulf, that is precisely how the Corps was used.

Historically, the Corps grew exponentially whenever there was a need for additional ground forces, in times of America's large conflicts. Only during the containment era was it allowed to size and equip itself for a role in a major war before the fact. Marine forces were earmarked for employment on the flanks of Europe, in Korea, and in the Aleutian Islands. This led to the strengthening of the two divisions and air wings based in the United States and the creation of Marine Expeditionary Force headquarters to deal with protracted land warfare. The end strength of the Corps leveled off to between 170,000 and 200,000—a comfortable range within which to maintain three active divisions and air wings.

As the threat of a World War III recedes, the scope of the Marine Corps will diminish. It will no longer have the funding or support to plan and structure for a global war, entailing the commitment of multiple divisions and air wings. The Corps will once more find itself in a battle with the larger services for a viable place in the strategy—a niche from which to justify appropriations and resources.

This situation is not new; the Marine Corps leadership has faced it after every major conflict. In 1867, and again in 1894, there were moves to disestablish the Marine Corps and transfer its functions to the Army. In 1932 President Hoover, with the full concurrence of the Army chief of staff, conceived the idea of transferring the entire Marine Corps into the United States Army by executive order. In 1946 the Army threatened to abolish the Fleet Marine Force and hand Marine aviation to the Army Air Corps. A brigadier general in the Army publicly described the Corps as "a small bitched-up Army talking Navy lingo," adding, "We are going to put those Marines in the Regular Army and make efficient soldiers out of them."[1] In 1949 Gen. Omar Bradley, then Chairman of the Joint Chiefs of Staff, perpetuated the Army line, admitting that he saw no need for Marine divisions and combined supporting arms. The aftermath of Vietnam witnessed yet another threat to the survival of the Corps. This time critics charged that the amphibious assault was obsolete in the face of modern weaponry; hence they questioned a need for the Marine Corps role and structure.

With the fading of the containment era, the pressures against the Marine Corps are rising anew. No one, at least at the present juncture, anticipates a move to abolish the Corps. This time the attack will more likely take the form of deprecating the value of the Marine Corps in the post-containment strategy.

The first shots have already been fired. The Army claims the leading role in the Contingency Response Force under the new Base Force Concept developed by the Department of Defense. Five active Army divisions would be retained for that purpose alone. Army forces also would be earmarked as the primary heavy components to deal with high-intensity conflicts. The Marine Corps, meanwhile, would be relegated to supporting maritime missions. Under this scheme, from the current structure of divisions and air wings, the Marines would shrink to light expeditionary brigades.

Past and current detractors notwithstanding, history has sided with the Marine Corps. In the second half of this century, Marine forces have seen action in every regional war in which the United States has been engaged: in Korea,

Vietnam, and the Persian Gulf. Beyond that there is a much longer roster of small wars and incursions in which Marines have participated; just a partial list includes such places as Lebanon (1958), Thailand (1962), Cuba (the missile crisis, 1962), the Dominican Republic (1963), Lebanon (1982), Grenada (1983), the Persian Gulf (1987–1988), and Panama (1990). Demonstrations of force, conducted with the Navy, have numbered in the hundreds. More recently, even while the massive U.S. buildup was proceeding in the Persian Gulf and virtually all available U.S. sealift and airlift were dedicated to Operation Desert Shield, Marine amphibious units were called upon to evacuate 2,609 American and other foreign nationals endangered by civil war in Liberia, and another 260 from Somalia.

History thus points the way. The Marine Corps will continue to be called upon to respond to limited and small wars, and to project U.S. military power along the maritime littorals of the globe.

FINDING A NICHE IN THE NEW STRATEGY

The major elements of the emerging U.S. defense strategy are: strategic deterrence and defense, forward presence, crisis response, and force reconstitution. Of these, crisis response will decide the size and capabilities of U.S. conventional forces. The new strategy aims primarily at rapid response to short-notice regional crises and contingencies that threaten U.S. interests.[2]

Every contingency probably will be unique. Gen. Colin Powell, the chairman of the Joint Chiefs of Staff, has spoken of the crisis nobody expected and the contingency nobody ever planned. Desert Storm confirmed that potential adversaries in the Third World are no longer trivial military problems. The uncertainties regarding future contingencies support the need for retaining a mix of light and heavy projection forces in the active structure. This concept is embodied in General Powell's basic force packages. The light components would be trained and organized to operate flexibly anywhere in the world. They should be able to move rapidly and sustain themselves once they reach their target areas. The heavy components provide the sustaining combat power, should deterrence fail or a conflict intensify.

The Navy–Marine Corps combination will commend itself to many as the premier rapid, power-projection force. Ever since the founding of the republic, the Navy and Marines have traditionally performed the task of projecting U.S. power and influence overseas. Naval task forces have been called upon as the first response to over 80 percent of the international crises since World War II.[3]

The Navy–Marine team offers unique advantages for crisis management. By design, Marine expeditionary forces, with their dedicated amphibious ships, are highly mobile and self-sustaining. They can be configured for a variety of missions. Amphibious forces can move to the vicinity of crisis as a deterrent while remaining afloat, uncommitted, in international waters. If intervention is called for, they have the organic means to land the measure of combat power required by the situation. In places where no friendly infrastructure exists ashore, the action can be supported from the sea. Subsequently, should the need arise, maritime forces can pave the way for joint or combined operations. Thus, in Desert Shield maritime forces were a major factor in the initial defense of Saudi Arabia and covered the later arrival of air and ground reinforcements.[4]

There is, of course, a comparable case to be made for maintaining Army forces in the contingency forces mix. All potential trouble areas do not lie along the seacoast. There will be a need for light Army strike forces, such as airborne formations and special operations units of the Army and Air Force. Air Force rapid-reactor tactical squadrons would be an essential part of the deployment package, to give air support to the army troops.

A sole Army–Air Force approach, however, is by no means the cure-all claimed by its advocates. Most of the world's population is concentrated within 50 miles of the sea.[5] Employment of Army forces involves an irrevocable decision to place them on foreign soil. Land-based air forces need air bases from which to operate. They must be sustained either from the United States or from forward, pre-positioned stocks. General Vuono, the former chief of staff of the Army, has cautioned, "Contingency operations in particular will demand a higher level of sustainment stocks than we currently maintain for that purpose."[6]

How many light, rapid deployment forces are needed, and/or affordable by the nation within declining defense budgets? The Marines maintain three divisions, from which they deploy expeditionary units and brigades for rapid deployment missions. The Army proposes five of its divisions for the same purpose: the 82nd Airborne Division, the 101st Air Assault Division, the 24th Mechanized Division, and the 7th and 10th Light Infantry Divisions. This smacks of "overkill."

Airborne and light infantry divisions are well suited for small operations, such as those that were carried out in Grenada and Panama. In a more intense combat environment, however, they have proven to be too light and in need of reinforcement. More often than not, in such situations Marine expeditionary units and brigades have been the chosen force. In the Grenada operation, for example, one Marine expeditionary unit captured the capital, St. George's, and the second-largest city on the island, Pearls, relying solely on the organic combat power embarked in the amphibious ships. Meanwhile, in the battle for the airport being constructed at Point Salines, Army Rangers and Special Forces units had insufficient firepower to overcome the opposition. Elements of the 82nd Airborne had to be airlifted in to get the job done.

The heavy component of contingency forces answers to a different set of criteria. These are the powerful sustaining echelons, the backup for conflict escalation. The Army and Air Force are the traditional custodians of heavy divisions and long-range tactical air forces, respectively. They are the practitioners of the high-intensity AirLand Battle. Operation Desert Storm would not have been accomplished successfully in a matter of six weeks without an air campaign involving nearly 1,300 United States Air Force combat aircraft and a

Marine Forces for the Future

sweeping ground envelopment executed by five-plus Army armored and mechanized divisions. The Army and Air Force demonstrated once again their preeminence in the heavy, high-intensity combat arena.

Even so, Desert Storm revalidated the role of the Marine Corps in that high-intensity arena as well. Marine formations, ground and air, supported by naval gunfire and carrier aviation, were key players in the campaign. Within three days, two Marine divisions in effect liberated Kuwait City. Gen. Norman Schwarzkopf described that as an "absolutely superb operation, a textbook, and I think it will be studied for many, many years to come as the way to do it."[7] Meanwhile, a Marine amphibious task force poised in the Persian Gulf served as a decisive strategic deception, forcing Iraqi commanders to divert at least six divisions to defend against an amphibious assault that never came.

The Gulf War thus confirmed the lessons of the Korea and Vietnam conflicts: Marines are as capable of a role in high-intensity combat as they are in executing missions in the lower range of the conflict spectrum. The lesson inveighs against any arbitrary division of service responsibilities into "light" and "heavy." Rather, the spectrum of conflict must be viewed as a continuum to which each service contributes relative advantages across the board. The Army and Air Force are primarily equipped for protracted land warfare. Marines are fundamentally oriented toward amphibious expeditions, but they have also fought alongside the Army in five wars. The Marines have the edge in deployment, with their dedicated amphibious ships. All, however, depend upon, and must compete for, strategic airlift and fast sealift. Army and Air Force formations require an extensive support structure to sustain their operations; once in place, however, those logistic funnels enable them to fight almost indefinitely. Marines, on the other hand, carry fifteen to thirty days of supplies with them for initial sustainment. When those stocks are depleted, the Marines must plug into an external support system. The Gulf buildup, starting in August of 1990, was the first real test of heavy force projection from the United States in response to a fast-breaking crisis. The Leathernecks distinguished themselves by quick response and versatility. In the four weeks following the president's decision to commit troops, the Corps deployed over 40,000 Marines to the region. They arrived fully ready for combat, with tanks, heavy artillery, and more than 100 combat aircraft. The First Marine Expeditionary Force was the first force on the scene fully capable of carrying out the mission. Furthermore, the Marine forces came prepared to take on a variety of missions. In Saudi Arabia approximately 33,000 Marines were in defensive positions to block an Iraqi advance southward from Kuwait. Concurrently, an expeditionary brigade, some 10,000 strong, stood off the coast ready to reinforce their comrades ashore or conduct an amphibious operation if the need arose.

Equally impressively, the Marines arrived with a month of sustainment. This was in sharp contrast with the Army 82nd Airborne Division, the leading elements of which came with only three days of support. The Central Command had to reallocate Marine stocks to tide Army units over until their supplies arrived. The Army forces, moreover, did not turn out to be as rapid as advertised. Of the divisions identified by the Army as the contingency force for rapid response, only the 82nd Airborne and the 24th Mechanized made it to Saudi Arabia in the first month of Operation Desert Shield. The 82nd carried insufficient combat power to serve as anything but a trip wire. As one senior officer succinctly put it, "Paratroopers don't fight tanks."[8] The 24th Mechanized Division, with its tanks and armored personnel carriers, arrived on the defensive line after the Marine expeditionary force had already dug in.

The bottom line is that a mix of service capabilities will be essential within both the light and heavy force packages. It would be imprudent, if not downright foolish, to suggest that one or two services can accomplish all the missions. Instead, as budgets shrink, care must be taken to maintain a balance among service capabilities relative to the potential requirements of global crises. That which is unneeded should be pared, rather than retained for the sole purpose of maintaining force structure or appropriations. If this yardstick is applied, the Marine Corps has demonstrated a solid case to maintain a viable structure.

SHRINKING MANPOWER

Traditionally, military planners like to imagine that national strategy and assigned missions determine the strength and composition of the individual Armed Forces. This has never truly been the case, certainly not with respect to the Marine Corps. The Corps has retained the roles and missions assigned by law, but the wherewithal to accomplish these tasks has waxed and waned. As one historian describes it, "The Corps shrank to fit federal budgets rather than expanding to fit contingency plans."[9]

What the Marines will have on hand to do the job will be determined largely by administration budgets and congressional appropriations, rather than by a new post-containment strategy. Theirs will surely be a smaller force than they have enjoyed since the Korean War. The question is, How much smaller?

Historically, the Marine Corps has suffered deep slashes in its strength at the end of every major war. In 1948, following World War II and before the full onset of the Cold War, the strength was 83,609, down from 485,053 at the height of the war. This was roughly comparable to the size of the Corps in World War I, which had been 75,101. Yet by 1958, subsequent to the Korean War, the total had only fallen to about 190,000. It dropped to this level again in 1979 following the Vietnam War.[10] This reflected the cushioning effect of the strategy of containment.

What will the end strength of the Marine Corps be by the year 2000? In 1990 Gen. A. M. Gray, the then commandant, argued that the Corps should not sink below 182,000. If history is a guide, the argument is probably futile. Marine commandants have long and consistently protested that the funding and manpower allocated to the Corps were not enough to enable it to carry out its assigned responsibilities. Their arguments for a sizable amphibious force in readiness to project power overseas, where and when the president might direct, have carried little weight. The U.S. public and Congress chronically have paid little heed to potential military entanglements of the future. In 1948, the commandant of the Marine Corps, Gen. Clifton B. Cates, believed that at least 114,200 Marines were needed by the Corps to carry out its postwar responsibilities. Instead he saw the Corps shrink from 92,222 to 74,279 by the spring of 1950.

Unfortunately, Gen. Carl Mundy, Jr., the current commandant, probably is destined to share the experience of his predecessors. A downward trend seems inevitable. The "notional" plan of 25 percent reductions in service end strengths, presented by the secretary of defense to Congress on June 19, 1990, would have sliced active Marine Corps strength from 197,000 to 148,000 by fiscal 1995-96.[11] The actual fiscal 1992-93 defense budget turned out to be less painful. Marine end strength was to be cut from 188,000 in fiscal 1992-93 to 171,000 in fiscal 1995-96.[12] Still, this represents a steep drop from the active force of 199,000 in 1987-88. And the end is not in sight. The Department of Defense has mandated a drop in the Marine Corps to a 159,000 active force by fiscal 1997-98.

The conclusion is painfully clear. The Marine Corps will go down to less than 160,000 by the mid-1990s. It could even drop below the Cheney figure of 148,000 by the end of the decade.

CUTTING THE FORCE

The possible loss of up to 40,000 Marines from the active force structure means that something will eventually have to go. With a funded strength of nearly 200,000, it was not difficult to maintain three full active divisions and air wings. "When the Marine Corps moves to the end strength range of 170,000s, it becomes very, very difficult to have three divisions and three wing teams as the law prescribed," according to former commandant Gray.[13]

The Corps will inevitably have to cut combat muscle to fit within the fiscal straitjacket imposed by a frugal Congress and by interservice competition. Where, however, should the line be drawn?

Secretary of Defense Dick Cheney has placed the strategic priority for the future on response to regional crises and contingencies. It follows from this that the maximum force required under the new defense strategy could be determined by examining the force levels actually employed by the United States in major, high-intensity regional conflicts. That maximum level should then suffice to also embrace the needed forces for lower-intensity contingencies and minor crises.

One Marine division and air wing fought in Korea. In Vietnam and in the Gulf War, the Marine Corps employed two divisions and the equivalent of two air wings. The conclusion derived from this admittedly simplistic methodology is that the Corps should not be reduced below the equivalent of two active divisions and two active air wings with associated combat service elements, plus support and overhead.

Even this "floor" is risky. Secretary Cheney has emphasized, "Because serious contingencies can arise quickly, a timely U.S. response would require mostly active forces."[14] The Marine Corps would be hard pressed to meet this criterion. The active sustaining base would be extremely austere. It would offer the bare minimum for satisfying the standing afloat deployments aboard the numbered fleets, while maintaining one ready fire brigade in the Atlantic and one in the Pacific.

Lt. Gen. Norman H. Smith, former head of Marine Manpower and Reserve Affairs, summed up the predicament. In fiscal 1990–91, when Operation Desert Shield began, the Marine Corps numbered more than 196,000 active-duty personnel. By the time the Desert Shield buildup was completed, 80 percent of the Corps was deployed outside the United States. Almost 50 percent, 94,000, were in Southwest Asia alone. A Marine deployment the size of Desert Storm would not be possible with 14,000 to 30,000 fewer Marines on active duty.[15]

Although the active strength of the Corps might fall to two division-wing team equivalents, the structure of three divisions and three air wings should be retained. Public Law 416, signed by President Truman on June 20, 1952, as an amendment to the National Security Act of 1947, provides that the Marine Corps "shall be so organized as to include not less than three combat divisions and three aircraft wings." For more than three decades this law has protected the existence of "fleet marine forces of combined arms, together with supporting air components" from attack by those who would reduce the Corps to what President Truman once described as "the Navy's police force."[16]

The law prescribes three divisions and three wings, but it does not set their strength. It is conceivable, therefore, to restructure the fleet Marine force into the equivalent of two divisions and two air wings while nominally retaining the three-divisions-three-wings identity. At worst, portions of the divisions and wings might be cadred. This would be in keeping with the "force reconstitution" element of the new strategy.

TRIMMING THE SAILS

It is within this constrained framework that the Marine Corps leadership will have to decide where to apportion the dwindling resources. The first order of business will be to conserve the muscle in the combat units to the maximum extent possible. This will entail a rigorous scrubbing of the lesser commitments and overhead that bleed resources from the fleet Marine force.

For example, does the Marine Corps need to continue providing the equivalent of two infantry battalions for State Department security guard detachments? Marine guards may be impressive decor at the entrances of American embassies abroad; seldom, however, are they called upon to exercise their martial skills in defending the facilities they guard. Ambassadors tend to shy away from use of force in the defense of their facilities: a conspicuous exception was the infamous takeover of the U.S. embassy in Teheran in 1979.

Marine Forces for the Future

Marine detachments aboard capital ships are similarly a relic of tradition—a throwback to the times when Marines fought in the fighting tops of sailing ships, maintained order among unruly crews, and conducted forays ashore. Today they function as honor guards, gun crews, and orderlies for admirals.

With dwindling funds, some bases may have to be sacrificed. Is there a need for logistic support bases on both the East and West coasts of the United States? Those bases are carryovers from World War II and the Korean war. Technology already has enabled the base at Albany, Georgia, to absorb many of the functions of the base at Barstow, California.

Then there is the Marine Corps Air Station at Kaneohe Bay, Hawaii, which is home to a Marine brigade. Proposals to close that base have surfaced periodically for years. The arguments have been on both strategic and fiscal grounds. The brigade is malpositioned; its lift is in California, while its target areas of deployment are Korea or southern Asia. The cost of living there is prohibitive for the troops. The real estate taken up by the base is among the most expensive and desirable on the north coast of Oahu. The cost of maintaining the base drains off construction and maintenance funds that could be invested in bases on the U.S. mainland. The brigade at Kaneohe is a conspicuous target in any force reduction, as is the base on which it is housed.

How many air stations can the Corps support in rough fiscal weather? Reductions in structure inevitably mean housing fewer active squadrons. On the West Coast, Marine aviation supports stations at El Toro, Tustin, and Camp Pendleton in California and Yuma in Arizona; the Tustin station already is slated for closure. There are three stations on the East Coast, at Cherry Point and New River in North Carolina and Beaufort in South Carolina.

In extremis, consolidation of recruit depots might be contemplated. If the end strength of the Corps is greatly reduced, will there still be sufficient annual inflow of recruits to justify maintaining a recruit depot in California as well as in South Carolina? The depot in San Diego has long been coveted by that municipality; it sits in the heart of the downtown area, adjacent to an airport in desperate need of expansion. Disposing over only 700 acres, it must rely on the large base at Camp Pendleton, forty miles to the north, for weapons and field training. Parris Island, in contrast, commands some 6,000 rural acres and is welcomed by the local communities. There may be a valid argument that both facilities will be needed in the event of mobilization for a major conflict; still, this rationale will be difficult to sustain amid a perceived decline of a threat of global proportions and the need to conserve precious resources in maintaining a credible Marine Corps.

MODERATION FOR MARINE AVIATION

There is a limit to the savings that can be realized from a paring of lesser missions and their support. Eventually there will be a squeeze on funds apportioned to the combat forces and allocated to modernization. In times of monetary stress, the internal debate in the Corps usually centers on a contest between the air and the ground components. Ground officers demand priority over aviation, while the aviators resist encroachments on their turf.

Aircraft are expensive to procure, operate, and maintain. Together with the ancillary aerospace hardware required to fight, control, and defend, Marine aviation can absorb a big chunk of the Marine Corps procurement budget. For example, an upgrade of the AV-8 Harrier fleet to the Harrier Plus could cost over $22 billion.[17] This magnitude of outlays, compared to the relatively lower costs for ground weaponry, is the bone of contention between the two camps within the Corps.

Fiscal factors aside, the air component is a precious asset to be preserved. The integrated Marine air-ground team has long been the envy of the Army and the bane of the Air Force. Fierce battles have been waged to retain the air arm as part of a Fleet Marine Force of combined arms. The defenders have been vindicated time and again; Marine aviation has proved itself to be an indispensable supporting arm for the infantry.

Desert Storm extended that legacy. The Marines deployed about 65 percent of their air fleet to the Gulf. The 3rd Marine Air Wing flew more than eighteen thousand combat sorties, including nine thousand during the ground phase of the operation. Attack aircraft, both fixed and rotary wing, delivered over 29.7 million pounds of ordnance on enemy armored vehicles, artillery pieces, and fortifications. When smoke and bad weather inhibited fixed-wing sorties, AH-1 Cobra attack helicopters took over in covering the advancing infantry. Transport helicopters moved troops and tons of matériel in support of the rapidly moving ground attack.[18]

In a time of retrenchment it is reasonable to ask how large a portion of ever scarcer funds should be directed to aviation. In many respects Marine aviation has emulated the Air Force, pursuing most of the functions for which the larger service is responsible: close air support, airlift, airborne operations, aerial photography, reconnaissance, air interdiction, and electronic warfare. The list extends to helicopter and light aircraft operations and surface-to-air missile defense organic to Army aviation and ground units. The implicit goal has been to create a stand-alone aviation component that can operate independently of tactical support from the Navy or Air Force. Such a goal, ambitious even in times of plenty, calls for a multiplicity of aircraft and equipment, which must be continually modernized. It adds up to heavy funds, causing consternation on the ground side of the house. In hard times, it becomes a pattern all the more difficult for the Corps to support.

Marine aviation will have to define its priorities more sharply. Support of the ground troops is the justification for its existence and must be the overriding objective. Close air support and tactical lift thus take precedence. This means less investment in high-performance aircraft to accomplish the air superiority and interdiction functions, along with reconnaissance and electronic warfare, and greater dependence upon the Navy and Air Force to fill gaps in those

Marine Forces for the Future 103

capabilities. The Corps may have to live with the present mix of F/A-18s and AV-8Bs, accompanied by a modest modernization plan. Those are the current weapons of ground support. It may be some time before follow-on systems exist that fit into the procurement budget.

Ground support should also guide the reduction in aviation structure. It means keeping active those aircraft essential to the close air support mission, while sacrificing those with capabilities that can be duplicated by the Navy or Air Force. At the same time, however, there is an opportunity to modernize the reserve air wing, which is still flying obsolete planes, such as the A-4 and the AH, that long ago were phased out of the active inventory. It would be useful to have a modern, albeit smaller, reserve aviation arm to back up the regulars.

BALANCE ON THE GROUND

Reducing Marine ground forces involves a different dispute, that of "light versus heavy." How should the remaining ground combat force be structured?

The 1980s were a golden decade for the Marine Corps. The total Marine Corps appropriation in 1986 jumped to $14.8 billion, from $4.6 billion in 1976. In his history of the Marine Corps, J. Robert Moskin described the transformation as follows:

The Corps returned to thinking about a worldwide role and the relationship of that role to possible future threats. This meant planning for swift insertion, battlefield mobility, concentrated firepower, over-the-horizon amphibious capabilities, better rifles and grenade launchers, swifter vehicles, tactical dispersion, large helicopters, VSTOL (vertical-short-takeoff-landing) aircraft, prepositioned supplies. And the Reagan Administration's bounty made it all possible.[19]

The intense pace of modernization and procurement was aimed at preparing the Marine Corps for combat at every level of conflict. This was fully in tune with the containment strategy and with integrating the Corps in that strategy, although it prompted rumblings of discontent. The Marine Corps, it was alleged, was becoming too heavy. The added new equipment and weapons exceeded the amphibious capability to move them. The Fleet Marine Force was in danger of losing its label as the premier rapid deployment force.

This line of argument was promoted, among others, by William S. Lind, a frequent lecturer at the Marine Corps command and staff college and contributor to the *Marine Corps Gazette*. He urged converting the Marine Corps to light infantry. Under his concept, Marines would learn to fight like guerrillas. They would live off the land and make maximum use of the small unit's own firepower. Overreliance on artillery or air support, according to Lind, slows tempo and brings the evils of centralized control. Light infantry would rely largely on ambushes carried out by many small units. It could have equipment or bases that it would have to protect. Large supply and maintenance areas, logistic lines, air bases, and road-bound equipment invite their own destruction.[20]

The Marine Corps prescribed by Lind would not have contributed to the resounding victory in the Gulf. In fact, it probably would not have been invited to participate. Rather, the Corps would have more closely resembled the small, readily available, lightly armed force that General Eisenhower espoused in 1946, justified solely by the mission of protecting American interests ashore in foreign countries.[21]

Indeed, in 1988 the Corps did begin to "lighten up." The shift was prodded by the fading threat from the Soviet Union, the reemergence of "small wars," and the national preoccupation with interdicting the narcotics traffic. The priority in Marine Corps planning shifted toward low- to mid-intensity conflict, with the stress on low. Purchase of the M1A1 tank was deferred to fiscal 1989 and 1990, with the numbers reduced from 476 to 221. This decision reflected the intent to "focus on the light end" of the contingency spectrum, according to Gen. John R. Dailey, former Assistant Commandant of the Marine Corps.[22] The M-109 and M-110, 155 mm and 203 mm self-propelled guns, were slowly phased out. Artillery was to be reduced in favor of a fourth rifle company. The infantry battalion was to become the building block for all force structure initiatives. Emphasis was given to the operational capability of light armored infantry battalions. Most of the afloat, forward-deployed expeditionary units were trained in special operations capabilities.

The record of the Gulf War should put an end to the debate. The Marine Corps was forced to borrow M-1 tanks from the Army. Central Command attached the 1st "Tiger" Brigade of the Army's 2nd Armored Division, with its 108 modern M1A1 tanks, to I Marine Expeditionary Force (I MEF). That brigade contributed signally to devastating an Iraqi mechanized division and securing the key road junction at Jahra, together with the critical Mutla Ridge. At the Kuwait International Airport, two battalions of Marine tanks successfully shot it out with an Iraqi armored division.

Marine Corps artillery fired some ten thousand rounds during Desert Storm. The 155 mm towed and self-propelled guns, some of which had been loaded onto the pre-positioning ships back in 1984, were never silent. They spelled the difference in the Battle of Khafji. Artillery raids from Marine positions marked the opening rounds of the ground war. Here self-propelled artillery was favored. The artillery units moved up, fired, and quickly displaced before the Iraqis could initiate counterbattery fire. Even then, Army MLRS had to be attached, providing a mobile, area-fire weapon that was lacking in Marine artillery. A rain of heavy artillery shells covered the break-in and triumphant advance of the 1st and 2nd Marine divisions. A mix of towed and self-propelled proved to be the right combination.

The Marines did well in the Gulf War because they had the tools for intense combat and knew how to use them. The lesson seems self-evident. Balance is the key. By moving too far toward a light, low-intensity ground structure, the Corps could effectively remove itself from the high- to mid-intensity combat arena, surrendering it entirely to the Army.

Marine Forces for the Future

The Marines need to maintain the fleet Marine forces of combined arms that their forebears wisely insisted upon four decades ago. It should be the force that Gen. P. X. Kelley, then commandant of the Marine Corps, described in 1985:

> The Marine Corps is what you want it to be. Amphibious operations are our primary mission and we have to be ready to cope with every level of conflict. We can make it light; we can make it heavy, because the whole concept is based on a "task" organization. Our concept is that you organize a division with all those things you can possibly foresee for an amphibious operation, and if you want to make it light, you can take away elements."[23]

Reduction of active Marine ground units thus ought to be symmetrical. The objective should be to retain, to the extent possible, a balance of combat capabilities for either low- or high-intensity conflict, enabling "task-organizing" for the specific mission at hand.

THE MARINE CORPS RESERVE

Operation Desert Storm was the first real test of the Marine Corps Reserve since Korea. Nearly 30,000 reservists answered the call in less than six months. Considering the urgency and compressed time, the mobilization went exceptionally well. Of those called up, over 99.5 percent reported. Fewer than 2 percent had disqualifying medical problems. Reserves accounted for 15 percent of the Marines in the theater of operations and 40 percent of the 2nd Marine Division.[24] The state of their readiness was exemplified by Company B of the 4th Tank Battalion; activated in November 1990, it was retrained on the M1A1 tank within 18 days, arrived in Saudi Arabia on February 19, 1991, and went into battle five days thereafter. In four engagements Company B destroyed 59 enemy tanks without losing a single one of its own tanks.[25]

The response was not a matter of luck. Over the years much planning and effort had gone into readying the Marine Corps Reserve. The organization was fashioned for insurance against the eventuality of global commitments or conflicts rising beyond the capabilities of the active force. The selected reserve was deliberately designed as a part of the total force, as a division-wing team structured to augment or reinforce the fleet Marine force. Of the 91,000 reservists, more than 40,000 are assigned to the 4th Marine Division, the 4th Marine Aircraft Wing, and the 4th Force Service Support Group. This foresight in structuring paid off in the Gulf War.

If the Marine Corps were to decline to less than three full active divisions and wings, dependence on the reserve should logically increase. In 1990 an active end strength of 196,500 necessitated the call-up of over 75 percent of the 4th Marine Division and almost half of the 4th Marine Aircraft Wing and 4th Service

Support Group.[26] It follows that an active strength of 171,000 or less would mandate almost full reserve employment for a similar or larger contingency. Yet reserve strength is projected to decline at about the same percentage as the active force.

The new U.S. defense strategy places the burden for initial response on the active forces, with reserves in a support role. According to Secretary of Defense Cheney, "reserve forces would initially provide airlift, sealift, and some other vital support for deploying forces. When longer preparation allowed, reserve components could provide additional support, plus combat units that would be needed for longer or prolonged deployments."[27]

The reserve component may have to be restructured as it shrinks. The guidance implies that the reserve division and wing would not be a scaled-down mirror of their active counterparts; rather, they would contain the types of units needed to sustain an initial operational surge and, when longer preparation allowed, units for additional support, expanded commitments, and larger or prolonged deployments.

The Gulf War offered a preview. The demand was for specific units and individual skills needed to flesh out shortages in the active units. Some reservists went to the battlefield; others replaced active units and personnel that were deployed to the Gulf. Much of the reserve was used to reconstitute the sustaining base. No doubt the reserves would have been the primary source of replacements had the war been extended or heavy casualties suffered.

If this is the guide, it may, in fact, help reserve readiness. The distribution and separation of the reserve ground units have been a vexing problem. Rifle companies are sometimes located hundreds of miles from their parent battalion headquarters. The same applies to regimental headquarters and subordinate battalions. The 4th Service Support Group is widely spread, sometimes fragmented into detachments in different cities. This works directly counter to unit cohesion and effectiveness. Training together once a year is not enough to remedy the problem. In fact, there is no ready solution, given the ruling hand of demographics. If the Gulf pattern is followed, only selected units—detachments, companies, battalions, and squadrons—would be mobilized during the first surge. The larger formations—regiments and air groups—could be activated for follow-on support, with additional training time allocated between mobilization and commitment.

The Corps was moving in this direction even before the Gulf War. Sixteen reserve rifle companies are assigned to train with and round out active battalions. Reserve tank companies will be equipped with the M1A1 tank to augment active tank companies. The active force plans to rely more on the reserve for specific combat service-support units.[28] It will take a bit of clairvoyance and some boldness to decide which reserve units to retain, establish, increase, or cut.

Reorganization may not be the only problem confronting reserve planners. There might be difficulties in recruiting the requisite numbers in the skills needed to man the reserve units, even though the numbers will be going down. Re-

Marine Forces for the Future

cruitment of prior-service Marines is already declining. With the active strength diminished, even fewer Marines will be leaving the service as candidates for the reserve. Moreover, those leaving active duty do not always settle in the vicinity of a reserve unit, and thus are lost to the cause. Even when a prior-service Marine is recruitable, the given reserve unit may not need his particular military skill, in which case he has to be retrained.

Non-prior-service recruiting also may face a challenge. Until now the Montgomery GI Bill has been a key factor in sustaining recruitment and retention of non-prior-service Marines. The future is less certain. The Gulf War may have a dampening effect on potential recruits who regard the prospect of fighting in a different light than simply earning an education by accepting a part-time job in uniform. Counteracting this, on the other hand, may be the afterglow of the rapidly achieved and overwhelming victory and the renewed patriotic fervor it generated. Time alone will tell.

Overall, the Marine Corps Reserve is in a good position to shoulder the new role assigned to it by the new defense strategy. The division, wing, and service support group offers an excellent framework within which to restructure. However, some difficult planning choices will have to be faced.

RESPONSIVENESS

Less manpower and diminished capability will not be the only challenges for Marine planners in the post-containment era. There is also the factor of response, but response is not an end in itself. As Gen. Al Gray has put it, "You have to be light enough to go where you want to go and heavy enough to win on the other end."[29]

As America brings her forces home and overseas bases shrink, the Corps will have to contend with projecting power from the U.S. mainland and relying less on forces forward-deployed. Cuts in operating funds will force the Navy to operate closer to U.S. shores and keep more ships tied up in port. Some of the amphibious and fire support ships, upon which the Marines rely, will be gone, transferred to the reserve or placed in reduced operating status for lack of black oil and crews to man them. As Senator Nunn has projected, "Funds will no longer be available to support all of the Navy's fleet at the operational tempo of the Cold War. Thus, the Navy will be faced with choosing between reduced operational tempos, including more ships in reserve status or a much smaller all-active Navy."[30]

There is some room for optimism, however. The cutback in combat forces and operating funds may have the effect of actually enhancing response.

The Marines have three active divisions and air wings, but there is only enough amphibious lift in both oceans to move one-third of the total force; the remainder depends on common-user airlift and sealift. In that regard those Marine units are no more mobile or deployable than their Army or Air Force counterparts. A reduced active combat structure might result in a Fleet Marine Force more closely aligned with the dedicated amphibious lift. Over time, forward deployments afloat will decrease in duration and frequency. Furthermore, the configuration will have to be tailored to available ships and units. This means new patterns in length and location of deployment, rather than the current fixed geographic orientation. The consequence will be flexible deployments to the vicinity of potential crisis areas, attuned to the shifting priorities of U.S. strategic interest. Those forward-afloat deployments would also be less onerous in operating costs and morale.

A draw-down in permanent basing overseas, such as Okinawa and Japan proper, may also result in raising overall readiness. Rotation of ground and aviation units to preserve this forward-deployed presence is costly and generates turbulence within the sending units. A cutback could allow those resources to be directed toward maintaining home-based units at greater combat strength, improving unit esprit and sharpening mission orientation.

PREPOSITIONING

The subject of prepositioning will be taken up in a subsequent chapter, but needs mention here in its relation to Marine Corps capabilities. Maritime prepositioning is a sound answer to the challenge of projecting power over great distances from the United States in the absence of overseas bases and forces. Afloat prepositioning was intended to complement rather than substitute for amphibious operations. It was designed to provide greater flexibility and improve strategic mobility, as well as to avoid the problems that afflict large, permanent U.S. bases in sensitive areas overseas. Unlike the Army's so called POMCUS program in Europe (described in Chapter 10), the Marine Corps took prepositioning to sea.

The Marine Prepositioning Program (MPS) took more than seven years to complete. Throughout there was vocal opposition. The program was expensive; the cost of building or modifying the ships and securing their use for twenty-five years was approximately $5.2 billion. The annual operating costs of the ships run to over $300 million. The MPSs have no assault capability and require a benign environment to offload.[31]

In the Gulf crisis, maritime prepositioning delivered everything the planners had promised. The prepositioning ships started moving on August 7, the day President Bush ordered the deployment of forces to the Middle East. It took the first ships about seven days to reach Saudi Arabia and another three days to offload. About 30,000 Marines from two expeditionary brigades flew in, joined with their prepositioned equipment and supplies, and gave Central Command a self-sustaining, mechanized force with supporting air at an early point in the operation.[32]

It would have required around 3,000 sorties to have moved just one fully equipped expeditionary brigade by airlift to the area, but only 250 sorties were needed under the afloat prepositioning system.[33] A decade of investment paid off. For the Marine Corps, maritime prepositioning was tested and validated.

INTO THE UNKNOWN

The close of the twentieth century brings uncertainty for the Marine Corps. A new national security strategy is still evolving. Old alliances are eroding. The world order is shifting, and the future role of the United States in that emerging order has yet to be established. Threats to U.S. national interests are changing. The confusion of transition obscures roles and missions, budgets, manpower, and resource allocation.

The Corps is moving into this uncertain terrain in a strong position. Nonetheless, two centuries of experience warn against complacency. "Change means movement, movement means friction, friction means heat, and heat means controversy."[34] The Marine Corps is synonymous with controversy, and the new round of challenges will be no different. The Corps must adapt, and its leadership will have to be on guard.

NOTES

1. Alan R. Millett, *Semper Fidelis: The History Of The United States Marine Corps* (New York: Macmillan, 1980), p. 461.
2. Dick Cheney, "Statement of the Secretary of Defense Dick Cheney before the House Armed Services Committee in Connection with the FY 1992–93 Budget for the Department of Defense," February 7, 1991.
3. Gen. A. M. Gray, Commandant of the Marine Corps, Annual Report to Congress, 1990, p. 4.
4. Lawrence Garrett III, Adm. Frank B. Kelso, and Gen. A. M. Gray, "The Way Ahead," *Marine Corps Gazette Supplement*, April 1991, pp. 4–6.
5. Garrett et al., "The Way Ahead," p. 4.
6. Quoted in *Defense Daily*, October 17, 1989, p. 84.
7. Deborah Schmidt, " 'Some Things Worth Fighting For'," *Navy Times*, March 11, 1991, p. 6.
8. John King, "First U.S. Ground Unit into Saudi Arabia Gets New Assignment," Associated Press, September 7, 1990.
9. Millet, *Semper Fidelis*, p. 465.
10. Ibid.
11. Rick Maze, "Cheney Unveils, Dismisses Plan to Cut Force by 25 Percent," *Navy Times*, July 2, 1990, p. 4.
12. Cheney, "Statement of the Secretary of Defense," p. 9.
13. General A. M. Gray, USMC, quoted in Elizabeth P. Donovan, "Stable Vision," *Navy Times*, January 14, 1991.
14. Cheney, "Statement," p. 9.
15. Deborah Schmidt, "Corps Leaders Warn of Strength Fall below 182,000," *Navy Times*, April 8, 1991, p. 16.
16. Millett, *Semper Fidelis*, pp. 419–97.

17. Charles Bickers, "Marines Seek Harrier Plus," *Janes*, August 11, 1990, p. 181.
18. Col. Norman G. Ewers, USMC (Ret.), "A Conversation with Lt. Gen. Royal N. Moore, Jr.," *Marine Corps Gazette*, October 1991, pp. 44–49.
19. J. Robert Moskin, *The U.S. Marine Corps Story* (New York: McGraw-Hill, 1987), pp. 759–61.
20. William S. Lind, "Light Infantry Tactics," *Marine Corps Gazette*, June 1990, pp. 42–47.
21. Gordon W. Keiser, *The U.S. Marine Corps and Defense Unification 1944–47: The Politics of Survival* (Washington, D.C.: National Defense University Press, 1982), p. 50.
22. "Marines Rediscover M-1 Abrams Tank," *Armed Forces Journal International*, December 1990, p. 20.
23. Quoted in Moskin, *U.S. Marine Corps Story*, p. 760.
24. Lt. Col. Mark F. Cancian, USMCR, "Marine Corps Reserve Forces in Southwest Asia," *Marine Corps Gazette*, September 1991, pp. 35–37; Maj. F. G. Hoffman, USMCR, "Reversing Course on Total Force?" *Marine Corps Gazette*, September 1991, pp. 37–40.
25. Department of Defense, *Conduct of the Persian Gulf Conflict* (Washington, D.C.: Government Printing Office, 1991), p. 11.
26. Hoffman, "Reversing Course?" p. 39.
27. Cheney, "Statement of the Secretary of Defense," p. 9.
28. Maj. Gen. Hollis E. Davison, USMC, Assistant Deputy Chief of Staff for Manpower and Reserve Affairs, "Active/Reserve Relationship Acts to Enhance Corps," *The Officer*, February 1991, pp. 68–72.
29. Donovan, "Stable Vision," p. 15.
30. Quoted in "A New Europe—A New Military Strategy," *Washington Post*, April 24, 1990, p. 25.
31. This section on pre-positioning is indebted to Commandant of the Marine Corps, "Events in the Persian Gulf and Southwest Asia," White Letter No. 9–80, April 22, 1980; Vernon A. Guidry, Jr., "The Promise of Prepositioning," *Military Logistics Forum*, September 1986, pp. 3–6; and Moskin, *U.S. Marine Corps Story*, pp. 715–18, 759–64.
32. Elizabeth P. Donovan, "It Worked! Prepositioning Practiced in Theory Deemed Success in Fact," *Navy Times*, October 15, 1990, p. 29.
33. Donovan, "It Worked!" p. 29.
34. Saul Alinsky, quoted in Charles Henning, *The Wit and Wisdom of Politics* (Golden, Colo.: Fulcrum, 1989), p. 28.

7

Strategic Forces for the Future

Gen. Larry D. Welch, USAF (Ret.)

In theory, of all the U.S. military forces, the strategic nuclear deterrent forces should be the most amenable to an orderly and rational process of force structuring—of defining national objectives and the threat to those objectives, formulating a strategy, and identifying the military tasks, capabilities, and forces required to underwrite the strategy.

In practice, however, the level and composition of U.S. strategic forces are strongly influenced by complex "surrounding issues." These issues include the inherent difficulty of defining and assessing the effectiveness of deterrent strategies, budgetary considerations, arms negotiations, perceptions of adversary intentions, and institutional and individual biases regarding defense priorities. Other subjective factors have come into play, such as persistent questioning of the morality of deterrent strategies, amid a general public antipathy toward nuclear weapons. Finally, there is the factor of prior investment in strategic systems and their long operational life, spanning successions of political leadership, changes in the international situation, and evolutions in strategy.

Therefore, any realistic projection of future U.S. strategic forces must consider both the central rationale for objectives, threat, strategy, task, capability, and forces, along with the political forces that influence them.

THE EVOLUTION OF U.S. DETERRENT STRATEGY

One of the main national security goals since the Soviets conducted their first nuclear weapons test in August 1948 has been deterrence of a nuclear attack on the United States or its allies. Yet other factors driving the strategy have evolved over time. Any projection of future U.S. strategic nuclear force structure must take those historical factors into account.

From the early 1950s to the late 1970s, U.S. strategic nuclear deterrent strategy evinced the sporadic search for a sustainable balance among credible deterrence, affordability, moral acceptability, and other complicating factors. In that quest, the declared strategy of the United States evolved, through several iterations, from "massive retaliation" to "flexible response." More recently, the search has returned to the conceptual beginnings of the age of nuclear deterrence: "minimum deterrence."

An informed student of strategy might properly argue that some of those evolutionary steps do not warrant the term "strategy." Defining the strategy has been complicated further by the lack of formal announcements of postural changes. More often than not, such changes have been inferred from statements and actions by principal players in the policy arena.[1] Furthermore, even when strategies were declared, they were not always in harmony either with unfolding events or available resources. For example, the early U.S. strategy of "massive retaliation," first publicly articulated by Secretary of State John Foster Dulles in a January 1954 speech, was difficult to reconcile with the facts of the day. Clearly, the "massive deterrent at a bearable cost" had not prevented the Korean War. The successful Soviet test of a thermonuclear weapon in 1953, followed by the first Soviet test of an intercontinental missile and the launching of Sputnik in 1957, all heralded the end of U.S. nuclear dominance, which was essential to the "massive retaliation" strategy.

Similarly, the shift in U.S. strategy, announced by Secretary of Defense Robert McNamara at Ann Arbor in 1962, from targeting Soviet cities to targeting Soviet military forces, almost immediately clashed with the reality of the U.S. defense budget. By 1967, this "counterforce" strategy had bowed to the lower-cost precept of "assured destruction," based on the ability of U.S. forces to absorb a surprise attack and survive with sufficient power to inflict unacceptable damage on the aggressor.

By 1971, continuing budget constraints and a growing Soviet capability led to Secretary of Defense Melvin Laird's doctrine of "strategic sufficiency" as the guiding principle for forces structured to provide the assured capability of a second strike, thereby reducing any incentive for the Soviets to launch a first strike. Force planners responded with requirements to improve the survivability of U.S. strategic nuclear forces, but again in the absence of any consensus as to how the needed resources to underwrite that strategy could be provided.

Whatever their ultimate credibility, however, declarations of strategy do serve as the basis for force planning and for assessing the adequacy of strategic forces. In fact, one of the difficulties in assessing declaratory strategy is that it is often primarily intended to set limits on the aspirations of force planners. As an example, Henry S. Rowen points out that in the strategy of "assured destruction," the stated goals of damage to be inflicted on the Soviet Union were intended more to limit U.S. forces than to define deterrent objectives. Even so, those goals were difficult to reconcile with Secretary McNamara's policy of avoiding attacks on Soviet cities.[2]

THE STRATEGY-RESOURCES MISMATCH

Another important aspect, which tends to be overlooked in the debate about "pure" strategy, is that "surrounding issues" have intruded on the central planning rationales throughout the process of strategy evolution. For example, long after earlier U.S. strategies had lost credibility, resources consistently fell short of those required to underwrite the more expensive "flexible response" strategy of the 1970s. A massive Soviet program of strategic forces development and deployment, dispersal and hardening, along with improved U.S. intelligence of these measures, constantly widened the gap between strategy and the means to underwrite it. A series of efforts to modernize strategic forces registered little progress through the 1970s. The B-1A bomber followed the path of the B-70 to early cancellation by the Carter administration. The MX missile became mired in chronic controversy over its basing mode. A long-planned new, smaller ICBM remained on the extended planning horizon, bereft of serious funding support. Hence, Soviet forces clearly exhibited the capability for mutually assured destruction, and lack of resources precluded endowing the credibility of "flexible response" with the needed counterforce element.

As a result, the "neglect of the 1970s" became a significant issue in the 1980 election campaign. The Reagan administration carried into office a perceived mandate to invest in the modernization of U.S. strategic forces, a conviction that arms reduction must inextricably be linked to such modernization, and a general policy of dealing with the Soviets from a position of strength.

Those perceptions, earnestly supported by the Department of Defense, initially supported by the public (with polls reporting up to 85 percent in support), and generally supported by the Congress, led to what quickly became known as the "President's Strategic Modernization Program." That program evolved into funded programs for improvements in command, control, and communications; two new bombers; two air-launched cruise missile programs; two ICBM programs; the Trident II ballistic missile submarine; and the D-5 Submarine-Launched Ballistic Missile (SLBM) programs; and a major enhancement of the air-refueling force with the KC-135R upgrade program. Together those programs were to modernize U.S. strategic forces across the board.

However, it quickly became apparent that, even with the heady defense budget expectations of the early 1980s, full-scale funding of the strategic modernization program would prove devastating to conventional forces programs. Some argued that conventional forces had been victimized even more by the "neglect of the 1970s" than strategic nuclear forces. Threats to U.S. interests in the Middle East, Southwest Asia, and elsewhere further strengthened the case for robust conventional forces. Alongside budgetary pressures came the growing commitment by the Reagan and Bush administrations to serious arms reduction nego-

Table 7.1
Strategic Force Modernization Expectations

System	Early 80s	End of 80s
Peacekeeper ICBMs (1)	100 missiles	0 missiles
	1000 missiles	500 warheads
Small ICBMs	500 missiles	extended development
	500 warheads	
B-1B bombers (2)	100 bombers w/cruise missiles	97 bombers missiles deferred
B-2 bombers	132 bombers	75 bombers
Advanced cruise missiles	replace all ALCMs	equip selected bombers
Trident II submarines	22+ boats	18 boats
Modern warheads	10,000+	6,500+

(1) Originally 200 -- dropped to 100+ small ICBM
(2) Originally 240 -- dropped for a mixed bomber force

tiations. Moreover, during Mikhail Gorbachev's tenure, from 1985 to 1991, the image took hold in the United States, and the West in general, of a Soviet leadership increasingly preoccupied with internal challenges and seriously seeking ways to divert investment from the military sector to economic development.

By 1986, this combination of budget pressures, arms negotiations, and perceived decline of the Soviet threat had significantly eroded the consensus for U.S. strategic force modernization. By that time as well, the public mood was reflected in polls that showed Americans to be concerned more with the threat from economic competitors than with a military threat. The defense budget was seen by some as a major cause of the budget deficit, by others as a likely source of help in its solution. Therefore, from 1985 onward, the resources available for strategic modernization fell short of what was required to support even a progressively reduced modernization program. Table 7.1 illustrates the gap between the expectations during the early 1980s and those at the end of the decade.

The discussion so far has illustrated the changes in expectations regarding modernization and the broad, continuing reasons behind these changes. As in the past, any sensible projection of the strategic forces for which the United States can realistically plan must take those complex and conflicting pressures into account.

Strategic Forces for the Future

ARMS REDUCTIONS MOMENTUM IN PERSPECTIVE

Fundamental in establishing the size and shape of future U.S. strategic nuclear deterrent forces is the criterion that such forces be adequate to ensure that no potential adversary can hope to derive gain from initiating an attack on the United States or its allies. Furthermore, persistent statements by the president and the secretary of defense have stressed that U.S. strategic nuclear capabilities must continue to be based on the assessed capabilities of a potential foe, in this case the Russian Federation, or the Commonwealth of Independent States (CIS). Judging by recent declarations by President Yeltsin, assessments of the potential adversary seem to indicate a cooperative rather than confrontational foreign policy agenda.

The Treaty between the United States of America and the Union of Soviet Socialist Republics on the Reduction and Limitation of Strategic Offensive Arms, signed in Moscow on July 31, 1991, is based on this principle of equivalent capabilities. This Strategic Arms Reduction Treaty (START) permits each side to deploy 6,000 "accountable" warheads, of which no more than 4,900 may be on ballistic missiles. As a result, the United States and what was the Soviet Union will reduce their total number of strategic warheads by about 25 and 35 percent, respectively, and their ballistic missile warheads by 40 and 48 percent. The limit on ballistic missile warheads will encourage both sides to move toward single-warhead ICBMs. In addition, by mandating a 46 percent cut in CIS aggregate ballistic missile throw-weight, START will substantially reduce the CIS potential to "fractionate," or load large numbers of extra throw-weight on its ballistic missiles.

By placing a cap on the throw-weight and the number of ballistic missile warheads each side may field, START complicates first-strike attack plans and severely limits the Russian, or CIS, capability of barraging large areas that may contain bombers, submarines, or mobile missiles. The treaty tightly constrains the SS-18 heavy ICBM force; this is the missile that the United States regards as the most destabilizing first-strike weapon in the CIS arsenal. No increase in the SS-18 throw-weight or number will be permitted. By counting ballistic missile warheads one for one, while heavily discounting the number of bomber-carried weapons, START will give the CIS a strong incentive to shift the relative emphasis of its strategic bomber forces from ballistic missiles to slower-flying bombers, which pose less threat of surprise attack. Overall, the already robust U.S. retaliatory capability will achieve even greater survivability, as Table 7.2 shows.

With that as a starting point, specific guidance with respect to post-START forces is found in the Soviet–United States joint statement issued on June 1, 1990, following the Washington, D.C., summit of President Bush and then President Gorbachev. Of the five points in the statement, the second dealt most directly with goals for arms reductions beyond START. It declared the overall purpose to be for the two sides to

Table 7.2
Survivability of U.S. Strategic Forces under START

Strategic Systems	Estimated Survival Levels in percentage	Total RVs/Warheads	Number of RVs/Warheads survivable
ICBMs (1)	10%	1,423	142
SLBMs (2)	67%	3,456	2,315
Heavy bombers (3)	30%	3,676	1,102
Heavy bombers (4)	36%	4,636	1,630
Totals		8,555 to 9,515	3,559 to 4,087

(1) Higher if mobile ICBMs are deployed.
(2) Excludes 880 nuclear armed SLCMs, a number of which would also survive.
(3) Fifteen B-2s and a 30 percent alert rate for the entire bomber force.
(4) Seventy-five B-2s at a 50 percent alert rate, with remainder on bomber force at a 30 percent alert rate.

Source: The Arms Control Association, Washington, D.C.

seek to reduce their strategic offensive arms in a way consistent with enhancing strategic stability. In the new negotiations, the two sides agree to place emphasis on removing incentives for a nuclear first strike, on reducing the concentration of warheads on strategic delivery vehicles, and on giving priority to highly survivable systems. In particular, the two sides will seek measures that reduce the concentration of warheads on strategic delivery vehicles as a whole, including measures related to the question of heavy missiles and MIRVed ICBMs.[3]

The June 1, 1990, Washington summit statement also stressed the need for effective verification "by national technical means, cooperative measures, and on-site inspection." Verification thus must be considered another important criterion in the shaping of post-START strategic forces, especially when central control of nuclear weapons on the territories of the CIS is far from assured.

Three rounds of arms reduction proposals, initiated by the United States, have created the potential for accelerated movement toward the post-START goals mentioned above. In September 1991, President Bush announced unilateral cuts in tactical nuclear weapons. At the same time, he also took off alert all ICBMs scheduled for deactivation under the terms of START and announced that he would speed up elimination of all systems covered under the agreement. The president terminated the development of the mobile versions of the Peacekeeper ICBM and the small ICBM, sought early agreement on steps to eliminate multiple-warhead ICBMs, and placed emphasis on a joint approach to strategic defense.

Strategic Forces for the Future

Table 7.3
Strategic Nuclear Warheads in Central Eurasia, January 1992

	ICBMs	SLBMs	Bombers
Russia	3,928	3,626	1,378
Ukraine	1,240	0	416
Kazakhstan	1,040	0	370
Belarus	72	0	0

Source: Arms Control and Disarmament Agency, Washington, D.C.

President Gorbachev reciprocated in the area of tactical nuclear arms and agreed to undertake similar steps to those proposed by Bush in the area of strategic systems. Gorbachev announced the termination of the development of a small-sized mobile ICBM and a freeze on the modernization plans for railway-based ICBMs, and indicated his intention to return all ICBMs to permanent bases. He also said he would reduce what was then the Soviet nuclear arsenal further than START called for and would propose even further cuts. Significantly, Gorbachev also was willing to discuss the U.S. proposal for non-nuclear antimissile defense systems, including the possibility of a joint system with ground- and space-based elements.

One rationale underlying President Bush's initiatives to pursue radical cuts was the threat of nuclear weapons proliferation among the republics of the former Soviet Union. Under the CIS agreement, the former Soviet strategic forces are still supposed to be centrally controlled, under a dual key arrangement between Russia and the other former republics. Nevertheless, the strategic forces that made up the Soviet nuclear arsenal are now located in four independent states— Russia, Kazakhstan, Belarus, and Ukraine. And, while the three latter states expressed their willingness to eventually eliminate strategic forces on their territories, the three have linked any such moves to reductions by other nuclear-armed states, especially Russia. The distribution of CIS strategic nuclear warheads is shown in Table 7.3.

Clearly, President Bush's September initiative was designed to help speed up the elimination of difficult-to-monitor tactical nuclear weapons throughout what were then the fragmenting Soviet republics and to begin an orderly transition, to the extent possible, toward post-START goals in the area of strategic forces. With the newly created CIS presumably in control of the strategic forces located in the four states listed above, Bush moved again in January 1992, this time to speed up cuts in the strategic arena. In his State of the Union message, he stated that the United States would end production of the B-2 bomber after twenty bombers were built, stop new production of the ten-warhead Peacekeeper ICBM, cancel the single-warhead small ICBM, end new purchases of advanced cruise missiles, and halt production of new warheads for sea-based nuclear missiles. Bush also proposed to Russia and the other nuclear-armed states in the CIS that land-based multiple-warhead nuclear missiles be eliminated. While President Yeltsin responded positively to this second major initiative, suggesting that long-range nuclear warheads be reduced to between 2,000 and 2,500 on each side, at this writing the complicated details remain to be worked out.

To place this in perspective, it will take Russia and the other nuclear states some time to eliminate tactical nuclear weapons and reduce their strategic arsenals to the START levels. Even if future negotiations between the United States and the four parties of the CIS concerned with strategic forces go smoothly, such negotiations are likely to take place during a time of tremendous social, political, and economic upheaval in all the successor states to the Soviet Union.

By December 1991, Gorbachev was out of power, the Soviet Union had dissolved, and as president of Russia, Yeltsin seemed poised to dominate the new Commonwealth of Independent States. Yeltsin continued to pursue an active arms control agenda. As a result of negotiations that started shortly after Yeltsin assumed power, on June 16, 1992, the United States and the Russian Federation were able to announce a new joint initiative. The two presidents agreed in principle to slash their nuclear arsenals to between 3,000 and 3,500 nuclear warheads apiece, which is approximately 8,000 warheads fewer than agreed upon under START. The agreement is to eliminate all land-based multiple-warhead missiles by the year 2003, meaning Russia will lose its SS-18s and SS-24s and the United States will lose fifty ten-warhead MX missiles and also have to reduce the number of warheads on its Minuteman IIIs from three to one.

Meanwhile, and despite statements by Yeltsin that Russian missiles would no longer be targeted against the United States, the strategic nuclear forces of the four territories of the CIS continue to be the only military forces that can threaten the continued existence of the United States as a nation. Of course, assessments of a potential adversary's intentions are important in gauging near-term risk, and may be a valid consideration in determining reductions in future U.S. strategic force posture. Given the long lead-times of strategic programs, however, the objective fact of CIS strategic nuclear capabilities, and not current political variables or expectations, must be the key guide to U.S. force-planning for the longer term.

The size and capacity of the nuclear forces that remain in the CIS arsenal exceed by far any requirement for covering targets in the United States, Europe, and China. Populations, industry, and military installations in the United States and Europe are heavily concentrated; key transportation, power distribution, and civil system communications nodes are easily identified; and only a small number of military facilities are hardened against nuclear blast. This means that the relationship between forces and targets leaves the CIS with a large reserve, and it seems willing to build down further, as the June 1992 agreement between Bush and Yeltsin indicates.

Any future negotiations, however, will have to take into account the factors

Strategic Forces for the Future

that helped to create the current CIS strategic force. In large part, it reflects the influence of the past SALT accords, as well as considerations of cost; both yield incentives that run counter to the purposes of START and the announced goals of follow-on negotiations. As the Soviets modernized their force over the years, the average concentration of warheads increased from 3.1 per ballistic missile to 7.6. At the same time, the average loading for ballistic missile platforms increased from 40 to 170.

The CIS forces also reflect a long-held priority on modernized ICBMs. The incentives that led the Soviets to concentrate on ICBMs in the early 1950s continue to weigh heavily. Geography and climate make bomber operations more difficult for the states in the CIS than for the United States. The southernmost bomber base in the CIS is subjected to harsher climatic conditions than the northern bases in the United States. Moreover, the former Soviet Union did not invest in the aerial tanker force required to sustain a larger penetrating bomber force.

Constrained access to the sea and lack of a "blue-water" naval tradition tend to limit the CIS ballistic missile submarine operations to "SSBN bastions" close to their coasts and even to their ports. These and other factors make for continued CIS resistance to shifting major strategic reliance away from ICBMs.

The current inventory of U.S. strategic forces, on the other hand, reflects the U.S. preference for a balanced triad, with quantitative emphasis on the maritime component. As with the Soviets, the SALT agreements and cost considerations have led to heavy MIRVing of U.S. ICBM and SLBM forces. In fact, the preponderance of highly MIRVed SLBMs makes the U.S. force heavier in warhead numbers overall than the CIS forces are—a point that is almost certain to be focused upon in follow-on negotiations.

THE FUTURE U.S. STRATEGIC NUCLEAR DETERRENT FORCE

A set of coherent objectives to guide the evolution of a future U.S. strategic nuclear force can be summarized as follows:

- Ensure a deterrent force adequate to convince a rational adversary that he has nothing to gain, and everything to lose, in initiating a nuclear attack. The force must also be adequate to deal with potential "third powers" armed with nuclear or other mass-destruction weapons whose behavior may be less rational.
- Increase stability by reducing the incentives for the first strike, reducing the concentration of warheads on strategic delivery vehicles as a whole, and giving priority to highly survivable systems.
- Reduce the cost of strategic nuclear deterrent forces.
- Reduce the incentive for destabilizing countermeasures.

A balanced triad, with each leg having significant deterrent power along with reduced concentrations of warheads and higher survivability, remains the best assurance of high-confidence deterrence. Such a force also incorporates the needed flexibility of capabilities adaptable to changing strategies, target bases, defenses, political factors, and other variables.

As an illustration of the need for that flexibility, the newest B-52 bomber is more than thirty years old. It was designed as a high-altitude penetrator to carry high-yield gravity bombs. Improved Soviet air defenses required that it be modified for low-altitude penetration. Technology and doctrine called for further modifications, to provide both standoff capability and accuracy in delivery. As suggested earlier, the operational lives of newer systems will similarly span generations of strategies, concepts, political leaderships, and doctrines. Therefore there is need for forces that are neither narrowly tailored nor driven by short-term considerations.

The foregoing discussion has been relevant to the composition of the U.S. deterrent force of the future, but less so with respect to its size. It does seem apparent that ultimately the force fielded by the United States will be significantly smaller than that permitted even by START and its follow-on agreement, for a number of reasons.

First, dramatic initiatives by both Bush and Yeltsin suggest that both sides are ready, at least in principle, to reduce their arsenals substantially and to further explore confidence-building measures, similar to those already advanced by Bush, Gorbachev and now Yeltsin, such as taking parts of the strategic force off alert.

Second, for a significant part of the 1980s, U.S. force plans were influenced by the "squeezers"—those who saw utility in the competitive pressures imposed by the U.S. strategic forces buildup on Soviet behavior both in arms negotiations and in their activities around the globe.[4] It may be argued that this approach had its intended effects.

And third, intense budgetary pressures presage a significantly smaller U.S. force.

To be sure, there are also strong considerations working to limit the decline in U.S. forces. There may well be a fundamental change in the Russian, or CIS, perception of the overall strategic position. From a Moscow perspective, the world has changed drastically since the Reykjavik summit, when Gorbachev indicated a willingness to eliminate all ballistic missiles. On balance, Russia or the CIS may now be contemplating a move from conventional superiority over potential opponents to inferiority, given the potential fragmentation of the centralized military. That shift would place a renewed premium on nuclear power as the "redressive" element among the CIS members that possess it.

OUTLINES OF A FOLLOW-ON FORCE

In light of all the factors, especially U.S. budgetary pressures, consideration must be given to post-START structure alternatives that meet the hard requirements of stable deterrence, but also the hard political and economic realities.

Strategic Forces for the Future

For cost reasons, the ICBM component of that force can be silo based. The single warhead per silo leaves the adversary with little prospect of altering the correlation of forces with a first strike on the ICBM force, since the exchange rate for the attacker will be worse than one for one. However, there is a margin of risk acceptance. The attacker could logically conclude that a rate of less than one for one still warrants a first strike against silo-based ICBMs, given the prospective combination of the value of damage to the opponent and the value of damage avoided by the preempting attacker.[5] If any comfort is still to be derived from reducing the opponent's prospects to worse than one for one, the latter's force must be small enough to demand economical targeting. Hence, while single-warhead, silo-based ICBMs are deemed less destabilizing than MIRVed missiles, it is important to keep in mind the overall deterrent equation. Until the Russian or CIS intentions become clear with respect to President Bush's proposal to eliminate MIRVed ICBMs, the Minuteman III ICBM can be reduced to a single warhead at minimum cost.

To reduce concentration of warheads on platforms in the follow-on force, the D-5 can be "downloaded" to five warheads each. That reduces the platform loading to 120 warheads versus 192, lowering the target value while sustaining a force of eighteen SSBNs. After the 1991 budget, the eighteen-vessel force will represent mostly cost already expended, and it is not economical to replace Ohio-class submarines (at just under $1.3 billion each)[6] with smaller submarines. This modification also drops the D-5 to a level below that challenged as "highly MIRVed" in previous negotiations. That, plus eventually eliminating the Peacekeeper, could eventually provide the United States with the tradeoff to persuade the Russian Federation or the CIS to give up at least its silo-based, MIRVed ICBMs.

The bomber remains the most stabilizing member of the triad, with high prelaunch survivability, no first-strike capability, and devastating retaliatory capability. Furthermore, as demonstrated by the range of uses over the more than thirty years of the B-52's operational life, the bomber provides great flexibility in the face of changing demands. Now that the number of B-2s planned has been reduced to twenty from seventy-five, some B-52H bombers should be retained in a cruise-missile carrier role and B-1B bombers in the penetrating role. If the B-2 force is fixed at twenty or canceled entirely, there is the obviously increasing risk over time of being forced either to abandon bombers entirely or to incur the cost of new bomber development.

The eight hundred silo-based, single-warhead Minuteman III ICBMs would offer reasonable security against a first strike due to their number and dispersal. Still, despite the president's decision to cancel it, it would be prudent for the United States to continue development of mobile basing for ICBMs. Mobility enhances not only survivability, but high-confidence deterrence across a wide spectrum of contingencies in an unpredictable global environment.

A more difficult, and disputed, question is whether the United States should (or better, will) continue development of a Strategic Defense Initiative (SDI). This subject will be explored in a broader context in Chapter 8.

STRATEGIC LOGIC AND AN UNPREDICTABLE FUTURE

There is little that is revolutionary in the thoughts and recommendations posited above. Instead, they reflect recognition that evolutionary changes are required. We have witnessed dramatic changes in the relationship between the United States and the Soviet Union and its successor states, along with an equally dramatic decline in the conventional threat to Western Europe. It remains to be seen whether these changes are lasting; meanwhile, however, there abides a constant: Russian or CIS strategic nuclear forces represent the capability to inflict devastating damage on the United States and its allies.

Compelling political and economic trends and pressures, together with changes in the strategic environment, seem to be pointing toward a future U.S. strategic posture characterized by reductions well beyond those contemplated in START and the follow-on agreement. Still, events in the world at large are moving rapidly. There is the prospect of changes in the newly created CIS of such scope that their consequences cannot be predicted. All this argues for time to absorb and understand the impact of global changes.

In the meantime, the basic planning framework for strategic forces still applies. The structure of forces for the twenty-first century should be shaped by strategic logic—that is, by definition of the national objective, of the strategy to achieve the objective, and of the military tasks, capabilities, and forces necessary to underwrite the strategy. The irreducible criterion for the force is that they must continue to be able to absorb some part of a first strike with surviving forces clearly capable of imposing unacceptable damage on the attacker. The declared and implied objectives for that follow-on force require that it be more survivable and less costly, and that it neither invite nor threaten a first strike.

NOTES

1. For a discussion of the evolution and practice of deterrent strategy, see Phillip Bobbit and Lawrence Freedman, *U.S. Nuclear Strategy* (New York: New York University Press, 1989); see also Stephen J. Cimbala, *Rethinking Nuclear Strategy* (Wilmington, Del.: SR Books, 1988).

2. Henry S. Rowen, "Evolution of Strategic Nuclear Doctrine," in *Strategic Thought in the Nuclear Age*, edited by Lawrence Martin (Baltimore, Md.: Johns Hopkins University Press, 1979), p. 146.

3. "Soviet–United States Joint Statement on Future Negotiations on Nuclear and Space Arms and Further Enhancing Strategic Stability," Washington, D.C.: June 1, 1990.

4. Arnold L. Horlick, "U.S.-Soviet Relations: The Threshold of a New Era," *Foreign Affairs* 69 (no. 1), pp. 51–69.

5. For a discussion on first-strike stability and target values, see Glenn A. Kent and David E. Thaler, *First Strike Stability—A Method for Evaluating Strategic Forces*, Rand R–3765-AF (Santa Monica, Calif.: Rand Corporation, 1989).

6. U.S. Department of Defense, "Department of Defense Budget for FYs 1990 and 1991," Washington, D.C.: January 9, 1989.

8

Coping with Global Missile Proliferation

Gen. John L. Piotrowski, USAF (Ret.)

The Iran-Iraq war was still in the early phase of what was to become an eight-year bloodbath of attrition. An E-3A AWACS, part of the contingent deployed to Riyadh, Saudi Arabia, since late 1980, was on patrol, executing racetrack orbits parallel to the Persian Gulf. Three weapons technicians aboard the aircraft were peering into the twinkling green-on-green displays, watching for Iranian and Iraqi aircraft that might pose a threat to Saudi Arabia. Suddenly the AWACS crew's boredom was broken by a rapid trace of processed radar returns on the screen. The crew had never before observed this unique pattern of closely spaced dots rapidly retracing themselves: they emanated from Iraqi territory and terminated near Teheran.

Upon landing, the AWACS crew was informed that the timing, location, and direction of the observed radar scope phenomenon correlated with an SS-1 Scud ballistic missile launched from Iraq into Iran. The "war of the cities" had begun, and with it the second missile bombardment of the twentieth century—the first since Hitler attempted to bring Great Britain to her knees with a rain of V-2 rockets.

The event was scarcely noted in the United States. After all, it transpired in a war remote from America's preoccupations at the time—a war, moreover, between two nations, neither of which drew much sympathy from Americans. No one could imagine at the time that, several years later, similar Iraqi Scuds would take on a different and very direct meaning for U.S. and allied forces deployed along the Persian Gulf, for Saudi citizens in Dhahran and Riyadh, and for the Israeli populations of Tel Aviv and Haifa.

In the Gulf War, the initial impact of this "terror weapon" was blunted (literally) by the remarkable performance of Patriot antimissile missiles, dramatized by the eventually almost routine spectacle of explosive flashes of missile intercepts in the night skies.

The Patriot missile system is designed for "point defense"—that is, the protection of fairly circumscribed military assets, such as airfields, command and control centers, and the missile batteries themselves, against incoming missiles. The Patriot missiles are shot upward to engage an incoming missile in its final approach to the target. The explosive fragments from the engagement, necessarily "close in," pose no significant problem in the case of defense of military targets located in thinly populated areas. For that reason, as well as because of their radar coverage, Patriots were not designed for the mission of defending dense population centers, let alone sprawling ones like Tel Aviv.

Fortunately for the coalition forces in the Gulf and the populations of Israel and Saudi Arabia, the Iraqi Scud missiles fired at them basically reflected Soviet missile technology of the 1950s, however improved and modified. They were relatively inaccurate, although accuracy with respect to the target is also a function of the explosive yield of the warhead on the missile. It would have been a different scenario if, instead of conventional explosives, the Iraqi Scuds had carried chemical or biological munitions, or worse, nuclear warheads. It is one thing to intercept and detonate high-explosive warheads several thousand feet over Riyadh or Tel Aviv; it would be quite another thing to engage and detonate in this way a 100-kiloton nuclear warhead. When a nuclear warhead is detonated at altitudes of several thousand feet, the nuclear blast, radiation, and fireball effects are enhanced, creating unimaginable damage over tens of square miles.

It would also have been a different story if Iraq had possessed and fired longer-range and therefore higher-velocity missiles. Longer-range missiles present two significant problems to Patriot defenses. First, they enlarge the geographical area of impact; hence the number of targets at risk increases geometrically. Short-range Patriot interceptors cannot protect the possible number of targets threatened by longer-range ballistic missiles, even if the Patriot could cope with the higher reentry velocities of those missiles. Second, a much faster ballistic missile, or one sophisticated enough to shed its warhead after rocket burnout, would severely challenge the Patriot's radar tracking capability, possibly even escaping radar detection altogether.

It was clearly in recognition of the threat dramatized in the Gulf war, as well as the limits of current defenses against it, that President Bush included in his State of the Union address of January 30, 1992, the following statement: "I have directed that the SDI program be refocused on providing protection from limited ballistic missile strikes, whatever their source. Let us pursue an SDI program that can deal with any future threat to the United States, to our forces overseas, and to our friends and allies." Recognition of dire threat is better late than never; in this case, it was long overdue.

The redirection of the SDI program to which President Bush referred has become known as the Global Protection Against Accidental Launch System, or

Table 8.1
Ballistic Missile and Spacecraft Launches, 1987–89

Year	U.S.	U.S.S.R.	Others	Totals
1987	90+	600+	100+	850
1988	90+	600	200+	950
1989	80+	600	1,000+	1,700

GPALS. More will be said below about the important distinctions between GPALS and the preceding Phase 1 SDI program.

THE TRAILS OF MISSILE PROLIFERATION

If the start and execution of Iraq's original missile war against Iran drew little attention in the West, the fact that Iraq eventually subdued Iran, in large part because of the carnage and terror unleashed on Teheran by the Scuds, was not lost on the leaderships of Third World nations. It certainly was not lost on the Soviet leaders who had made the missiles available to their Iraqi ally, or to Soviet "advisors" working with Iraqi missile crews. The Soviets apparently were so impressed with the results of their missile exports that they built upon that experience in the subsequent war in Afghanistan.

Indeed, the ominous prospect of a worldwide proliferation of ballistic missile capabilities is finally gaining attention, as the threat it poses becomes more obvious. Take as one indicator the number of missile and space launches conducted in the world each year. The number of such launches in 1987–89 is shown in Table 8.1. In 1987, militarily relevant missile and space launches throughout the world totaled approximately 850, of which Soviet missile tests and space launches accounted for well over 600. Comparable U.S. firings of missiles and space boosters amounted to less than 100. The remaining launches were attributed to other nations, including France, the United Kingdom, China, and India.

In 1988, the total number of launches climbed to approximately 950. The number of Soviet firings declined somewhat, reflecting the near completion of testing of new-generation Soviet ICBMs and SLBMs: the MIRVed, silo-based, and rail-mobile SS-24; the single-warhead, road-mobile SS-25; an improved SS-18; and longer-range and more accurate SS-N-21s and SS-N-23s. The increase in the total was caused by the firing by Iraq of roughly 200 extended-range SS-1 Scuds, attempting to bombard Teheran into submission.

The cessation of hostilities between Iran and Iraq did not bring about a decline in the worldwide total of missile launches in 1989. To the contrary—the Soviets shifted the focus of their missile exports to Afghanistan, where their puppet government, with the assistance of Soviet advisors, launched hundreds of Scuds against Mujahideen strongholds. By the end of 1989, the sum of missile and space firings nearly doubled that of the preceding year. Spurred by Iraq's success against Iran, a race was on for missile capabilities among Third World nations.

The basic incentives in this race among Third World countries are clear. Ballistic missiles offer a shortcut toward military power and prestige, particularly to nations that have neither the means nor the technological base and infrastructure to build large, modernized armies. The range of the missiles makes their possessor a "regional" military power. Once one aspirant for regional hegemony acquires the missiles, rival neighbors feel compelled to answer with comparable capabilities. The whole process is fueled by the progressive ease of acquiring such capabilities on the international marketplace of arms, particularly by entering into a client status with such heretofore liberal suppliers as the Soviet Union, now Russia, and Communist China. Once rudimentary missile capabilities are acquired, they can be improved and expanded through indigenous efforts or contracted foreign expertise. Again, Iraq is a perfect case in point.

The process of proliferation is both accelerating and spreading. Table 8.2 lists countries either possessing ballistic missiles or known to have them under development. It will be noted that most of those states inhabit a broad arc along the periphery of the Eurasian landmass, from North Africa through the Middle East and Southwest Asia to Northeast Asia. All of them bear the scars of revolutionary upheavals and regional rivalries and conflict. But the proliferation trails are also extending elsewhere, into southern Africa and even into the Western Hemisphere.

Giving this picture its ominous cast is the marriage of missile capabilities with warheads of mass destruction—nuclear, chemical, and biological. Judge William Webster, the former director of the CIA, shocked Congress with his estimate that by the turn of the century some twenty nations will have stockpiled warheads of mass destruction.

Ballistic missiles are not the only long-range delivery means of such warheads. Desert Storm showed the effectiveness of the United States Navy's Tomahawk cruise missiles, fired from vessels in the Gulf at targets deep inland. The record of their performance undoubtedly heightened the interest of would-be "proliferators" looking for relatively inexpensive means of delivery.

Indeed, the availability of GPLAS or Global Orbiting Navigation Satellite System (GLONASS) satellite navigation receivers, and the combination of such receivers with jet engines, or even with the autopilots of unmanned jet aircraft loaded with explosives, brings cruise missile capabilities increasingly within the reach of a number of nations. It may be true that uncoded GPLAS and GLONASS signals provide a potential accuracy of only some 40m to 50m. Still, such precision parameters are more than sufficient for striking at population, industrial, and cultural targets.

Moreover, cruise missiles offer several advantages over their ballistic counterparts, particularly as weapons of terror. For one, their launch (takeoff) signature is too subtle for detection by current sensors, allowing room for "plausible

Table 8.2
Third World Ballistic Missiles

Country	Missile	Range (km)	Warhead (lbs)	Status
Argentina	Condor I	100	880	developing
	Condor II	900	1,000	developing
Brazil	MB/EE-150	150	1,100	in testing
	SS-300	300	2,200	in testing
	SS-1000	1,200	2,200	R&D
	MB/EE-350	350	na	R&D
	MB/EE-600	600	na	R&D
Egypt	Frog-7	70	1,000	used 1973
	Scud-B	300	1,100	deployed
	Saqr-80	80	50	deployed
	Improved Scud	300	2,200	production planned
	Badr-2000	900	1,000	developing
India	Prithvi	150-300	1,100-2,200	tested 1988
	Agni	2,500	2,000	tested 1989
Iran	Frog-7	70	1,000	Iran-Iraq War
	Frog-B	300	1,100	Iran-Iraq War
	Al-Husayn	600	420	Iran-Iraq War
	Iran-130	120	na	Iran-Iraq War
Iraq	Frog-7	70	1,000	Iran-Iraq War
	Scud-B	300	1,000	Iran-Iraq War, Gulf War
	Al-Husayn	600	420	Iran-Iraq War, Gulf War
	Al-Abbas	900	na	tested in 1988
	Condor II	900	1,000	developing
	Fahd	250-500	1,000	R&D
	3-Stage Rkt	1,800	na	tested 1989
Israel	Lance	110	600	deployed
	Jericho I	500	680	deployed
	Jericho II	1,450	na	tested 1987
Libya	Frog-7	70	1,000	deployed
	Scud-B	300	1,100	used in 1986
	Otrag	490	NA	development
North Korea	Frog-7	70	1,000	deployed
	Scud-B	300	1,100	deployed
Pakistan	HATF I	80	1,100	tested in 1989
	HATF II	300	1,100	tested in 1989

Table 8.2 continued

Country	Missile	Range (km)	Warhead (lbs)	Status
Saudi Arabia	CSS-2	2,200	4,500	deployed
South Africa	unknown	na	na	tested in 1989
South Korea	Korean SSM	180-250	na	deployed
Syria	Frog-7	70	1,000	deployed
	Scud-B	300	1,100	deployed
	SS-21	120	1,000	deployed
Taiwan	Ching Feng	120	na	deployed
	Sky Horse	960	na	R&D
Yemen	Frog-7	70	1,000	deployed
	Scud-B	300	1,100	deployed
	SS-21	120	1,000	deployed

Sources: IISS, SIPRI

denial'' by the aggressor nation. At the same time, the narrow cross-section of cruise missiles makes them difficult to distinguish by radars. By dint of their long range (1,500 nautical miles or more), cruise missiles can be launched along a circuitous trajectory, thereby compounding the problem of identifying the source of aggression. All of these considerations call urgently for the development of detection and tracking systems capable of coping with cruise missiles and "digging them out" of routine air traffic.

OPTIONS FOR COUNTERMEASURES

The broader problem, missile proliferation and its implications, was placed in sharper relief by the Gulf War, where the shadow of the missile threat extended over U.S. forces in the field, as well as over allied forces and populations. This kind of experience may well be repeated, with much more disastrous consequences than occurred during Desert Storm. Beyond that, however, the day may not be too remote when U.S. territory and population centers themselves become prey to missiles armed with warheads of mass destruction in the hands of powers other than the CIS and Communist China. Memories are fading of the Cuban missile crisis of 1962 and its traumas. The nuclear armed projectiles then aimed at U.S. cities were Soviet medium-range missiles, and the crisis was resolved in the context of a potential superpower confrontation. But if they had been Cuban missiles, what might have been the outcome of the crisis?

Possible countermeasures against the evolving threat fall into basically three categories. The first is deterrence through the threat of retaliation against the offending nation. However, deterrence rests on the indispensable twin pillars of (1) credibility—the believed intent and the ability to carry out the retaliatory threat—and (2) rationality, meaning calculus on the part of the would-be aggressor of potential gains versus risks and consequences. Deterrence may have worked in the U.S.-Soviet confrontation. As the crisis in the Gulf demonstrated, rationality, and therefore deterrence, are likely to be far more elusive elements in Third World scenarios. Moreover, as possession of warheads of mass destruction and the means to deliver them spread to an increasing number of countries, credible deterrence calls for another vital prerequisite: namely, the assured ability to pinpoint the source of a missile launch and thus positively identify the transgressor.

A second category of possible countermeasures is that of preemption—a disarming strike launched against the offending state's means of mass destruction. Again there is the issue of credibility. A nation like Israel, which considers itself in a state of continuous war with its Arab opponents, has shown a willingness to reach for this option, as it did in the raid against the Iraqi nuclear reactor in 1981. The U.S. punitive attack on Libya in 1986 notwithstanding, it staggers the imagination to picture the United States deliberately embracing a strategy of preemption across the board. Moreover, the issue of willingness becomes somewhat academic in light of the question of operational feasibility. The lessons of the Gulf War, and its aftermath of efforts to pinpoint and destroy Saddam Hussein's surviving capabilities and programs of mass destruction weapons, are all too clear in that respect as well. It is difficult enough to pinpoint the locations of a country's nuclear, chemical, and biological weapons facilities and to eliminate these via aerial strikes, especially to the extent that these are widely dispersed and/or hardened. It is all the more difficult to detect and target mobile missiles already armed with mass-destruction warheads.

That leaves the third category: a comprehensive defense shield designed to intercept any such missiles, irrespective of where they are launched and at whatever targets they are fired. As has already been noted with respect to the Patriot, terminal defenses alone cannot aspire to that task, even though, as will be brought out later in this chapter, they do have a role to play. What is needed, and practicable, is a space-based missile defense "against all comers." That is what President Bush presumably had in mind when he called for a redirection of the SDI program.

THE PHASE I STRATEGIC DEFENSE INITIATIVE (SDI)

Notwithstanding the obstacles of myopic politics and increasingly meager congressional funding, SDI has made substantial progress since it was first announced by President Ronald Reagan in March 1983. There is no space here for a detailed history of that progress. Suffice it to note that the practicable concept of a comprehensive Ballistic Missile Defense (BMD) emerged from the program; it has been dubbed Phase I SDI. This concept will be discussed here first in the context of its central rationale: a defense against what was then a potential Soviet missile attack upon the United States. Subsequently, we will explore how Phase I SDI might be applied to the broader problem.

The concept is relatively simple. Ballistic missile launches are easily and instantly detectable through state-of-the-art satellite technology (Figure 8.1). An ICBM, for example, at launch generates as much heat and light as a small city at night, and thus a commensurate "infrared signature." U.S. Defense Support Program (DSP) satellites have been detecting and reporting on a wide range of ballistic missile launches for more than a decade. These infrared-sensing satellites, in geosynchronous orbit, provide overlapping coverage of most of the earth's surface. They have proven highly reliable in providing data on detected and tracked ballistic missile and space launches. This writer had personally been involved in the assessment of more than three thousand ballistic missile and space launches detected and processed by the DSP system. Those assessments indicate origin of launch, trajectory, and likely area of impact. They thus perform the first three steps of a five-step process of ballistic missile defense.

Further technological advances are certain to yield rapid and positive identification of even the types of missiles launched. Thus, vastly improved sensors and Very-Large-Scale Integrated Circuit (VLSIC) processors will ensure that even missiles with shorter burn-time and lower heat signature rocket motors will be detected, tracked, and characterized. A large number of successful tests conducted under the sponsorship or direction of the Strategic Defense Initiative Office (SDIO) have erased any doubt about the U.S. aerospace industries' ability to manufacture the sensors, as well as the ground- and space-based interceptors required to mount an effective BMD.

Those space-based interceptors are the much-publicized Brilliant Pebbles (BPs) (Figures 8.2 and 8.3), conceived in the Lawrence Livermore Laboratory under the genius of Edward Teller and the stewardship of Lowell Wood. Tests have demonstrated the effectiveness of these small, hypervelocity projectiles in destroying a missile in thrusting flight. It has been estimated that an orbiting shield of approximately 7,000 Brilliant Pebbles could provide the wherewithal of a strategic defense, not only against a missile attack from the nuclear-armed republics of the CIS, but also for contingencies elsewhere on the globe.

As concerns the CIS, taking into account the limitations imposed by START, and pending further reductions in the strategic offensive forces of both sides, a major ICBM/SLBM attack by the CIS might consist of between 4,000 and 6,000 warheads atop anywhere from 500 to 700 boosters. Approximately 15 percent of the orbiting constellation of 7,000 BPs—some 1,050— would be positioned to engage the attack. The booster is highly vulnerable to BP intercept as it pushes its payload of deadly warheads through the atmosphere and into space and ballistic flight, where the boost vehicle coasts for several minutes before releasing up to 12 warheads on individual trajectories.

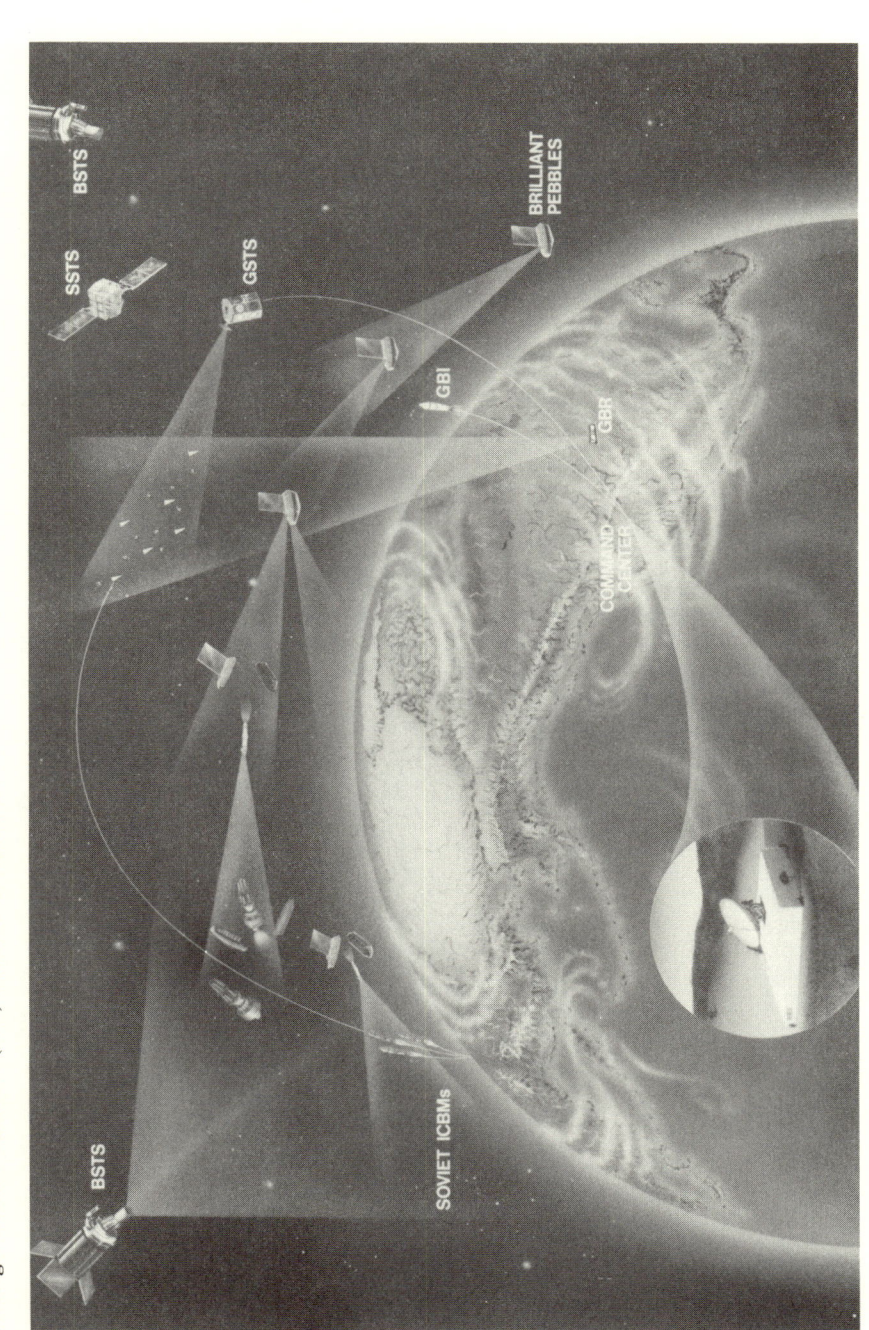

Figure 8.1
Strategic Defense Initiative (SDI) Planned Architecture

Figure 8.2
Brilliant Pebble, in Life Jacket

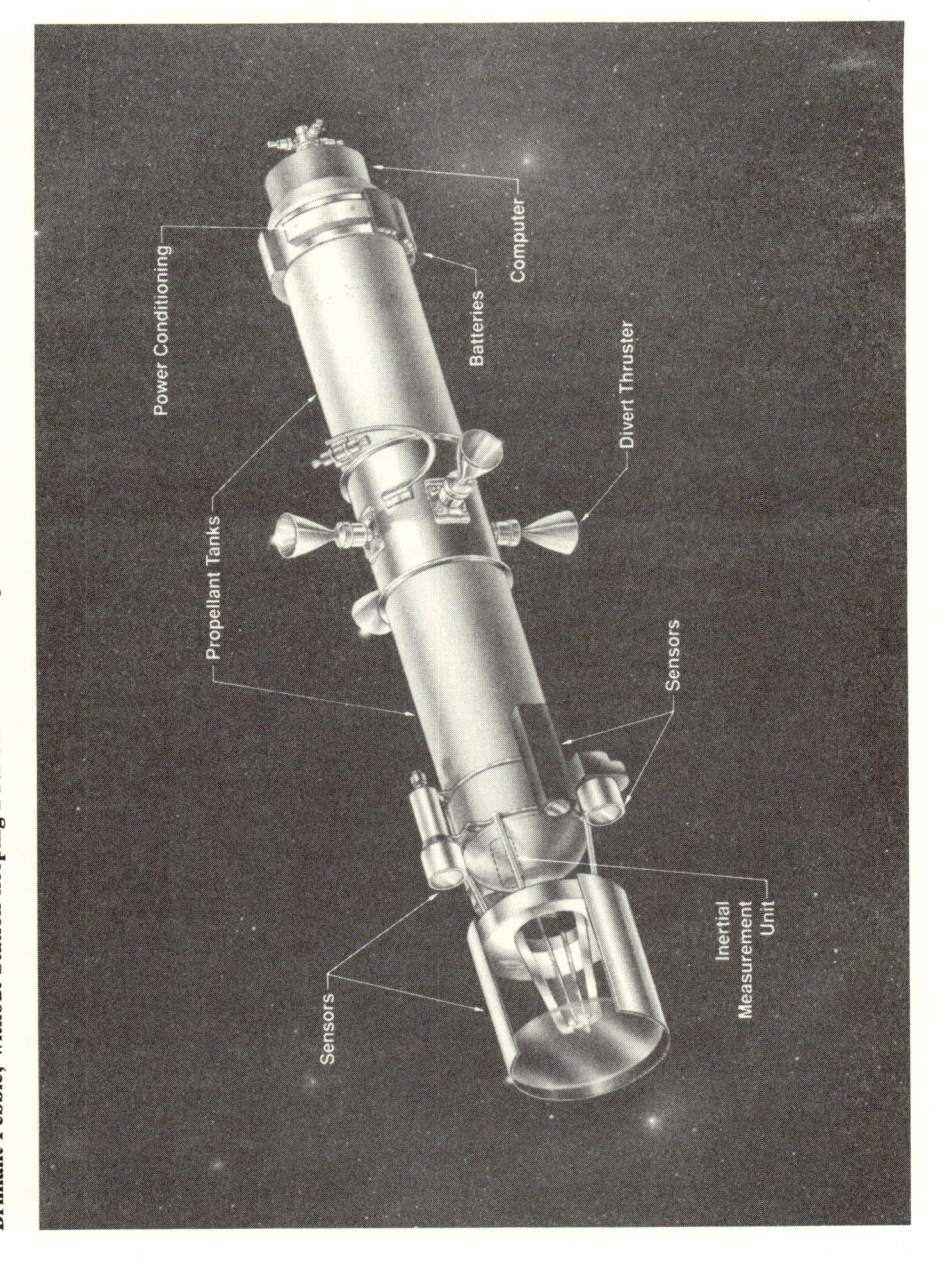

Figure 8.3
Brilliant Pebble, without Station-keeping Fuel Tanks and Life Jacket

133

These boost, post-boost, and "busing" phases can take anywhere from three to eight minutes, depending on the launch location, missile type, target area, and target dispersal.

Not all of the 1,050 BPs positioned to engage boosters would be successful. Yet the favorable ratio of BPs to boosters permits the individual targeting of a large percentage of the initial attacking force of missiles with two BPs apiece, thereby increasing the probability of their destruction from 90 to 99 percent. Altogether, the initial spasm of 500 to 700 boosters could thus be reduced substantially. This could still leave large numbers of warheads hurtling toward their targets in the United States. Those would be engaged, in turn, by BPs in their midcourse flight and by ground-based interceptors in their late midcourse and terminal phases.

What is being described is a layered strategic defense. In the postulated "worst-case" scenario, in which the United States must confront the full force of the CIS nuclear arsenal, it would by no means be a "leak-proof" defense. Some warheads would still penetrate to their targets, wreaking devastating damage. Even the most passionate advocates of SDI have never realistically aspired to a perfect defense. What they have pursued, rather, is essentially twofold: (1) buttressing of deterrence through defense, rather than endlessly amassing offensive capabilities in search of a "delicate balance of terror," and (2) creation of safeguards whereby, even in the worst "unthinkable" case, the United States might be able to survive as a functioning society.

It is being argued that all this belongs in the past tense—that the disappearance of the Soviet Union, along with the prospect of cuts much beyond the limits set in START, obviated the rationale for strategic defense. Unfortunately, the reverse is true; the arms reductions, real or anticipated, tend to elevate that rationale.

Uncertainty of CIS Control

No one can predict with any confidence the likely outcome of the turmoil in the Russia-dominated CIS. Though the Russian president, Yeltsin, has suggested that he and Marshal Y. I. Shaposhnikov control the nuclear button, Yeltsin has also stated that the other three republics with strategic forces on their territories—Ukraine, Belarus, and Kazakhstan—have some form of veto over a decision to launch. How that would play out in practice cannot be calculated with any certainty, and the elimination of strategic nuclear weapons from the territories of these three republics, which their leaders have pledged, is equally uncertain.

In the meantime, the essence of what was at the heart of the Soviet nuclear threat is still in place. In fact, there is strong evidence to the effect that the Strategic Rocket Forces and their supporting (vertically integrated) industrial complex have remained steadfast in the pursuit of modernization, including the "third generation" of nuclear weapons. Moreover, it is not difficult to imagine how important, from the standpoint of military power, the CIS (and eventually Russian) nuclear forces are, especially if conventional forces have

Coping with Global Missile Proliferation

been withdrawn from forward-deployed positions and dismantled. That "nuclear credential" arguably becomes more valuable to a Russian Federated Republic, as the principal or potentially the sole "nuclear successor power."

But will strategic weapons in the CIS be responsive to the control of a single authority? As of 1992 there is no way to know, for instance, whether the nuclear-armed republics will actually give up their weapons and place all strategic nuclear power in the hands of the leader of the Russian Republic. The CIS already seems to be viewed by Yeltsin as Russian controlled, a sentiment not shared by republic leaders contemplating doing away with strategic nuclear forces on their territories.

Given the ever more strident assertions of sovereignty and independence, one can also envisage the emergence of several nuclear successor states. Take Ukraine. As an independent state, if Ukraine should assume possession and control of the strategic nuclear weapons deployed on its soil, it would command a nuclear arsenal far greater than that of the combined forces of Great Britain and France.

The Problem of Residual Nuclear Capabilities

The reduction in U.S. and CIS strategic offensive forces under START, possibly to be followed by even deeper mutual cuts, cannot resolve the fundamental dilemma of the residual nuclear capabilities that could be employed by the several republics. In fact, the lower the numbers of strategic forces on both sides, the greater the rationale for strategic defense, (1) as a hedge against "cheating" with respect to agreed-upon force levels, and (2) on the grounds that it becomes increasingly effective against fewer numbers of offensive forces.

It must also be noted that there is an ironic "side effect" to drastic drawdowns in the U.S. and CIS strategic arsenals: namely, the additional incentive that it may provide to other potential "proliferators" to build up their own nuclear forces. Let us assume, for example, that the United States and the CIS, or its nuclear successor state(s), finally agree to reduce the strategic nuclear inventories on both sides to the 2,000–2,500 deliverable warheads that President Yeltsin proposed to President Bush. This might then establish a clear and practicable goal of "parity capabilities" in the nuclear arena, certainly for China, but also for other aspirants for nuclear weapons, such as India. Paradoxically, therefore, the U.S. and CIS reductions may ultimately result in greater numbers of nuclear weapons worldwide.

In the meantime, the turmoil in the CIS increases another danger: namely, that of accidental or unauthorized launch of ballistic missiles. It may be difficult to assign a probability to that risk; it is unfortunately easier to project the result of an occurrence. The impact of just one multi-megaton warhead on an American city would result in hundreds of thousands of casualties and enormous devastation.

The intent here is not to paint "scare scenarios." Rather, it is to underscore a point: If there was a rationale for ballistic missile defense in the era of mutual

Table 8.3
Comparing the Strategic Defense Initiative (Phase I) with the Global Protection against Accidental Launch System (GPALS)

	Deterrence and Damage Limitation Phase I	Protection
Attack nature	deliberate	accidental, unauthorized, deliberate
Attack size	5,000+	200 warheads, or less
Detection capability	modest	very high
Engagement success	modest	very high
Number of interceptors	very high, 7,000-plus	modest to low, 1,000
Discrimination	designed to meet a responsive threat	modest, current threat
Allowable leakage	high, above 60%	very low, below 10%

deterrence between two confronting superpowers, that rationale becomes even more compelling in an era of confused and dangerous transition—an era, moreover, in which the spread of weapons of mass destruction, and the means of their delivery, projects the picture of a "multipolar world," with potentially disastrous implications. There is but one available insurance policy in the face of this precarious future: a comprehensive defense against the means of mass destruction.

AN EXTENDED BALLISTIC MISSILE DEFENSE

What might be the basis of such an extended defense, as implied by President Bush's call for a redirection of SDI? Although it would be an ambitious and complex undertaking, its fundamental "architecture" is already suggested by the "Brilliant Pebbles" concept described earlier. The architectural and operational differences between SDI Phase I and GPALS are outlined in Table 8.3.

Within the United States, GPALS also calls for a ground-based component, to be deployed at Grand Forks, North Dakota. A Ground-Based Surveillance and Tracking System (GSTS) would complement the "Brilliant Eyes" sensors deployed in space. Initially, 100 Ground-Based Interceptor (GBI) missiles would be deployed at that site.

Beyond the immediate defense of the United States, let us assume that space-based BPs, once their development is completed, are deployed by the United States in orbits inclined at roughly 40 degrees relative to the equator. This orbital parameter would hold the BPs in a band overlooking the Earth, between 40 degrees north and south. In this way, they would be positioned to engage missiles launched from locations as far north as Iraq and North Korea, and as far south as South Africa and Argentina. This 80-degree swath of mid-latitudes encompasses the vast majority, if not all, of the Third World nations currently on the list of possessors, producers, and aspirants of missile capabilities and warheads of mass destruction.

With the emergence of a crisis, the space-based interceptors would be directed by the National Command Authority to focus on the given area. Deployed in low earth orbit 400 km above the planet, they would be aimed flexibly and accurately to engage missiles in flight, even Scuds such as those that Iraq fired into Israel and Saudi Arabia, which have a relatively low trajectory. Moreover, they would intercept those missiles at altitudes at which the explosion of the latter's warheads would pose no real residual danger to the earth below. The kinetic energy released at impact would vaporize the missile. Any nuclear (radioactive), chemical, or biological material would be dissipated above the atmosphere, and explosive debris would burn up upon entering it.

Indeed, analysis undertaken after Desert Storm indicated that a modest deployment of BPs (some 1,000) would have achieved better than 85 percent effectiveness against the Iraqi Scuds fired against Saudi Arabia and Israel in the course of the Gulf War. A larger constellation of BPs, or even the 1,000 deployed in optimal orbit, would have destroyed all the launched Scuds.

Again, the space-based shield might not prove perfect. Also with Desert Storm sharply in mind, the shield should be linked with rapidly deployable ground-based systems of sensors and interceptors, to provide complementary terminal defenses for U.S. contingency operations overseas, incorporating substantial improvements over the present technology represented by Patriot systems.

Under the president's GPALS program, the Patriot is to be upgraded, work is to continue on the Israeli Arrow antimissile program, and a number of promising technologies are to continue to be developed, including the Extended-Range Interceptor (ERINT) missile and the Theater High-Altitude Area Defense (THAAD) missile. Under this planning, upgraded Patriots are to be on line in fiscal year 1993, ERINTs in fiscal year 1994, and Arrow and THAAD missiles by fiscal year 1996.

One can also envision, for example, the design of mobile land-based systems that could be made compatible with the vertical launch tubes (VLTs) of Aegis cruisers and other vertical launch-configured ships. These could be stationed off the U.S. coastlines, adding depth to the territorial defense of the United States but ready to be moved to the vicinity of crisis areas abroad.

The all-embracing concept that has been outlined here may evoke the by now standard responses of incredulity, stereotyped by the derogatory "Star Wars" label that has long been applied to SDI by its opponents. But if the war in the

Gulf—the "video war"—has yielded a central lesson, it is that technology has wrought enormous, seemingly incredible advances in modern warfare. Those advances have been demonstrated in televised images of the pinpoint accuracy, and effect, of the offensive forces. They apply in equal, if "laggard," measure to the means of defense. In short, these images attest to the historically validated axiom that "for every offensive weapon, there will be (in due course) a defensive weapon." The difference, in the modern era of mass-destruction weapons, relates to the urgency of mastering that defense.

OVERCOMING THE OBSTACLES

Aside from incredulity and derogation in the United States, SDI thus far has faced two major hurdles: (1) political-ideological opposition, which has focused its attention on U.S. obligations under the 1972 ABM treaty with the former Soviet Union, which constrains the development, let alone deployment, of missile defenses, and (2) the costs of erecting such defenses, particularly in a period of an increasingly limited U.S. defense budget.

As far as the ABM treaty is concerned, there are some ready, compelling answers. No treaty among nations is permanent. All apply to the objective circumstances covered by the given treaty. Those circumstances change. For that reason, most treaties entail provisions for abrogation or renegotiation in light of changed circumstances. The ABM treaty is a perfect example. Since it was signed two decades ago, in the avowed interest, illusory or not, of "mutual, stable strategic deterrence" between the United States and the Soviet Union, the world, and its strategic landscape, have changed drastically. The circumstances of the bilateral equation have changed, and may be altered even more by new arms agreements. Meanwhile, the reality of a larger global problem is also intruding into the bilateral arrangement.

The ABM Treaty, in short, is an anachronism. Unilateral abrogation of the treaty, no matter how warranted, may be alien to the American tradition. What is warranted, however, is at the very least an easing of the "strict" interpretation of the treaty and optimally its renegotiation. First of all, the diffusion of sovereignty in the CIS already presents a myriad of questions about the continued status of previously concluded treaties.

Perhaps even more important, a variety of signals from President Yeltsin, including his call for the creation of a joint U.S.-Russian global system of missile defense, suggests a great deal of rethinking about the relevance of a ballistic missile defense in a dramatically revamped global environment. Yeltsin also recognizes that his territory is within easy reach of other potential nuclear successors of the old Soviet Union.

Furthermore, the GPALS would mean, in effect, a fundamental redirection, at least initially, of the SDI effort away from the old U.S.-Soviet context. An orbit for Brilliant Pebbles inclined 40 degrees each way from the equator would exclude all the CIS land-based ICBMs and dockside SLBMs, as well as its

Coping with Global Missile Proliferation

SLBMs deployed in northern oceanic regions. In its basic import, in other words, the concept should evoke no logical allegations from Moscow about a U.S. threat aimed squarely at the territories of the CIS.

There is thus every reason to anticipate that the old "Soviet obstacle" to a comprehensive missile defense—and with it the barriers of the outdated ABM treaty—can and will be overcome. Meanwhile, against the background of global trends of missile proliferation, such a defense augurs as an imperative not only for the safeguarding of the United States and its forces deployed abroad, but also for the future of U.S. alliances and its coalition diplomacy.

Already the aftermath of the Gulf War has indicated how sharply the experience of even the crude Iraqi missile attacks has penetrated overall security concerns. As one telling example, in the fall of 1991 the Bush Administration discussed with its Desert Storm coalition partners the option of new military actions against Iraq for its failure to comply with the terms of the ceasefire, particularly those applying to freedom of movement for the UN inspection teams. Reportedly the Saudi government immediately requested the emplacement of additional Patriot missile systems in Saudi Arabia as a prerequisite for even considering such actions. Especially with the progression and proliferation of ever more powerful, accurate, and longer-range missile capabilities, one can confidently project that the "safeguard condition" will be an essential part of any coalition against a missile-armed transgressor in the future.

A comprehensive defense will be expensive. One broad estimate suggests the figure of $11 billion, expended over a period of five years, for a program deploying some 4,000 Brilliant Pebbles and their associated support, another $10 billion for the theater segment, and $25 billion for the ground-based segment. Even if those figures rise, the ultimate level of cost pales in comparison with astronomical figures that have become commonplace in the U.S. budgetary debate, such as the hundreds of billions of dollars in penalties accruing to U.S. taxpayers from the savings-and-loan scandal. Moreover, the funding that went into operations Desert Shield and Desert Storm may set a logical precedent: Shouldn't other nations, especially those much more vulnerable than the United States to the rapidly evolving threat, be expected to contribute toward the common security?

Indeed, what is at stake is a national—and universal—insurance policy against incalculable disaster. The premiums to be paid for the insurance policy may be subject to the wranglings of the marketplace. At this juncture, however, the need of such a policy should be beyond any reasonable debate.

9

The Pivotal Elements: Airlift and Sealift

Gen. Duane Cassidy, USAF (Ret.), and Vice Adm. Albert Herberger, USN (Ret.)

In the afterglow of victory in the Gulf War, a number of confident assertions were made about the military stature of the United States in the world. A popular one is that the United States now remains "the only superpower." This verdict reflects not only the demonstration of strength in Desert Storm, but also the perception of the economic and political difficulties afflicting the Russian Federation. The latter's status as a "former superpower" seemed confirmed by its essentially passive stance in the Gulf crisis.

Whether or not the verdict is premature, it begs a definition of "superpower." Basically, that term has been used in the past four decades to denote military power with two credentials: (1) massiveness and (2) effective global reach. In the popular mind, the term has been associated primarily with nuclear weapons and the means of their delivery. The Gulf War, however, is a reminder that much more complex factors are at work. Indeed, only by looking back to what is now alluded to as the "Cold War era" can we gain a clearer understanding of the military posture and strategy of the United States as they have evolved over the past four decades, and of the newly emerging challenges to that posture and strategy.

The Soviet Union emerged from World War II as the dominant power in Eurasia—the region the geopolitical thinker Halford MacKinder designated as the "heartland" of global power competition. Although weakened by the conflict, the Soviet Union, under Joseph Stalin, stood poised to exploit its geopolitical position toward the conquest of, or at least hegemonic sway over, the Eurasian landmass as a whole, particularly the rich industrial prize represented by Western Europe. In pursuit of this goal, the Soviet Union could look not only to the massive formations of the Red Army, but also to the inherent advantages of interior lines of communication that enabled Soviet power to be shifted easily and brought to bear along a wide arc extending from northern Europe to northeast Asia.

The postwar leadership of the United States, on the basis of the bitter and costly experience of two European conflicts, determined that the nation could not allow a new, hostile power to establish its hold over Eurasia. Accordingly, the United States adopted a strategy of containment of the Soviet Union. As this strategy evolved over time, it came to rely on the following essential elements: (1) deterrent forces (primarily long-range nuclear ones) directed squarely at the Soviet Union proper; (2) U.S. ground, air, and naval forces forward deployed at pivotal points along the peripheries of Eurasia; (3) multilateral alliances that both sustained and augmented those forward deployments of U.S. military power; and (4) a strategic reserve in the Continental United States (CONUS) to reinforce the forward-deployed forces in a major contingency.

Against the Soviet advantage of interior lines of communication, the United States—as the "world island" power, according to MacKinder's geopolitical atlas—pitted its advantages of "global strategic mobility," based on control of lines of communication by sea and air, to link the forward-deployed elements with one another and with the sources of national power in the United States proper. Backed by enormous technological advances, the "glue" that held this posture together was strategic mobility across the sea and in the air.

It is perhaps ironic that only relatively late in the strategy of containment, in 1987, was responsibility entrusted to a unified U.S. military command, the newly created United States Transportation Command (USTRANSCOM). The four short years since that command's establishment have brought far-reaching global change, and adaptation of the U.S. military posture both to the emerging challenges of the "post-containment era" and to the constraints of declining defense budgets. This adaptation was foreshadowed through the progressive retrenchment, or scheduled withdrawal, of substantial numbers of U.S. forces from their forward positions in Europe and Asia, leaving behind what can best be described as a forward presence. At the same time, the network of overseas logistical bases and facilities that grew in support of the erstwhile forward deployments is shrinking. Projection of U.S. military power must rely ever more heavily on physical transportation of fighting men, their weapons, their materiel, and their sustenance from CONUS.

The capabilities of sealift and airlift loom as the pivotal element in the ongoing shift of U.S. military posture and strategy. The Gulf War imposed the first demanding test upon this pivotal factor. Judged by the outcome of the conflict the test was successfully met.

What lessons can be drawn from Desert Shield and Desert Storm for the timely projection of U.S. power? The emphasis here is on "timely projection." Iraq's invasion of Kuwait graphically demonstrated the little prior warning with which challenges to U.S. interests can arise halfway around the globe, in areas remote

The Pivotal Elements: Airlift and Sealift 143

not only from forward-deployed U.S. military forces, but also from their logistic lines of support.

Moreover, in contrast with the era of containment, when U.S. military planning could be focused on several key regional theaters of potential combat, the emerging map of such "theaters" literally covers the globe. Therefore, are the lessons of the Gulf War transferable to possible contingencies elsewhere? What gaps and shortfalls in timely lift capabilities were revealed? What is needed to overcome them?

THE U.S. MILITARY TRANSPORTATION SYSTEM

As was noted above, the USTRANSCOM was established in 1987 with the task of overseeing and marshalling the strategic life capabilities relevant to all the U.S. military services. What has made the command's mission both unique and challenging is that it covers not only assets under the direct control of the Department of Defense, but also, and for the most part, civilian, commercial assets designated to be pressed into service at time of crisis.

USTRANSCOM's structure and operations bear some outlining here. One element is a command center, operated around the clock, which monitors political and military developments throughout the world, as well as the readiness of the command's component units. Through its command, control, communications, and computer (C4) systems, USTRANSCOM constantly tracks the hundreds of ships and aircraft that comprise the command's "organic" and "contracted" transportation assets as they move about the globe. In this way, the command is able to provide the National Command Authority and the other relevant military commands with timely advice regarding the status of lift capabilities at the onset of crisis, and is prepared to implement the mobilization of those capabilities rapidly once the decision is made.

USTRANSCOM directs the transportation effort through three component commands: the Military Airlift Command (MAC), Military Traffic Management Command (MTMC) and Military Sealift Command (MSC). When fully mobilized, MAC's current airlift capability comprises over 550 active-duty, reserve, and Air National Guard aircraft and some 700 Civil Reserve Air Fleet (CRAF) aircraft.

The responsibility of MTMC includes mustering, manifesting, loading, and moving troops and cargo within CONUS. Working in close coordination with unit-level transportation staffs and USTRANSCOM headquarters, MTMC ensures that the proper mix of trucks, trains, buses, and aircraft is available to transport people and materiel to their posts of embarkation.

In any major sustained operation, such as Desert Shield, airlift transports the majority of military personnel. At the same time, MSC's sealift operations are expected to deliver approximately 95 percent of all the dry cargo and 99 percent of all the petroleum products that are transported.

Table 9.1
Four-Engined Airlift Aircraft, Excluding Support Aircraft

Four-Engined Airlift Aircraft	C-5	C-130	C-141	Total
Charleston	-	-	52	52
Dover	35	-	-	35
McGuire	-	-	50	50
Pope	-	46	-	46
Rhein-Main	-	16	-	16
21 AF Total	35	62	102	199
Yokota	-	20	-	20
Dyess	-	26	-	26
Elmendorf	-	10	-	10
Little Rock	-	74	-	74
McChord	-	-	36	36
Norton	-	-	48	48
Travis	35	-	32	67
22 AF Total	35	130	116	281
Altus	6	-	16	22
Total	76	192	234	502

U.S. AIRLIFT CAPABILITIES

What makes USTRANSCOM unique among U.S. military commands is its embrace of both military and (designated) civilian capabilities. That applies to what is collectively referred to as the Airlift Force. The airlift capabilities available to the Department of Defense consist of an Organic Force of military transport aircraft and CRAF.

The Organic Force is composed of two parts: an active duty component and an air reserve component, comprising the Air Force Reserve and the Air National Guard. Tables 9.1 and 9.2 depict the current inventory of primary (four-engine) airlift aircraft assigned to the active and reserve components, and the Air Force bases from which they operate.

So far, this total force has acquitted itself in exemplary fashion in the contingencies in which it has been called upon. From smaller operations, such as in Grenada, to the massive Operation Desert Shield, the Airlift Force has demonstrated rapid and flexible responsiveness to demand. In fact, by dint of its performance in the past, the force has earned the ultimate compliment of largely being taken for granted.

The Airlift Force faces two major problems: (1) an aircraft inventory marked by technologically aged planes and (2) air crews burdened by high turnover and consequent high training demands. The "newest" aircraft in the force are the

The Pivotal Elements: Airlift and Sealift

Table 9.2
Military Airlift Command, Gained Aircraft Inventory

Aircraft Inventory Locations	C-5A	C-141B
Air Force Reserve		
Kelly AFB, TX	14	-
Westover AFB, MA	14	-
Andrews AFB, MD	-	8
Air National Guard		
Stewart IAP, NY	11	-
A.C. Thompson Fld., MS	-	8

C-5Bs, the last of which was delivered in 1988, although the design essentially dates back to the early 1960s. While redesigned and newly manufactured parts and systems make the C-5B more reliable and maintainable, there has been no change in its basic airframe, engine design, and performance. It may have been fortunate for Operation Desert Shield that the decision was made in the 1980s to procure an additional fifty C-5Bs. In the context of modernization requirements, however, the decision may not have been the optimal one.

The C-141 has been the workhorse of airlift for over twenty-five years. It also holds the distinction of being the most heavily flown airplane in the history of the U.S. Air Force. Its airframe was originally designed for an operational life of 30,000 flying hours; this was extended to 45,000 hours when the airplane was "stretched" in the late 1970s. The average C-141 airframe life now exceeds the originally stipulated 30,000 hours, and the age and stress of both flying time and changing missions are beginning to take their toll. This is not to suggest that the C-141 has completely outlived its usefulness, but that the aircraft increasingly demands more attention and maintenance. With additional passage of time, the cost of its utilization will rise substantially. The C-141's aging technology, minority engines, and avionics cry out for modernization.

The C-130 is another story. It was procured as a tactical airlifter, but was pressed into service for a period as a strategic lift aircraft while the C-141 was coming on-line. Its range and load capacity are limited, but well-suited for shorter-range, high-sortie rate operations. The aircraft has been in continuous production since 1955; no other airplane in history can lay claim to that longevity. It, too, is in obvious need of modernization, and efforts are underway to accomplish that.

Several missions of airlift are performed by specialized airplanes, such as the C-9, the C-21 and the C-27, augmenting the "big three." They underscore the continuing need for airlift in a wide variety of missions, many of which are still to be defined in adaptation to the changing demand.

Beyond the aircraft themselves, the principal factor of airlift capacity resides in the crews that fly them. In fact, ever since the advent of turbine power for aircraft, the crews have figured more significantly with respect to lift capacity than the aircraft themselves. In order to maximize the utilization rate of the available airlift aircraft, they are flown by both active-duty and reserve crews. The Air Force Reserve Associate program furnishes up to 30 percent of the air crews in normal times; in a mobilization of reserves, that share rises to some 60 percent. It should be noted that crews in the combined force of active and reserve in the airlift mission average more flying hours than other Air Force crews; nevertheless, their safety and reliability levels have been the best on record.

A substantial portion of total airlift capacity is comprised of CRAF. This air fleet enshrines a unique relationship established some thirty-five years ago between the Department of Defense and the commercial airline industry in the United States. The relationship has reflected recognition of the vast potential in a crisis of commercial airlift capabilities, allowing the country to forgo the huge costs of building and maintaining a military fleet dedicated to that purpose. This fleet consists of three stages (groupings) of passenger and cargo aircraft: 39 aircraft in Stage I, 193 in Stage II, and 475 in Stage III. The numbers and types of aircraft in those stages are adjusted annually in response to airlift requirements. Stages I and II were activated for the first time in the Persian Gulf crisis. From November 1990 to January 1991, an average of 77 such commercial aircraft were utilized daily.

U.S. SEALIFT CAPABILITIES

The sealift capability of the Department of Defense resides in a government-owned and chartered fleet of approximately 301 ships (see Table 9.3) manned by civilian mariners. Other sources of sealift shipping are U.S.-flag commercial vessels, Effectively U.S.-Controlled (EUSC) "flag-of-convenience" shipping, and other foreign-flag vessels, depending upon the circumstances of the contingency. The government-owned fleet is maintained by two organizations, the Navy's Military Sealift Command (MSC) and the Department of Transportation's Maritime Administration (MARAD). Let us describe them in turn.

THE MILITARY SEALIFT COMMAND

The fleet under the aegis of MSC is presented in the first section of Table 9.3. It consists, first of all, of eight Fast Sealift Ships (FSSs). These are high-speed container ships purchased by the United States Navy and converted into roll-on/roll-off vessels for carrying combat equipment. Fitted with an onboard crane, a self-contained ramp, and a helicopter deck, each ship can be loaded or

Table 9.3
Government-owned and Chartered Fleet as of May 1, 1990

Type	Number of Vessels
MSC CONTROLLED	
Fast Sealift Ships (FSS)	8
Maritime Prepositioned Ships (MPS)	13
Afloat Prepositioned Ships (APS)	12
Aviation Support Ships (TAVBS)	2
Hospital Ships (TAH)	2
Dry Cargo (chartered)	9
Tanker (chartered)	20
Subtotal	66
READY RESERVE FORCE (*)	
Auxiliary Crane Ship (TACS)	8
Breakbulk	49
Lighter Aboard Ship (LASH)	4
Seabee (Barge) Ship	3
Roll on/Roll off	17
Seatrain	2
Tanker	9
Offshore Petroleum Discharge Ships (OPDS)	2
Subtotal	94
NATIONAL DEFENSE RESERVE FLEET (*)	
Victory Ship (Dry Cargo)	75
Other Dry Cargo	37
Tanker	20
Troopships	7
Subtotal	139
Total Fleet	301

(*) Maritime Administration Controlled.

offloaded in a single day. Together the eight ships, each some 946 feet in length and capable of a speed of 33 knots, can carry the equipment for one Army mechanized division. The vessels are maintained in 96-hour readiness status with 12-man cadre crews.

Also under the control of MSC are thirteen Maritime Prepositioning Ships (MPSs), divided into three squadrons, deployed in the Atlantic, Pacific, and Indian oceans, respectively. Each squadron of four or five vessels can carry the equipment and combat supplies to support an expeditionary brigade of 16,500

Marines. In addition, twelve Afloat Prepositioning Ships (APSs) are on permanent station in the Indian Ocean. They will be discussed in greater detail in Chapter 10.

Rounding out the capabilities under the MSC are Two Aviation Logistics Support Ships (TAVBs)—converted merchant ships that carry equipment and personnel for maintenance support for Marine Corps Aviation—and two hospital ships (TAHs), each of which provides 1,000 beds and twelve operating rooms. The vessels in both of these categories are maintained in a five-day activation status. Finally, the MSC administers some twenty-nine "common-user" vessels (nine dry cargo ships and twenty tankers). These are not government-owned, but under long-term charter for point-to-point delivery of materiel and supplies to defense department forces worldwide.

The second major category of government-owned sealift embraces the reserve capabilities under the jurisdiction of MARAD. The numbers and types of vessels in this category are listed in Table 9.3.

The National Defense Reserve Fleet (NDRF) consists of an inactive pool of ships under MARAD's control. As of September 1989, the NDRF listed approximately 139 mothballed vessels located at James River, Virginia; Beaumont, Texas; Suisun Bay, California; and several other U.S. ports. The types of ships in this fleet are dry cargo (including seventy-five World War II–vintage Victory vessels), tankers, and troop ships. Factors of age, size, and condition cast doubt on the utility of this fleet. Conservatively speaking, sixty to ninety days would be required to activate many of these vessels and to train the needed numbers of mariners to operate their steam-driven propulsion plants and cargo-handling equipment.

There is also the Ready Reserve Force (RRF) of ships maintained by MARAD contractors (ship managers) in a 5- , 10- , or 20-day activation status. On August 2, 1990, there were ninety-six such vessels. In addition to the standard types of sealift ships, this fleet includes auxiliary crane ships—modified container ships fitted with twin-boom rotating deck cranes that have enough outreach to offload non-self-sustaining container ships moored alongside Offshore Petroleum Discharge Ships (OPDS).

U.S.-CONTROLLED MERCHANT VESSELS FOR SEALIFT

The government-owned fleets described above may be considered the "spearhead" of the nation's sealift capacity in time of crisis. Clearly, however, for any major contingency, such as the Gulf War, the sealift strategy of the United States continues to depend critically on privately owned ships and their crews to carry the bulk of the effort. These include, in descending order of reliance, (1) U.S.-flag vessels, (2) foreign-flag vessels under U.S. ownership, and (3) whatever foreign-flag ships under foreign ownership may be available in the given contingency.

As of May 1, 1990, the privately owned merchant fleet under U.S. flag consisted of 272 active vessels (as reflected in Table 9.4). This number marks

The Pivotal Elements: Airlift and Sealift

Table 9.4
Privately Owned Merchant Fleet, Active Ships, as of May 1, 1990

Type	Number of Vessels
Dry Cargo	
Breakbulk	9
Container/Breakbulk	16
Container Roll on/Roll off	4
Container	84
Roll on/ Roll off	19
LASH (Lighter Aboardship)	5
Subtotal	137
Tanker	131
Passenger (*)	4
Fleet	272

(*) Includes school ships

Source: Military Sealift Command

a steady downward trend in the U.S. merchant marine industry. The decline is confirmed by relevant statistics in nearly every sector of the industry. Thus, for example, it is startling to discover that this nation, with its proud maritime history and heritage and its abiding status as the largest trading nation in the world, has a merchant marine that carries a mere 3.9 percent of its oceangoing trade. It is no less unsettling that in 1992 only one commercial oceangoing ship was on order to be built in a U.S. shipyard. Moreover, the total number of U.S. merchant seamen, who man our commercial and military sealift ships, has dwindled by 60 percent since 1970, to a current level of 25,600—and that number is projected to plunge to some 12,000 by the turn of the century.

In its 1989 study, the presidentially appointed Commission on Merchant Marine and Defense Support concluded that "our commercial maritime fleet and its supporting industrial base are deteriorating at a rate sufficient to compromise our ability to preserve our national interests." Indeed, the condition of the U.S. maritime industry is tantamount to a national tragedy. That tragedy not only affects military sealift capabilities, but makes the United States almost totally dependent on foreign-flag shipping for importation of raw materials essential to the nation's industry.

Also accessible by the MSC are vessels in the category of "Effective U.S.-Controlled Shipping" (EUSC)—merchant ships manned by foreign crews and

Table 9.5
Effectively U.S.-controlled Fleet

Ship Type	Number of Vessels
Barge carrier	4
Breakbulk	4
Car carrier	1
Chemical tanker	8
Container (NSS)	6
Container (SS)	2
Crude tanker	28
Oil/bulk/ore	3
Passenger	13
Product Tanker	53
Reefer	13
RO/RO	4
Total	139

Source: U.S. Department of Transportation Maritime Administration, Washington, D.C.

registered under "flags of convenience," with an open registry country designated by the Department of Defense. Current EUSC registries are in Liberia, Panama, Bahamas, Honduras, and the Marshall Islands. To qualify, the vessel must be more than 50 percent owned by a U.S. citizen. Considered effectively under U.S. control by virtue of ownership and prior agreement, those vessels can be requisitioned during a presidentially declared national emergency.

Of the 300 U.S.-owned, foreign-registered ships in the EUSC fleet, however, only about 139 can be considered militarily useful in a national emergency (see Table 9.5). That category includes only thirty-four dry cargo ships, fifty-three product tankers, and thirteen passenger ships, while the remaining designation of crude tankers and bulk cargo carriers could be used for U.S. raw material imports. Since the passage of the Tax Reform Act of 1986, which repealed the deferral of tax on income of a controlled foreign corporation that was reinvested in shipping operations and modified foreign tax credit limits and deficits rules, the EUSC fleet, too, has been in steady decline. Without a change in the tax law, U.S. ownership in foreign-flag shipping is expected to drop still further.

The shrinkage in U.S. merchant shipping affects more than just the physical capacity of military sealift. Mention has been made of the steep decline in the number of U.S. merchant mariners. MSC depends on the merchant marine labor pool to man the reserve sealift ships described earlier. This pool has dwindled, not only quantitatively but also in skills relevant to military sealift. The commercial fleet, while declining in number, has shifted toward diesel-driven, non-self-sustaining container ships featuring smaller crews and greater automation. Because of their militarily useful characteristics (breakbulk, self-offloading), many of the former steam-driven, manpower-intensive ships disdained by com-

Table 9.6
Airlift in Desert Shield/Storm/Sortie

Strategic Airlift (From August 7, 1990 to May 1, 1991)

18,900 missions (20% commercial)
512,000 passengers (62% commercial)
602,000 tons of cargo (27% commercial)

Intra-Theater Airlift Flown by C-130s

14,500 missions
364,900 passengers
199,000 tons of cargo

Redeployments (Desert Sortie) from March 1 to May 1, 1991

3,400 missions (28% commercial)
287,000 passengers (82% commercial)
107,000 tons of cargo (40% commercial)

TON-MILES MOVED: APPROXIMATELY 4.37 BILLION TON-MILES

mercial fleets were procured by the government for its reserve fleets. In the process, however, there has emerged a growing shortage of mariners with steam-propulsion plant experience and the operational skills to rig and operate the cargo-handling booms and winches on the older, breakbulk-type vessels of the reserve. This problem became conspicuous in the early phases of the Desert Shield buildup.

AIRLIFT IN THE GULF WAR

U.S. military airlift performed in splendid fashion in the three operational phases of the Gulf War: Desert Shield, Desert Storm, and Desert Sortie, the latter covering military redeployments after the termination of hostilities. The scope and size of the effort, measured in missions, passengers, and cargo, is reflected in Table 9.6. A simple comparison, expressed in ton-miles, begins to put that effort in perspective. The historic airlift to blockaded Berlin in 1948–49 featured 697.5 million ton-miles over a period of fifteen months. The comparable figure, covering some nine months of the Gulf operation, was 4.37 billion ton-miles.

In the initial deployment phase of Desert Shield, MAC mustered an average of approximately 65 mission offloadings in Saudi Arabia every day. After the U.S. forces were in place in their defensive positions and in a sustainment mode, that average dropped to 45 per day. In Desert Shield Phase II, in response to the president's order for additional troop deployments, that number rose to nearly

100—and to approximately 125 at the start of Desert Storm, with an aircraft landing every eleven minutes.

The massive effort was a tribute not only to the air crews flying the largely aging aircraft of the MAC fleet, but to the full spectrum of personnel involved, including transporters, air police, the airlift control element, maintenance experts, rescue specialists, weathermen, and aeromedical specialists. They labored through long days and nights, often in thirty-hour duty shifts. The Air Force Reserve and Air National Guard were full partners in the effort. When Desert Shield was initiated, some 1,300 reservists and guardsmen were voluntarily serving on extended active duty alongside the MAC regulars. Following the first activation on August 23, 1990, more than 18,000 reservists and Air National Guard personnel answered the call.

The Gulf War also provided validation of a number of concepts that had long been developed and refined within MAC. These include time-phased inspections of airplanes, and maintenance concepts that stress quality maintenance yet minimize maintenance man-hours per flying hour. The proven maintenance concepts assure the ability to generate wartime (surge) utilization rates over prolonged periods of time. MAC's peacetime mission provides the unique combination of a built-in readiness posture of continuous airborne alert, along with realistic mission training. The war also revalidated a crew management system that stages rested aircrews for available aircraft.

Successful though the total effort proved to be in meeting the operational requirements of this particular contingency, it also served to post warning signals about the ability of military airlift to respond to the demands of future contingencies in requisite time and capacity—especially compressed demands of response time. A key issue in this context is again the limitations of aging aircraft in the airlift fleet.

The best way to spotlight the problem is via a comparison of existing airlift capabilities with those of the new C-17 cargo aircraft, procurement of which has been mired in the past in controversy over funding priorities. In the critical twelve initial days of Desert Shield, the C-17 could have delivered about fifty percent more combat forces—fighter squadrons and light infantry brigades—than were airlifted in that span. It took forty-five days to deliver all of the airlift-designated troops, supplies, and equipment for the first phase of Desert Shield. On C-17s, the same forces could have arrived ten days earlier. Notwithstanding the large Saudi airfields, ramp space was congested due to the hundreds of fighter, bomber, reconnaissance, and tanker aircraft operating in-theater. The C-17 can carry the load of two C-141s, while requiring the ramp space of only one.

Moreover, the greater maneuverability of the C-17 gives it access to a substantially higher number of airfields in potential contingency areas abroad than could be utilized by the present airlift fleet. In Chapter 5 of this book, addressed to U.S. tactical air forces, Gen. John L. Piotrowski speculates about how Desert Shield and Desert Storm might have fared if Saudi air bases had not been

The Pivotal Elements: Airlift and Sealift

Table 9.7
Desert Shield/Desert Storm Delivery (in percentage of short tons)

	Fleet	In Shear Tons	In Percentage	Percentage per Category
Government Fleet	MPS	164,328		4.8
	APF	116,328	3.4	
	FSS	321,940	9.4	
	RRF	707,529	20.6	38.0
U.S. Flag Commercial	U.S. CHARTER	495,209	14.4	
	SMESA	951,016	27.6	42.0
Foreign Flag	ALLIED CHARTER	681,797	19.8	20.0
Total		3,438,147	100.0	100.0

Source: Military Sealift Command

available, reducing options for forward-deployed U.S. airpower to (possibly) Turkish facilities, plus an inadequate base in Egypt and three airfields in Oman and Bahrein. Not only could that have drastically shifted the fortunes of the air campaign, but it would have imposed inordinate difficulties for any U.S. military buildup in the region, particularly the critical airlifted first line of defense and presence. In fact, one can legitimately question whether, given those postulated circumstances and obstacles, the decision for Desert Shield would have been made in the first place. The main point here, in any event, is that C-17 aircraft promise to boost the speed and capacity of U.S. airlift capabilities, while also expanding the flexibility and range of response to potential contingencies that may not feature the "hospitable" aspects of the Gulf War.

SEALIFT IN THE GULF WAR

If airlift was a critical factor, particularly in mounting the first line of deterrence and defense in the Gulf crisis of August 1990, sealift had to convey the bulk of the subsequent military buildup, as it is destined to do in any major contingency. What has been deemed a record-setting performance in short tons of cargo moved, between August 1990 and mid-April 1991, is shown in Table 9.7.

Nothing can, or should, be said in detraction of the impressive magnitude of that effort. Nevertheless, especially with an eye to the future and its unpredictable demands, we must take into account some significant circumstantial factors that helped make the record-breaking performance possible. The ships enjoyed free transit through the Suez Canal—an all-important variable bearing upon time, distance, and cost in any Middle East contingency operation. They were able to offload in large, modern, and well-equipped seaports in Saudi Arabia. The operation benefited from substantial quantities of locally supplied subsistence and fuel, along with the distribution of that fuel by some 5,000 Saudi trucks. Above all, the sealift was not subjected to hostile interdiction. Similar benefits may not be available in future contingencies.

Such favorable circumstances notwithstanding, the operation proved the wisdom of Department of Defense investments in surge sealift capabilities in the 1980s. The available MPSs and FSSs enabled sizable ground forces to be emplaced in Saudi Arabia soon after the president's decision to act. During the first phase of Desert Shield, the FSSs delivered 392 million pounds and 20 percent of the total sealift dry cargo. Overall, by the end of January 1991, 250 vessels in 360 offloadings had carried 14 billion pounds of equipment and petroleum products to U.S. and coalition forces in the Gulf.

Key elements of the effort were surface transportation and seaports. Active and reserve units of the MTMC marshalled the equipment and supplies for sea shipment, while coordinating loading operations at twenty-eight ports worldwide. By mid-April 1991, 1.2 million tons of cargo had been transported by more than 27,000 commercial trucks and 16,000 rail cars. This massive and time-sensitive undertaking inevitably encountered problems of congestion, spot shortages of skilled longshoremen, and deficiencies in heavy-duty equipment. Overall, however, the transshipment operation was managed with remarkable smoothness.

The total effort produced what came to be called "the steel bridge" between the United States and the Persian Gulf. A "snapshot" of ship activity under MSC control at the end of December shows the following: 132 ships inbound to Persian Gulf ports, 28 vessels loading or offloading their cargoes in ports, and 44 ships returning from the Gulf.

NEGATIVE AND WARNING LESSONS

Notwithstanding the record-breaking magnitude of the sealift in support of Desert Shield and Desert Storm, and the ultimate verdict of success pronounced by victory on the battlefield, a number of gaps and shortcomings were bared by the effort. In the main, they pertained to initial surge capability. Beyond the above-mentioned favorable circumstances that aided the overall undertaking, its principal benefactor was—or better, turned out to be—that of time. Because the United States and its coalition partners were able to retain the initiative, particularly with respect to the timing of Operation Desert Storm and its air and ground phases, the earlier gaps and shortfalls in sealift could be overcome. It might have been a different story, however, had Saddam Hussein not been so obligingly passive militarily, especially during the critical initial phase of the Desert Shield buildup. The aggressors of the future are bound to draw their own lessons from the Gulf War in that critical respect.

One conspicuous problem immediately encountered by the sealift was a lack of readily available ships to haul the heavy unit equipment (tanks, vehicles, etc.)

The Pivotal Elements: Airlift and Sealift 155

called for by initial surge requirements. Ideal for this function are roll-on/roll-off (RO/RO) vessels equipped with a series of ramps that allow large numbers of tracked vehicles to be driven onto and off the ship. When Desert Shield was ordered, only seven such vessels remained in the U.S.-flag fleet and were made available by their operators, along with seventeen in the Ready Reserve Fleet. An additional nineteen RO/RO ships had to be chartered from foreign-flag fleets. Those vessels became the optimal workhorses of sealift in the crisis, given the priority demand for large numbers of heavy combat and combat-support equipment and the availability of modern ports for offloading them. A big question for any future contingency is whether both conditions—foreign-flag ships and ample, modern port facilities—will again be available.

Overall, only thirteen of the first forty-eight RRF ships mobilized met the five-day activation call. By the end of February 1991, seventy-one of the ninety-six RRF ships ordered were activated. Of that force, some 30 percent missed their activation targets by ten or more days, due primarily to poor material conditions and manning problems, particularly a shortage of steam propulsion plant engineers. The force proved to be somewhat less than "ready." After that inauspicious beginning, this fleet of old vessels (averaging twenty-four years in age) did deliver over .7 million short tons, 20 percent of the dry cargo needed, by mid-April. Again, however, a future crisis may not allow so much time for overcoming a rocky start.

Militarily useful, "handy-size" (about 30,000 deadweight tons, or .2 million barrels, capacity) product tankers were not an issue in Desert Shield because of the availability of fuel in the immediate Gulf region. Thereby obscured was a growing shortage in available tankers, particularly their handy-size version. That problem could become more acute against the background of a continuing decline in the U.S.-flag tanker fleet—a decline prodded by a number of factors, including a dwindling intercoastal trade, shrinkage of the Alaska North Slope oil reserve, growing importation of foreign oil carried by foreign-flag tankers, and the phasing-out of single-hull tankers in U.S. waters beginning in 1995, as prescribed by the Oil Pollution Act.

IMPLICATIONS OF DESERT SHIELD FOR FUTURE LIFT REQUIREMENTS

Several lessons have been drawn from the Gulf War, lessons not only of victory, but also of urgent requirements for the future. As far as strategic mobility is concerned, the focus should be on timely sealift.

Perhaps the best way to place current sealift shortcomings into perspective is in terms of the stated United States Army requirement, noted by Gen. John W. Woodmansee in Chapter 2, to "close" within thirty days two heavy Army divisions as part of a corps-sized rapid reaction force in a remote contingency area. It is instructive to contrast this requirement with what was actually deployed by sea within the first 30 days of Operation Desert Shield, from August 7 to

September 7, 1990. During that period a total of twenty-four sealift vessels arrived in Saudi ports. They included nine MPSs, delivering combat equipment and thirty days of ammunition, supplies for two (airlifted) Marine Expeditionary Brigades (with 33,000 personnel); ten APSs with Air Force and Army stocks; and six FSSs, carrying about two-thirds of the Army's 24th Mechanized Division. This was far short of the projected requirement. Closing the gap will entail a substantial increase in numbers of ships in the forward (afloat) prepositioning and fast sealift deployment modes.

The sealift capacity of the United States, even though aided by a variety of favorable circumstances, was stretched to the limit in the Gulf War. Brought sharply into question is the prudence of continuing reliance in deployment planning on the rapid activation of a large number of aging ships, many of which have been laid up for years, lacking even a nucleus cadre of engineers familiar with their operation. The early phase of the sealift also highlighted a glaring shortcoming: the inadequacy of the U.S. mariner work force with respect to a short-term, high-volume "surge" effort.

Requirements for the future call for a restructured Ready Reserve Force of militarily useful vessels in the RO/RO, LASH, heavy lift, and product tankers categories. A more general requirement is for a government fleet maintained at a higher state of readiness, with a civilian merchant marine manpower reserve program to fill any gaps in the maritime labor pool. The size and composition of this fleet must be closely tailored to the envisioned mix of heavy and light U.S. contingency forces.

To enhance timely deployment, from origins at depots or factories to destinations in the contingency area, a greater measure of containerization is needed for accommodating ammunition and smaller vehicles and equipment. Another major trouble spot bared during the conflict was the delayed delivery of combat support equipment. Despite the large, modern Saudi seaports, the limited availability of motor and rail transport inland placed a critical premium on trucks, "heavy haulers," and support vehicles to move troops and their equipment to their initial defensive lines, and subsequently into their offensive positions. In future contingencies, additional sealift capacity will have to be reserved for such equipment during the early, surge phase. Combat support equipment and nonperishable supplies and ammunition should also be candidates for forward afloat prepositioning, in order to minimize long-haul sealift requirements.

There are some bright spots in the picture. The Transportation Command stands to benefit greatly from the introduction of information technology being developed for the civilian transportation industry's integrated logistics systems and internodal operations. Application of this technology will make for higher intransit visibility of priority cargoes, providing military logisticians, as well as combat commanders, with the flexibility to adjust the transportation flow.

The visible shortcomings do not apply solely to early deployment and build-up, however. A growing requirement portended by Desert Storm for both airlift and sealift is timely transport, following the initial surge, of war materiel produced on an accelerated basis by industry, to fill combat needs as the battle progresses. "Just-in-time logistics," which have dramatically increased in the U.S. civilian sector for economic reasons, became part of the Gulf War experience as a consequence of declining equipment inventory and stockpiles of "smart" weapons and munitions. This requirement looms large for the future, because shrinking defense budgets are likely to limit the stockpiling of ammunition, spare parts, and supplies.

Finally, the most pressing overall need is for a robust U.S. merchant fleet to join in the requisite surge-and-sustainment shipping in crisis and to provide skilled mariners to man the reserve fleet. Admittedly this paramount requirement is more easily stated than implemented. As matters stand, however, an inconsistent, outdated U.S. government approach to the maritime industry not only has failed to arrest the seemingly relentless decline in U.S. commercial shipping, but has placed in grave danger the "maritime muscle" that is indispensable to the nation's security and ability to act in the world at large. The National Security Sealift Policy, signed by President Bush in October 1989, points a promising direction, but needs to be vigorously and concertedly pursued in the face of opposition by special interests in both industry and government.

POWER AND ITS PROJECTION

There has been a tendency, in the wake of the Gulf War, to equate the conflict with the "worst-case" contingency likely to confront the United States in the post-containment era. Implicit is the convenient notion that the magnitudes of forces and matériel invested in Desert Shield/Desert Storm have set a rough upper boundary for sizing U.S. military posture requirements for the years ahead.

As far as U.S. military airlift and sealift capabilities were concerned, the Gulf War certainly was a demanding contingency. Indeed, as has been pointed out, those capabilities were stretched nearly to their limit. Compounding the severity was lack of warning time prior to mobilization of the massive lift operation. Nevertheless, the challenge was mastered. Without the needed means of transporting forces and matériel to the scene of quickly moving crisis in a region halfway around the world, there could have been no Desert Storm victory, let alone one in the astounding manner in which it was accomplished, with minimal American casualties. Arguably, absent the needed means of conveyance, Operation Desert Shield might not have been undertaken in the first place.

But does the Gulf War really signify the worst case of possible military challenges to the United States? Leaving aside the question of whether the erstwhile threat from the Soviet Union has permanently vanished, it is not difficult to conceive of worse cases than the Gulf War scenario. In fact, the Gulf crisis itself could easily have taken turns that would have substantially heightened the military task for the United States and its coalition partners, perhaps materially changing the outcome.

While the Gulf War represented a rigorous test in terms of response and volume, one can—without much effort in imagination—paint a picture of future contingencies that would impose even harder demands. In Chapter 2, General Starry undertook a general "risk assessment" on a global scale. He alluded persuasively to potential scenarios with conflict of no lesser intensity than that faced by the United States in the Gulf War. From the vantage point of strategic lift requirements, many of those scenarios would also involve logistic problems far more difficult than those the military had to cope with during the Gulf War, with its relatively "hospitable" environment. More realistic planning schemes have to reckon with greater difficulties, such as more limited access to fewer, less spacious, and less modern airbases and port facilities; remoteness from pre-positioned stocks; greater distances and greater obstacles to inland transport; and lack of in-theater sources of supplies (notably fuel) and distribution means.

Projections of the future military posture of the United States are predicated on the assumption of substantial withdrawals of U.S. military forces, along with their supporting bases and means of sustainment, from their present forward positions in Europe and Asia. It follows logically that the more that is withdrawn from abroad, the heavier will be the burden on redeployment of those forces from the continental United States in response to crises.

The United States is in the process of shifting from a forward-deployed posture to one of increasing reliance on power projection from CONUS. "Power" and "projection" are inseparable. Without the needed means of projection—of the requisite capacity, responsiveness, and modernization of airlift and sealift—to meet the fuller range of foreseeable contingencies affecting the vital interests of the United States, U.S. military power, however adequate it may be deemed in terms of manpower and arms, risks irrelevance.

10

The Need for Forward Prepositioning

Gen. Joseph Went, USMC (Ret.)

In Chapter 9, Gen. Duane Cassidy and Adm. Albert Herberger marked "strategic mobility" as the key to a viable shift from a U.S. military posture primarily reliant on forward-deployed forces to one increasingly dependent on power projection from CONUS. It is important to point out, however, that there is one element of strategic mobility that will continue, by definition, to be forward deployed. That element is prepositioning—the emplacement and storage of military equipment in strategic locations, ready for use by U.S. forces.

Indeed, strategic lift (by air and sea) and prepositioning are integral parts of a single strategic mobility equation. How those parts overlap and interact was demonstrated in Operation Desert Shield. On August 7, 1990, nine Maritime Prepositioning Ships (MPS) and five Afloat Prepositioning Force Ships (APF) set sail toward the Persian Gulf from their stations in the Indian Ocean and the Western Pacific. On the same day, the order was also given to deploy eight Fast Sealift Ships (FSS) from the United States. There were substantial differences between those two forms of deployment. The MPS and APF vessels were at sea, fully crewed and ready to sail upon order. The FSSs, on the other hand, were located in various ports on the U.S. East Coast, manned by skeleton crews and maintained so as to be able to be underway within ninety-six hours of the order to deploy.

The prepositioning ships reached the Persian Gulf almost two weeks before the first FSSs. On August 9, an additional twelve AFPs, loaded with Army and Air Force equipment and supplies, were ordered out of Diego Garcia. Once the ships of the MPS and APF fleets discharged their original cargoes in Gulf ports, they either joined the continuing, massive sealift effort or served as sea-based logistic ships for storage of selected ammunition stocks and heat-sensitive supplies.

The principal effort of the early movement of MPS ships was early deployment of two brigades of U.S. Marines in Saudi Arabia, fully equipped and ready for combat. Other U.S. forces had been rapidly airlifted to the scene, but it was weeks—in some cases months—before those units were fully constituted and prepared for sustained operations. Meanwhile, in the early phase of the Desert Shield buildup, the food, water, and fuel carried by the MPS and APF vessels were vital in sustaining the forces being assembled.

The Gulf War underlined the value of pre-positioning in general, and of maritime pre-positioning in particular. Pre-positioning is intrinsically valuable, even critical, in enhancing the early combat readiness of forces deployed abroad to meet any contingency that calls for more than light insertion forces. (Light insertion forces were all that were needed in the intervention in Panama in 1989.) Unfortunately, the Gulf War served as a preview of the likely geographical remoteness of future contingencies, principally in the area of chronic turbulence extending from the Middle East to Northeast Asia. It also illustrated the kind of mid- to high-intensity conflict environment that U.S. forces are likely to confront again.

In the broader context of the conduct of such contingency actions, the value of prepositioning is also relative to that of U.S. strategic lift capabilities—airlift for rapid transport of personnel and equipment to the crisis arena, and sealift, in particular for hauling the materiel needed by heavy forces for sustained combat. In other words, prepositioning is in a "trade-off" relationship with the alternative of transporting materiel from the continental United States. Factors other than purely military and logistical ones bear on this trade-off relationship, including the comparative costs of stockpiling and the security and reliability of the stocks, not to mention a host of political considerations on either side of the equation.

The value of prepositioning is likely to rise relative to strategic lift, as well as in intrinsic combat readiness. The United States faces sharp inadequacies in available sealift—inadequacies that were exposed to one extent or another in Desert Shield. Despite the national security interests affected by those deficiencies, they are not likely to be redressed in the foreseeable future.

Meanwhile, the demand on sealift capacity appears to be strained even more as U.S. forces are withdrawn from their past emplacements overseas. It follows that the greater the number of forces pulled back, the heavier will be the lift requirements for returning U.S. power to meet contingencies over the globe. Prepositioning, on land or sea, thus emerges as a pivotal element in rapid and effective response to contingencies. Before exploring future dimensions and options, however, it is useful first to examine past experiences.

THE POMCUS PROGRAM IN EUROPE

The program that became known as POMCUS—the acronym stands for "Prepositioning of Matériel Configured to Unit Sets"—was initiated by the Joint

The Need for Forward Prepositioning 161

Chiefs of Staff following the Berlin crisis of 1961. It was aimed at reducing the time required by reinforcements from the United States to take their battle stations on the NATO Central Front. It was also intended to ease the strain on transportation assets in time of crisis.

As the program's designation suggests, POMCUS supplies and equipment are stored by unit sets—in company- and battalion-sized packages—rather than by commodity, as is the rule in most supply depots. The concept allows U.S. reinforcing units to be rapidly outfitted once they arrive in the theater. There are seventeen POMCUS storage sites located under NATO arrangements, in Germany, Belgium, the Netherlands, and the United Kingdom.

A major effort in the POMCUS program has been to store matériel in humidity-controlled warehouses in order to keep it in optimal operational condition and ease maintenance requirements. But lack of adequate facilities in that regard has forced some storage outdoors. All matériel in POMCUS is vigorously maintained and constantly monitored to allow for introduction of new equipment and the modification or replacement of older items in stock. The maintenance is carried out in the various locations by cadres of active U.S. Army support units and civilian labor forces from the respective host nations.

POMCUS stocks are a part of U.S. war reserve assets; they cannot be added to United States Army acquisitions. War reserves are predetermined quantities of matériel that are acquired and stored in peacetime for the event of a major war, to serve as sustaining stocks in the initial phases of conflict until new production and procurement can offset matériel losses suffered in combat and training. POMCUS stocks include most major items of equipment, but not, on the one hand, such large or complex ones as aircraft, radars, missiles, or high-cost electronic equipment or, on the other, individual equipment for soldiers, shelf-life items, or ammunition. In general, POMCUS is made up of the items placing the heaviest demand on transportation. The basic aim is to create conditions whereby, in the event of a major deployment of forces to Europe, the airlift from the United States would embrace only personnel and minimal equipment, and subsequent sealift requirements would be eased as well.

In its early years the POMCUS program was the target of substantial criticism about shortcomings in maintenance and readiness. Considerable effort was expended in remedying those problems and bringing about general improvement. Exercises practicing the return of U.S. forces to Germany have played an important part in testing the effectiveness of the prepositioning concept and the readiness of the equipment.

Over time, and with reductions in the number of U.S. units forward deployed in Germany, the requirement for additional prepositioning has grown. POMCUS has expanded from its original two division-sets of equipment to six division-sets, along with their associated support units. The total amounts to prepositioning for a corps-sized force. One way of measuring its full extent is by the amount of strategic lift that would be needed to move the matériel (some 340,000 short tons) across the Atlantic. It would take on the order of 5,000 C-5 aircraft loads and approximately 50 FSSs.

POMCUS has proved to be a viable middle way between the alternatives of massive stationing of U.S. forces in NATO's Central Region and substantial increases in U.S. strategic lift capabilities. In the thirty years since its inception, the program has been an integral part of NATO's posture of deterrence and defense in Europe, as well as a key link in the trans-Atlantic relationship in the alliance. Paradoxically, however, the first true application of the program came in the context of conflict outside Europe.

During Operation Desert Shield, a substantial number of POMCUS stocks, including tanks, Bradley Fighting Vehicles, matériel-handling equipment, and transportation items, were moved from their storage sites in Europe to the Middle East. Once they arrived in the Persian Gulf, the equipment and supplies were used to outfit the assembling forces or as sustaining stocks. They were allocated wherever needed, rather than in accordance with the unit principle of the POMCUS concept.

The future of the POMCUS program is very much at the mercy of the changing political and military scene in Europe. By 1995 the total U.S presence in Europe is slated to be reduced to almost 150,000. The CFE treaty will directly impact the stockpiles of conventional military hardware by, most notably, reducing the numbers of tanks and fighting vehicles. Against the backdrop of those prospects and other uncertainties, the whole POMCUS program is under review. One possible course of action is movement of the residual stocks in prepositioning sites more relevant to contingencies in the Middle East and South Asia.

U.S. PREPOSITIONING IN NORWAY

The Norway prepositioning program contrasts with POMCUS in that it has been substituted entirely for the peacetime presence of U.S. forces in that country. A NATO initiative, directed by the U.S. Department of Defense, the program emerged from a bilateral U.S.-Norwegian study in the late 1970s and a subsequent Memorandum of Understanding between the two countries, signed in January 1981. Under its terms, Norway, with NATO support, provides storage facilities, airbase reception facilities, operating airbases, common user items of equipment, security and maintenance of equipment and supplies, and infrastructure to support the deployment of U.S. forces. For its part, the United States committed itself to contingency deployment of a Marine Expeditionary Brigade (MEB) of approximately 13,000 troops and 155 aircraft, trained and equipped to fight in the terrain and climate of Norway. The Marine units would be structured as a mobile, rapid-response defense force.

The Norway program offers a unique prepositioning mode, in which equipment and supplies are stored in six granite caves tunneled into the mountains along the Norwegian coast. The stores include ammunition, howitzers, rolling stock, engineering items, rations, medical material, and repair parts. Aviation ground support equipment and bulk fuel are stored in other facilities. Aircraft are not stationed, but are to arrive as part of the fly-in element. The design is for enough stored stocks to support the MEB in full combat for thirty days.

Even more unique is the fact that the program is operated almost entirely by the host country. No Marine units are stationed in Norway in peacetime. All storage maintenance and service is carried out by a Norwegian labor force, while the Marine Corps is responsible for providing repair parts and any special tools or testing equipment needed, as well as maintenance training of Norwegian personnel. Norway also provides a support battalion, to operate with the brigade once it is committed.

Prepositioning of supplies began in 1982, and the program achieved initial operational capability in 1989. In contrast with POMCUS, equipment and supplies procured for the Norwegian program do not fall under war reserve requirements.

The Norway program was undertaken in response to the perceived vulnerability of NATO's Northern Flank against the backdrop of a Soviet naval buildup in the late 1970s and early 1980s. The heightened Soviet strategic interest in the Baltic Sea and the much-publicized Soviet submarine probes along the Swedish and Norwegian coasts necessitated such a buildup. Like POMCUS, the program, and the commitments behind it, will be reassessed in light of political and military changes in Europe and as part of the broader ongoing review of NATO strategy and force posture.

EARLY MARITIME PREPOSITIONING INITIATIVES

Prepositioning at sea is not a recently minted concept; a version of it was explored prior to the Vietnam War. Aimed at reducing the deployment time of Army units in response to contingencies in the remote reaches of the Pacific Basin, it was dubbed "fast forward prepositioning" and involved storing heavy equipment and supplies for an Army brigade on dehumidified ships. The concept was even tested in an exercise at Okinawa. Although the experimentation yielded some useful experience and data, the concept was soon overshadowed by the much more massive demands of the Vietnam War.

The genesis of the current maritime prepositioning program goes back to the late 1970s. The U.S. inability to rapidly resupply Israel in the 1973 Yom Kippur War prompted rising concern in the U.S. defense establishment over shortcomings in U.S. strategic lift capabilities. In 1979 the advent of the hostage crisis in Iran and the Soviet invasion of Afghanistan gave new urgency to the problem, highlighting the need for rapid deployment of U.S. forces into areas, such as Southwest Asia, that were remote from U.S. forward-deployed forces and logistic infrastructure.

In August 1979 the secretary of defense, Harold Brown, proposed the development of the Maritime Prepositioning Ships (MPS) program, with the objective of enhancing the mobility of Marine forces on a global scale. The overall concept called for the Marine Corps to muster three 17,000-man brigades that would be structured, equipped, and trained for rapid deployment into crisis areas as a preemptive force or to provide reinforcement to forces already committed. The Marine units were to be capable of insertion in the absence of port facilities and prepared for thirty days of operations without local or external support.

In quest of this capability, the United States Navy was directed to provide the ships for three pre-positioned task forces (now commonly referred to as squadrons). The Defense Department called for long-term leasing of thirteen privately owned commercial vessels, as well as procurement of a full suite of Marine Corps equipment. The development effort represented a new and added dimension to the nation's capabilities of contingency response, rather than a reallocation of existing resources. It was to be fully implemented over a four-year period.

During the early months of 1980 the Joint Chiefs of Staff looked for a "quick fix" to the problem of more rapid projection of substantial U.S. forces worldwide, with emphasis on the Persian Gulf area. They settled on storing existing stocks of equipment and supplies aboard chartered commercial vessels, to be positioned near the island of Diego Garcia in the Indian Ocean. The effort became known as the Near-Term Prepositioned Ships (NTPS) program.

The Marine Corps was directed to form and provide a mechanized brigade, with the associated materiel. Three roll-on roll-off vessels and one breakbulk ship were to hold the Marines' equipment and supplies. Three additional ships were joined to the flotilla: a breakbulk ship carrying Army and Air Force supplies; a petroleum, oil, and lubricant tanker; and one water tanker. Within six months, through the efforts of the four services, coordinated by MSC, all of the sevens ships were on station in the Indian Ocean.

A year later, six more ships were added to the NTPS fleet—five to carry additional Army and Air Force supplies and one to augment the prepositioning for the Marines. Overall, the support was mustered for one Air Force wing and an Army brigade of 5,000 troops. The additional ship enlarged the Marine component to some 12,000 troops. The ships involved in the effort underwent little modification, and the bulk of the equipment and supplies was drawn from existing stocks.

Over the course of the subsequent six years, as the 1979 MPS decision was funded and implemented, the initial ships chartered for support of the Marines were phased out and replaced by a fleet of thirteen specially configured ships, either newly constructed or converted. An entire suite of new equipment to outfit three brigade-sized Marine Air-Ground Task Forces (MAGTFs) was procured and embarked on the new fleet, replacing the original NTPS equipment. Nine ships of the Marine-support fleet were the first to reach the Persian Gulf in Operation Desert Shield.

Meanwhile, the afloat pre-positioning of Army and Air Force materiel, initiated under NTPS, continued apace, with periodic maintenance and introduction of new equipment. Those ships and their stores, growing to a total of twelve, became known as the Afloat Prepositioning Force (APF). As was noted earlier, this entire fleet set sail on August 9, 1990, from Diego Garcia in support of Desert Shield.

THE MARITIME PREPOSITIONING SHIPS (MPS) PROGRAM: UNDERLYING RATIONALE

The MPS program, which has emerged from the 1979 initiative, deserves to be discussed in closer detail here because of its rising significance as a prepositioning option for the future. The underlying concepts of the program were laid down in a Memorandum of Agreement signed by the chief of naval operations and the commandant of the Marine Corps in April 1983. Central to that agreement was recognition of the complementary nature of maritime prepositioning and amphibious operations. The agreement remains in force today. There are five essential elements of the MPS concept.

Rapid response. The agreement established the goal of putting a MAGTF of brigade size ashore in any target area on the globe within ten days of the order given. Upon receipt of warning of a crisis entailing potential intervention, ships would be positioned in such a way that the major constraint on achieving the ten-day goal would bear on airlift rather than on the time it would take the relatively slow (16 to 20 knots) ships to close. It is interesting to observe in retrospect that since the initial positioning of the MPSs, they have never been ordered to relocate by the national command authority upon warning signals of a crisis and in advance of the order to proceed to the target area. In the case of Operation Desert Shield, the squadrons of MPSs stationed at Diego Garcia and Guam sailed directly to Saudi Arabia five days after Iraq's invasion of Kuwait.

Global capability. The 1983 agreement stated that the MPS must provide the needed flexibility for either simultaneous or sequential deployment of the Marine task force worldwide. This would include the ability to mass all MPS assets in a single theater. In Desert Shield this was achieved when the Atlantic squadron sailed in December 1990 to join the other squadrons from Diego Garcia and Guam in Saudi Arabia.

Employment capability. Inasmuch as the MPS task force would be most vulnerable during the period of offloading and build-up, the supporting Navy fleet had to be responsible for combat support and protection until the MAGTF was sufficiently constituted and ready to assume its normal mutual-support role with the fleet. As the program has progressed, it has become apparent that, although the Navy retains the prime responsibility for protection during the transitional phase of deployment, protection might also be provided by other U.S. service components and friendly forces, as needed.

Command relationship. It was stipulated that operational control of each MPS squadron would be exercised by the appropriate Navy fleet commander, with administrative support provided by MSC. Once the MAGTF was employed in a contingency, operational control would continue to reside with the naval commander unless passed ashore to a unified commander. This was the case in the Gulf War, when the Marine force was responsive to General Schwarzkopf as CINCCENT. The important point regarding the command relationship is that MPS (although it relies for strategic airlift on MAC) is essentially a naval program.

Sustainability. It was projected that the combination of prepositioned materiel and airlifted elements would allow a capability for sustaining the MAGTF in combat for thirty days. Two Aviation Support Ships (TAVBs) would provide intermediate maintenance to deploying Marine aviation elements, augmented by blocks of aviation spares to be flown to the target area. In the Gulf War, both existing TAVBs, the *Curtiss* and the *Wright*, were activated and operated in-theater.

BROADER CHARACTERISTICS OF THE MARITIME PREPOSITIONING PROGRAM

From its beginning, the MPS concept was conditioned by three basic assumptions, which remain valid to this day. (1) The ships would have freedom of (unopposed) transit to the objective area. (2) The MPS forces would be deployed to a "benign" environment, that is, a secured area for off-loading and joining the forces with their equipment. (3) A suitable airfield would be available close to the port of debarkation in order to facilitate coordinated off-loading of ships and arrival of MAGTF personnel and flown-in elements. All three conditions existed in Operation Desert Shield.

Those assumptions equate to operational constraints on the MPS concept. They add up, first of all, to the fact that it should not be thought of in terms of a "cutting edge," forcible entry capability, such as that possessed by amphibious naval forces. The concept is keyed to the following types of missions:

- Support and/or reinforcement of an amphibious operation.
- Reinforcement for a threatened allied or friendly nation prior to the outbreak of hostilities.
- Establishment of a sizable force ashore in preparation for, or support of, a land campaign.
- Crisis management and deterrence of aggression through the "signaling" function of ships being positioned and associated Marine forces alerted.

The second and third of the missions listed were carried out in exemplary fashion in Operation Desert Shield. It is not relevant whether the fourth function was also in play, or to what extent the activation of MPS impacted on possible options contemplated by Saddam Hussein to follow up the occupation of Kuwait with an attack on Saudi Arabia. As has been pointed out, the Marine forces associated with MPS were the first to be constituted in full combat readiness on the ground in Saudi Arabia.

SHIPS AND FORCES OF THE MARITIME PREPOSITIONING PROGRAM

It is useful to offer some detail regarding the specific composition of the forces involved as a prototype of afloat prepositioning.

Let us consider, first of all, the ships. Of the thirteen extant MPSs, five are newly constructed. The remaining eight are commercial carriers—container roll-on/roll-off ships—that have undergone extensive modification. In the aggregate, the vessels are capable of the following functions: direct loading and offloading of rolling stocks; carrying breakbulk equipment such as ammunition, refrigerated rations, and general cargo; storage and pumping of petroleum, oil, and lubricant; and furnishing deck space for landing craft, cargo lighterage, warping tugs, as well as platforms for heavy-lift helicopters. Fuel and water can be discharged as far inland as two miles. The ships hold the wherewithal for fueling the embarked equipment and berthing Marine and Navy offloading teams aboard. Each ship is capable of self-sustained offloading, both pierside and "instream."

Although they were not part of the original MPS concept, two types of sealift vessels round out the overall prepositioning concept: aviation logistic support ships TAVBs and hospital ships TAHs. These vessels are maintained on reduced readiness status in U.S. ports and can be activated within ninety-six hours. They were deployed in the Gulf War.

The three brigade-sized MAGTF is specifically designated and trained to operate in conjunction with the MPS stocks. These integrated, combined arms teams are built around three full infantry battalions supported by tanks, amphibious assault vehicles, field artillery, and light armored vehicles. The aviation element of the force consists of transport, attack, and command and control helicopters, as well as fighter-attack fixed-wing aircraft. It is complemented by aerial refueling and all-weather aircraft and guided by automated air command and control.

The Navy provides support elements from naval beach groups and port groups, to handle both pierside and instream off-loading. This Navy contingent includes trained cargo handlers, ship-to-shore lighterage operators, a special warfare detachment, and beach control personnel. Maintenance of the embarked equipment is performed under contract at Blount Island, Florida. The maintenance program includes upkeep and regular servicing, rotation of shelf-life items, and introduction of new equipment reflecting the up-to-date items in the Marine Corps inventory. The goal is 100 percent serviceability of the entire range of stock. The MPSs are periodically rotated on a sequential basis to undergo the maintenance cycle.

The airlift to carry personnel to ships and equipment is managed by MAC. Marine aircraft that are self-deployable fly directly to the scene of action. It takes approximately 250 strategic airlift sorties to move the personnel and "fly-in" materiel of a single Marine expeditionary brigade, compared to the more than 3,000 sorties that would be required in the absence of prepositioning.

THE STRATEGIC MOBILITY EQUATION

Strategic mobility, ever more important in an era of retrenchment from forward-deployed military power, can be described in terms of an equation: Airlift + Sealift + Prepositioning = Global Mobility. The formulation is useful both in denoting the need for a balanced approach and in suggesting that the left side of the equation can only be tampered with only so long as the sum on the right side does not fall below stipulated, overall requirements.

Those requirements tend to be both quantitatively and qualitatively different with respect to such specific variables as the distance over which power is to be projected, the parameters of needed reaction time, the intensity of combat, and the sustainment requirements in a given contingency. By the same token, the interaction between prepositioning and airlift, on the one hand, and sealift, on the other, changes in accordance with contingency requirements.

Airlift is the costliest of the three mobility elements, but it is essential for (1) initial, rapid deployment of personnel and high-priority cargo to the contingency area; (2) movement of personnel to join with prepositioned supplies, if and where available; and (3) as the battle progresses, continuing conveyance of personnel and equipment on a priority basis. Aside from fiscal restraints, there are inherent limits to what airlift can deliver, in terms of the bulk and volume of the forces and equipment. Airlift can satisfy, or come close to satisfying, the requirements of "light" contingencies, such as the U.S. intervention in Panama in 1989. However, when U.S. heavy armored forces are required within a sustained high-intensity combat environment, such as in Desert Storm, the estimated operational volume that can be moved through the air comes to only some 5 percent of the total.

The remainder, again with emphasis on the equipment for armored forces, as well as heavy and bulky items more generally, has to be moved by sea. As a general proposition, sealift from the United States offers advantages of relative cost and reliability. The disadvantages relate to reaction time and limits on available shipping.

The lack of reaction time became obvious in Operation Desert Shield. The eight SL-7 fast sealift ships under MSC performed generally as expected. Nevertheless, it took roughly a month for the first U.S. heavy forces, of the 24th Mechanized Division, to reach port in Saudi Arabia. Units of the second heavy United States Army force, the 1st Cavalry Division, arrived only in early November, some three months after the initiation of Desert Shield. It is at least

The Need for Forward Prepositioning

questionable whether such luxuries of build-up lead-time will be available to the United States in a future contingency.

Moreover, sealift is a lower-cost option of strategic transport only when enough of it is available to do the job. Recall that the sealift demands of Operation Desert Shield could be met, not only because of the buildup time, but also because of the relatively wide latitude the United States enjoyed in the charter of foreign-flag shipping. Depending on its international political ramifications, that latitude may not be there in a future crisis.

In short, airlift, sealift, and prepositioning must be looked upon not so much as distinct options of strategic mobility, but rather as elements in a synergism of capabilities, each of which has its own unique contribution to make toward achievement of the given objective. The relationship of the elements will vary in accordance with the demands of the contingency. There will be margins of tradeoff among them. In looking ahead to the overall demands on a U.S. power-projection posture relying primarily on the conveyance of military power from CONUS, one critical denominator stands out: reaction time. For all the reasons that have been brought out above, that critical denominator puts a continued, even growing premium on U.S. prepositioning abroad.

LAND-BASED VERSUS SEA-BASED PREPOSITIONING

Accepting the continuing, even rising, value of prepositioning still begs the question of how it might optimally be pursued. The choice comes down essentially to one of land-based as against afloat prepositioning. That choice is conditioned by a host of factors and variables. Although these may differ in specific application, they can be examined according to cost, commitment, and flexibility and mobility.

Cost

Considerations of cost alone clearly favor land-based over sea-based prepositioning options. Fixed warehouses and storage facilities are less expensive to construct, operate, and maintain than ships. Moreover, it has been the general rule of such land-based prepositioning agreements in the past that the host nation has relieved the United States of a substantial share of the costs entailed. Major maintenance and upkeep is easier and cheaper at fixed bases than on ships, which must put into port for that purpose, with the port fees and equipment-handling costs involved. By the same token, periodic exercises and testing of equipment is substantially easier in land-based facilities, which offer a full range, from selective testing to major exercises. In contrast, exercising sea-based equipment requires off-loading in port or "instream": the major effort involved tends to limit the frequency of exercises and to enlarge their scale when they are conducted.

Commitment

Land-based prepositioning sites have the advantage of constituting a direct U.S. commitment to the host country. In addition, the stockpiled equipment may serve to strengthen alliance ties through use in joint exercises and even through contingent availability to host-country forces in an emergency. Sea-based prepositioning does not signal a commitment in such a direct and tangible sense.

At the same time, however, the commitment symbolized by land-based stocks tends to be largely restricted to the direct defense of the given country or alliance. If the United States uses those stockpiles for out-of-country or out-of-area contingencies, the host countries must agree to the "extended role" prior to its use. The United States may encounter difficulties in reaching such agreements. Moreover, depending on local politics, a military presence can turn from an asset of assurance into a liability in relations with the host country, complicating its politics and becoming a convenient target for radical opposition groups and even terrorist attacks.

Flexibility and Mobility

The inherent advantages of afloat prepositioning over its land-based counterpart lie, of course, in the flexibility of uses to which the stored materiel may be put and the broad geographical range of its potential application. That use is relatively unhampered by a need for prior agreement and arrangements with other nations; its exercise is restricted only by definition of international waters.

Sea-basing allows freedom of ultimate decision and action. Deployed into the vicinity of a crisis area, afloat prepositioning can serve as a deterrent to aggression and as a tool for crisis management without committing the president to a set course of action. Once the decision to commit military forces is made, sea-based prepositioning permits substantial forces to be deployed more rapidly than by any other means, and with the needed sustainment to prevail on the battlefield.

This flexibility of commitment promises to become more important in the unfolding post–Cold War environment. To a considerable extent, U.S. on-land prepositioning programs abroad, as exemplified by POMCUS, are the legacy of the multilateral alliances forged by the United States over the past forty-five years. Although those traditional alliances retain residual value in safeguarding against a potential resurgence of a Russian threat and in terms of broader stability considerations, the ongoing process of diffusion and differentiation in the global threat environment portends a commensurate fluidity in future U.S. alliance relationships. The improvised nature of the coalition that was put together by the United States in the Gulf War may have served as a preview in that respect. This prospect, too, argues for maximum control over, and flexibility in, the application of military assets offered by sea-based prepositioning.

THE TRIAD OF STRATEGIC MOBILITY

The above should not be mistaken for a proposal that the United States abandon its existing land-based prepositioning programs. It would be unwise to unilaterally alter the nature or scope of POMCUS and the Norway program in support of NATO, until an overall alliance agreement is arrived at in that regard. At the same time, however, there would seem to be little rationale for initiating new land-based prepositioning programs abroad. The one possible exception is the Middle East, where U.S. military stockpiles might have the benefit of continued reassurance of Saudi Arabia and other friendly regional nations, and might enhance a stabilizing U.S. role in the area.

As far as the locations of sea-based prepositioned stocks are concerned, no basic changes in the current deployments of existing assets seem to be called for. The MPS sittings in the Atlantic, South Pacific, and Indian oceans proved their strategic value in the most recent conflict. Similarly, there does not appear to be an alternative to the facilities at Diego Garcia, for locating Army and Air Force APF assets. The immediate priority is to reconstitute those assets, rather than relocate them.

The question of location is more relevant with respect to new ships and associated materiel. This question will become ever more salient as the nation reviews the levels of forward-deployed forces in Europe and Asia within an overall scaling down of the U.S. armed forces. The variable of continued base rights overseas also has a strong bearing on where new afloat assets might optimally be positioned.

While questions of specific location may occupy military planners, in an overall sense the problem is not a difficult one if the need for sea-based prepositioning is acknowledged. Sea-basing permits flexibility and mobility over a broad range of potential sites, as well as subsequent relocation in adaptation to changing global conditions and strategic requirements.

As the United States moves from a forward-deploying to a forward-projecting military posture, recognition must be given to the growing importance of strategic mobility. Strategic mobility has been described here as the function of the triad of airlift, sealift, and prepositioning. As shown by the Gulf War, the problem of elongated distances for power to be projected, in tandem with compressed warning and reaction times, places a growing premium on forward prepositioning. Still, what is called for is a balanced and concerted enhancement of all three arms of the strategic mobility triad.

11

The U.S. Defense–Industrial Base

Gen. Alfred G. Hansen, USAF (Ret.)

Historically, the United States has heavily relied on its industrial base to meet the demands of major military conflicts and provide the nation with an intrinsic advantage in the prosecution of war. The tradition is that of a hemispheric power that, protected by the moats of two oceans, has enjoyed both time and relative safety in mobilizing its robust industrial resources for the challenge of conflict.

World War II stands out in that tradition. Even after the punishing blows delivered on U.S. military power at Pearl Harbor, once U.S. industry was mobilized and geared to war-production priorities, the military leadership could look to a virtually endless conveyor belt of materiel to sustain whatever strategies and campaigns are selected.

The experiences of the Vietnam War reinforced this traditional reliance on industrial capacity to rise to the challenge of conflict. It also provided the notion of a "shortcut" offered by the high-technology era: the concept of capitalizing on American qualitative superiority in the high-tech arena by fashioning weapons systems that could "out-trump" a numerically superior military opponent. In this way, surge production in response to an emergency could be fine tuned and selectively concentrated in certain sectors of what had emerged as a full-fledged defense industry, without unduly disrupting the society's pursuit of both guns and butter. Essentially the same approach prevailed during Desert Shield and Desert Storm.

It would seem that the overwhelming victory in the Gulf War validated the "limited surge" mobilization strategy as a continuing safeguard for the future. That lesson, however, is deceptive. In point of fact, in the Gulf War the United

States was able to "draw on past accounts"—to cash in on the technological edge and military-industrial assets amassed in the context of the U.S.-Soviet confrontation. Will that technological edge, along with the needed industrial capacity, be maintained and be exploitable for future contingencies? The question becomes more insistent in light of what is seen as a progressive decline in the U.S. industrial base relevant to defense.

BACKGROUND

The fact of that decline drew attention in the 1980s, during the early years of the Reagan Administration. An effort was made then to pull together various government agencies to explore the problem and chart a redressive strategy. This led to an impressive organizational structure, but little in the way of a viable strategy to deal with the problem. As is chronically the case with respect to broad and long-range initiatives in the U.S. government, the high-level leadership, preoccupied with the issues of the day, failed to follow through with the needed attention and funding. The committees met infrequently and accomplished little.

In the 1980s some coordinated action was directed at two specific problem areas: machine tools and semiconductors. The alarming decline in the U.S. machine tool industry prompted President Reagan to declare a temporary moratorium on machine tool imports, in the hope of giving American industry the needed breathing space to regear and become competitive again in the world market. Noteworthy about the episode is that it was probably the first time that the Department of Commerce enlisted the support of the chairman of the Joint Chiefs of Staff. The latter's demands for a machine-tools capacity for the U.S. defense effort were pivotal in the presidential decision.

Concern was also focused on the U.S. semiconductor industry, which was in danger of becoming extinct in the face of advances in development and production made abroad. In fact, only two U.S. manufacturers of semiconductors remained, and both of them were on less than firm financial legs. Recognition of the importance of semiconductors to the defense industry and the prospect of reliance on foreign sources of supply led to a joint government-industry effort, joined in by Congress, to do something about the problem. Following the recommendation of a Defense Science Board study on the subject, a Semiconductor Manufacturing Technology (SEMATECH) program was started in 1987 to boost development and demonstration of advanced semiconductor manufacturing techniques. The federal government provides $100 million per year, with matching funds coming from industry. After a slow start, the program has registered some momentum.

Two other government-sponsored industrial modernization efforts, also initiated in the 1980s, are the Industrial Modernization Incentives Program (IMIP) and Manufacturing Technology (MANTECH) program. These broad-gauged initiatives, however, have been meagerly funded and have lacked the necessary infusions of strategic direction and planning.

In all, thus far the record of efforts to shore up the conspicuously sagging defense industrial base, even in high-tech areas where the United States was once the acknowledged world leader, has hardly been impressive. The initiatives undertaken have been desultory, underfunded, and addressed at best to small parts of the overall problem. Still, even that poor record indicates that governmental initiative, particularly by the Department of Defense, could make a difference, given the needed investment of resources and sustained leadership.

NEW ECONOMIC REALITIES

It is important to see the problem in a larger context. The economic map of the globe, and the place of the United States on that map, have changed drastically in the four decades since World War II, when the nation could put full and deserved reliance on its prodigious industrial resources in meeting any challenge to its security. The principal and interrelated salients of change are globalization, foreign ownership of U.S. industry, the impact of foreign competition, and the loss by the United States of its former technological dominance in key industrial areas.

Globalization describes the progressive interlocking of world economies. National economic self-sufficiency is a phenomenon of the past. Increasingly, the United States is dependent on foreign sources, not only for the basic raw materials that drive its industries, but in some significant sectors on foreign technology and products manufactured abroad. Indeed, any number of indicators attest to a progressive decline in U.S. technological proficiency, relative to such competitors as Western Europe and Japan.

At the same time, it has become evident that the long-time policy of strategic stockpiling of huge supplies of the raw materials needed for a total mobilization of the industrial base in a national emergency is no longer affordable. Particularly in response to the national debt problem, the strategic stockpiles have been quietly but substantially drawn down. With the exception of oil, the stockpiling focus has narrowed on "exotic" materials associated with high-tech defense endeavors.

The drop of the U.S. dollar in international currency markets has accelerated the phenomenon of foreign ownership of industry in the United States. The Japanese incursion into the U.S. automobile industry, through the acquisition of existing plants or the building of new ones, is just one case in point. There may be merit to the well-publicized claims of the overall benefits to the American economy flowing from the greater productivity, high quality, and satisfied work forces generated by the "Japanese way" of production. Rarely noted, however, is the potential loss of the manufacturing capacity involved to U.S. wartime production of trucks, tanks, and other fighting vehicles.

For their part, U.S. defense industries, eager for short-term profits, are increasingly looking to overseas ventures. The magnets that draw them out of the country are lower labor costs, less stringent environmental and safety requirements, and subsidies from foreign governments intent upon modernizing their own industries. In some cases entire factories have been acquired or built by U.S. firms abroad: notable examples are the General Dynamics and General Electric plants in Turkey, which produce F-16 aircraft and jet engines, respectively. Such modern facilities, incorporating the latest in American know-how and technology, represent not only a net loss to the manufacturing capacity in the United States, but also increased pressure on the U.S.-based industry, which, burdened by higher labor and operating costs, has difficulty competing even with U.S. industrial transplants abroad.

More generally, foreign competition is beating U.S. industry across a broad range of products. The cutting edge of that foreign competition is an emphasis on quality and productivity that generates goods superior in reliability, durability, and costs. The Japanese started their "quality revolution" more than a decade ago, but today such a revolution is still being debated in the United States. Although some individual U.S. firms have made progress in rising to the challenge, in general U.S. industry has a long way to go in re-optimizing the efficiency of its manufacturing processes.

Part of the problem is a general lack of appreciation of the magnitude of the problem. Most Americans, having been reared with the image of the United States as the industrial giant of the post–World War II era, have difficulty accepting the fact of a loss of this erstwhile dominance. In this respect the Gulf War, with its dazzling display of advanced U.S. military technology, performed a disservice by reinforcing the old image. Obscured was the fact that the weaponry, which performed so splendidly on and over the sands of Desert Storm, reflected the investments of past decades. The future looks much less promising.

A deeply disturbing indicator, particularly with respect to technological modernization, is the rate of investment in research and development. Already in 1989, a study by the United States Air Force Association noted that the United States spent less on research and development than most other industrialized nations, and that the rate of increase in such investments was similarly lower.[1] Research and development is the life-blood of a modern national technology base. If this failure to invest continues, a future contingency comparable to the Gulf War is likely to find the United States in a much less confident, let alone commanding, posture—if, indeed, the intervening erosion of our technology base has not progressed to the point where the national leadership will be reluctant to risk our fighting men in a new, major military contingency abroad.

The U.S. defense industry is a prime victim of the unfolding trends. On the one hand, foreign penetration of such key defense-related industries as machine tools, semiconductors, and precision optics is sapping the ability of the defense industry to respond to high-priority military security needs. At the same time, shortsighted government policies and practices are exacerbating the overall decline and obstructing the application of remedies. Myopic government policies have had a debilitating impact on defense industry; they include excessive ov-

The U.S. Defense-Industrial Base

ersight, fixed-price development contracts, changes in the tax law, profit limitations, and cost-sharing with respect to new development programs.

Within the dwindling U.S. defense budget, the impact of such policies and restrictions is sharpening. Already the termination by the Pentagon of "big-ticket" weapons programs, such as the Navy A-12 fighter aircraft, has dealt heavy blows to defense contractors, who have made heavy investments in funds and resources in expectation of contracts. More generally, the fact and continued prospect of a dwindling "market" is turning the competition among contractors, which was intense even when there was an abundance of funding options, into a battle for survival. They face, at the very least, lower incentives on the part of capital investors and higher costs of borrowing money. Some will go out of business. Those who survive will "hedge their bets" by diversifying into broader, nondefense commercial pursuits. In the process, they will endeavor to lighten the risk burden by spending less on research and development, concentrating on low-risk technological solutions and generally cutting back on modernization investments.

The common denominator of trends is a drastic shrinkage of productive capacity relevant to defense. The production lines, once closed, will not easily be reopened in response to a national emergency, especially in light of the rapid march of technology, which calls for constant innovation and modernization. Already the laggard pace of modernization in U.S. industry is implicit in statistics attesting to aging plants. The average age of U.S. industrial equipment is in excess of seventeen years, as contrasted with eight years in the case of Japan.

As far as the mobilization base is concerned, the picture is exacerbated by new management techniques, such as "just in time" production, designed to reduce inventories and minimize in-plant resources. Such techniques were of good avail during the Gulf War in supporting the "desert express" of rapid manufacture and shipment of materiel in response to selective and specific requirements stated by the commanders in the field. Still, reduced inventories mean less stocks available for "surge" mobilization in the first place.

Moreover, there is the all-important human side of the equation. The large-scale layoffs of technicians and trained workers probably represent permanent losses to the defense industry, which will not easily be replenished in time of emergency. Not only are skilled personnel, once displaced and retrained, unlikely to be attracted back to their old jobs—or to perform readily with their former effectiveness—but there is general agreement that the U.S. education system is failing to produce adequate numbers of technicians ready to enter the work-force with the necessary job qualifications.

The industrial "arsenal of democracy" that generated the huge and timely mobilizations of World War I, World War II, and Korea is history. In fact, many believe it is unlikely that the nation's industrial base could rise again to the challenge of a conflict comparable in its demands to the Vietnam War. The problem resides not only in a decline of the U.S. industrial base generally, and its defense-related sectors in particular, but also in the "jump-starting" means. The mobilizations of the past required massive infusions of public money. Especially in light of the growing national deficit, there is scarce prospect that the needed financial resources will be available in a future emergency.

INDUSTRIAL PLANNING

A number of studies undertaken during the past several years have identified gaping inadequacies in the ability of the U.S. industrial base to meet the requirements of military commanders in the event of a major conflict. Proposed remedies have covered a broad and diverse spectrum of recommended action; virtually all, however, have stressed the need for active and concerted industrial planning. Yet the search for such planning solutions has generally been frustrated by the sheer magnitude of the problem.

In the mid–1980s several initiatives were generated in the Joint Chiefs of Staff to deal with the problem. What distinguished those efforts was that, rather than trying to come to grips with the industrial base and its inadequacies as a whole, they focused on the requirements side—specifically the critical wartime requirements of theater commanders-in-chief. The various theater commanders were asked to identify their "war stoppers." The Joint Chiefs logistic staff then consolidated and prioritized the lists of requirements.

The top twenty of these requirements all fell into the category of precision-guided munitions (PGMs). A joint "warfighting group" was established, with representation from the office of the secretary of defense, the Joint Chiefs of Staff, the military services, the Federal Emergency Management Agency (FEMA), the Department of Commerce, and the precision-guided munitions industry (both prime and subcontractors). The group was given the mandate of assessing the ability of the PGMs industry and its subcontractors to meet critical warfighting requirements by surging production. It thus represented the first effort to identify and correct deficiencies in a single sector of the industrial base.

The study's major finding was that it was feasible to obtain a surge capability to meet the theater commanders' stated requirements of precision-guided munitions on the basis of existing capacity. No additional "brick and mortar" would be needed. Instead, additional PGM production could be accomplished by reallocating priorities, working additional shifts, and making long-lead-time resources available. The long-lead-time resources were characterized as rolling inventory. In effect, during the first year of production, 200 percent of inventory would be procured. This inventory cost would have to be funded up front under development as "surge insurance," but the investment would be recoverable in later years of production. The PGM study concluded that, although dependence on some foreign sources posed a problem, advance planning could assure that the needed resources would be available or that ways could be found to work around the problem.

Although that study effort addressed a specific sector of the industrial base, it pointed the way to a broader remedy by showing that surge production was possible, and affordable, by rigorously advancing industrial planning, which entailed identification of critical materiel requirements and investment in rolling inventory.

The PGM study and its high-level endorsement led to revived interest in the process of Joint Industrial Preparedness Planning and Service Production Base Analysis. Unfortunately, the military services, anticipating a low likelihood of congressional authorization of the necessary funds for industrial planning and rolling inventory, generally sat on their hands. The entire initiative, while spotlighting the problem and possible remedies, has wrought little in the way of significant change.

Another attempt at energizing industrial preparedness came shortly after the Packard Commission gave birth to the new acquisition structure in the Department of Defense. The under secretary of defense for acquisition was given direct responsibility for manufacturing policy and guidance in the acquisition of defense systems. It was envisaged that the program executive officers and program managers would give due consideration to industrial base requirements, as well as to post-production mobilization and surge requirements, in the development of new weapons systems. Toward this end a manufacturing guide was even issued to provide program managers with better understanding of the industrial base. Yet this initiative also foundered, because program executive officers and program managers tend to concentrate only on peacetime production parameters and efficiencies. They are reluctant to burden their programs with warfighting requirements and the associated costs of maintaining a healthy industrial base.

In 1988, the under secretary of defense for acquisition directed an examination of the industrial base and its problems. The review engaged more than three hundred government policy makers, industry leaders, academicians, and representatives of professional organizations and industry associations. The subsequent study, completed within a year, came up with the following major conclusions:

- Industrial planning is obstructed by frequent government policy changes, shifts in requirements, and budget/program instabilities.
- There are poor profit incentives for quality performance and reduction of unit costs.
- Layers of bureaucracy and the cumbersome nature of the contract administration process increase the costs to industry of doing business with the Department of Defense and bear responsibility for huge inefficiencies.

Implicit in the discussion of these problems, but never specifically addressed in the study report, is a common cause: lack of requisite leadership on the part of government. As a consequence of the study, three new institutions were created with direct reporting responsibilities to the under secretary of defense for acquisition. A Defense Manufacturing Board, modeled after the Defense Science Board, was to recommend policies for research, development, and acquisition pertinent to improving manufacturing quality and efficiency. A Manufacturing Strategy Committee was to give advice with respect to long-range manufacturing issues. Finally, a Production Base Advocate would provide a focal magnet for criticisms and recommendations from industry.

The initiative followed its predecessors into inertia and ultimate failure. While the three newly established "functions" presaged badly needed bridges between government and industry, they were never really given a chance. The Defense Science Board tended to view them as encroachments on its responsibilities. Because of the board's opposition, and lack of support from the newly appointed under secretary of defense for acquisition, the experiment was aborted after only a year.

The history thus traced shows a prevalent theme. Sporadically, the Department of Defense has faced up to the problem of the declining industrial base and its implications for the future wherewithal of U.S. defenses, particularly the requirements for surge mobilization of industrial resources in a national emergency. In piecemeal fashion, initiatives have been mounted to do something about the problem. Some of these initiatives, with emphasis on the aforementioned effort on precision-guided munitions, have pointed to promising ways of dealing with the problem. The answer clearly lies in industrial planning. But there has to be catalyst for such planning, and it has to come from those charged with assessing and projecting the hard and enduring requirements of safeguarding the defense of the nation.

THE DEFENSE INDUSTRIAL BASE

The prerequisite for effective industrial planning in the interest of the nation's defense, let alone for assertion of leadership in that process by the Defense Department, rests in a cooperative relationship between government and the defense industry. There can be no question that this relationship has, if anything, deteriorated in the past two decades.

The deterioration has had to do with broader societal factors, notably a long-standing popular stereotype of the U.S. "military-industrial complex" as a conglomerate of cynical forces seeking windfall profits at the expense of the taxpayer and disdainful of true national interests, especially the overall health of the nation's economy. The stereotype was magnified in the 1980s by media reports of alleged transgressions, spearheaded by such isolated examples as the infamous "$670 toilet seat" and "$9,600 Allen wrench." There were plausible explanations for these high costs, and rational ways to deal with them, but they were ignored in a general outcry against the defense industry in general, and against the Defense Department in particular, for the way in which they conducted business. The emotional waves swept into Congress, triggering an avalanche of legislation that added layers of oversight to the defense procurement process and forced even greater competitiveness in the award of defense contracts.

Competition is the lifeblood of a market economy. But in the case of an "exacting consumer" like the Defense Department, which must place a strong premium on product quality relative to product costs, there is a point at which competition brings diminishing returns. Thus, the pressure to move away from proven "sole-source" contractors has led the department to accept the bids of unproven manufacturers, who may either fail to deliver or deliver substandard goods. Not only have items not been supplied in time, but inefficient manufacturing processes have led to ultimately higher costs. The institution of firm, fixed-price development contracts had induced defense contractors to make overly optimistic cost projections and unrealistic pricing quotes. These have resulted, in some cases, in massive write-offs by industrial firms, shaking the confidence of their stockholders and undermining the financial foundations of the given firms.

This picture, already emerging in the 1980s, of government-industry relations in the United States was in stark contrast with that of other industrial nations. While the governments of those nations were actively engaged in developing, subsidizing, and nurturing their industries, the U.S. government, in effect, was in a state of confrontation with U.S. industry.

In the late 1980s the situation and its implications was recognized by many analysts in and out of government, including those on the Packard Commission, who urged for a new era of government-industry cooperation. Voices in industry issued somber warnings about the impact of congressional legislation on industry in general, and the defense industry in particular.

A report by the Mac group entitled *The Impact on Defense Industrial Capability of Changes in Procurement and Tax Policy*, issued in 1988, projected that the substantially reduced profits—by an average of 23 percent—in defense business would be inadequate to sustain the shareholders' stock values, and thus would inhibit bids for defense contracts.[2] Those companies continuing to bid would be forced to borrow heavily in order to meet cash requirements. The report predicted that, feeling the squeeze on available capital, these contractors would have to cut back on research and development, thus drying out the seedbed of industry-developed ideas. In the process, they would forfeit their ability to attract top-flight scientists and technicians, who would drift toward more rewarding industrial sectors. More generally, lowered capital investments would result in decreased productivity and higher costs.

The report painted a more generally bleak picture for the defense industry—that is, for those segments of industry still willing to confront the rising risks in that sector. They will try to contain those risks by focusing on "proven" defense programs, eschewing investments of money and brainpower in innovation and modernization. Hedging against the risks would prompt new industrial mergers, thus narrowing the competitive arena. The net consequences would be a loss of U.S. technological prowess and an industry increasingly vulnerable to foreign competition, along with less competitive spark within the industry itself. The report predicted that the impact of those trends would become visible within a period of two to three years.

That 1988 forecast has proven prophetic—all the more so because it did not anticipate the full measure of precipitate drops in U.S. defense spending and the radical changes in defense programs that have occurred since the report was issued. As was suggested earlier, the entire defense industry in the United States is reeling in a state of confusion and uncertainty. In the absence of longer-range industrial planning, instability imposes a well-nigh intolerable burden upon industrial firms accountable to their investors. It is at least questionable whether the Department of Defense, engrossed in adapting to the new U.S. military posture and strategy and to shifting priorities at home, has recognized the full impact of the radical changes in military programs and funding on the defense-industrial base.

IMPROVING QUALITY

Any discussion of the defense-industrial base must deal with the problem of the declining quality of U.S. industrial output. As was noted earlier, the problem pervades U.S. industry much more than it does its global counterparts, as in Japan. Quality improvements hold the potential for huge savings that can yield the needed funds, for example, for long-term investments in research and development and in modernization.

There has been broad recognition of the problem within the Department of Defense, reflected in the creation of the office of an assistant secretary for Total Quality Management (TQM). Organizational answers, however, are only the beginning. Basic to remedies of the quality problem are reforms in the ways in which government and industry conduct business with one another.

An obvious first line of attack is to encourage the many efforts undertaken in industry to improve quality performance, and to remove obstacles to such performance. In 1989 a group of Defense Department officials and industry representatives convened to address the problem. The group identified twenty-six impediments on the road to quality improvements and came up with specific recommendations for overcoming those obstacles. The more fundamental of those recommendations called upon the Department of Defense to forsake its emphasis on inspection, to elevate criteria of quality relative to those of cost, to recognize the importance of quality training, and to establish long-term and cooperative relationships with contractors. The common denominator of the recommendations was the clear expectation that the defense industry will perform more efficiently, with higher-quality output at lower costs, once it is relieved of the stultifying burden of multiple layers of direction and oversight exercised by the Department of Defense.

WHAT CAN BE DONE?

Admittedly, a large and complex problem has been compressed into the preceding pages. The defense industrial base of the United States is an intrinsic part of the nation's industrial establishment, and of its vitality as a whole. For reasons that have been described, in an era of intensified global competition, the overall capacity and productivity of U.S. industry have been in a state of decline relative to that of other nations. The ongoing trends offer alarming implications for the industrial and economic health and future of the nation, let alone for its erstwhile technological-industrial dominance in the world at large.

Clearly, however, the trend is especially sharp in the defense industry. In peacetime there may be reasonable room for debate about the positive or negative economic ramifications of foreign incursions into U.S. industry, or about reliance by U.S. industry on specific items manufactured abroad. With respect to wartime requirements, however, the result is clear: a net loss in U.S. industrial mobilization capacity.

Moreover, the defense industrial base is battered by the dislocations resulting from steep drops in U.S. defense spending, compounded by uncertainties about future funding. The already visible consequences are shutdowns in plant capacity and layoffs of qualified personnel, amid a more general tendency by firms that have concentrated on defense-related enterprises to diversify into the general consumer market. That industrial capacity, once lost, is not likely to be easily reconstituted at a time of national emergency. In the meantime, the technological wherewithal of such future mobilization is being compromised by dwindling investments in research and development.

These trends are unfolding, paradoxically, against the background of unremitting signals of conflict and instability on a chaotically changing world stage, as heralded by the Gulf War. The United States is in the process of sharply reducing its standing military forces, and its warfighting inventories, in response to a dwindling of the former threat from the Soviet Union—and in response to domestic economic forces. This means that in meeting any future military challenge to its vital interests, let alone to its direct defense, the nation will be all the more reliant on requisite and timely mobilization of military manpower and resources.

Already it is generally acknowledged that the scope of mobilization that ensured victory in World War II is no longer within reach. At present, the United States only has the industrial capacity for achieving a "selective surge mobilization," which can barely meet a few of the most critical requirements of conducting a modern war. Yet even this more modest objective calls for concerted measures of institutional adaptation and, above all, long-range industrial planning and guidance. The following recommendations are advanced to meet this goal:

- A defense–industrial base policy group should be established in the president's National Security Council, with the mandate of focusing on the defense-industrial base as a strategic element vital to the nation's security, and therefore as a national priority. Its continuing task would be to monitor the ability of the industrial base to meet national security objectives.
- The Department of Defense, the Joint Chiefs of Staff, and the respective military services

should create offices with specific responsibility for industrial preparedness planning. "War-stoppers" should be identified, resources provided, and the needed planning with industry undertaken to ensure the capability for sustained surge production of critical warfighting materiel.
- The Department of Defense should take the lead in monitoring the health of defense industries, raising the warning flag when problems are discerned, so that appropriate remedies can be designed and acted upon in time. An overall strategic plan should be developed in this behest.
- The Department of Defense should make the requirements of the defense industrial base, including post-production support and surge considerations, an integral part of the acquisition process.
- The Department of Defense should consider reinstating the Manufacturing Board, Manufacturing Strategy Committee, and Production Base Advocate to strengthen support to and communication with the defense industrial base.
- In general, policies should be weighed for their encouragement of modernization, technology investment, and other initiatives, to enhance the competitiveness of the U.S. industrial base with its counterparts abroad.
- The Department of Defense should assume an active leadership role in quality management and strive to remove "non-value-added" requirements and other impediments that stifle industry's quest for greater quality of its products. This is an indispensable step toward restoring a more general sense of cooperative partnership in government-industry relations and dispelling the confrontational climate that is all too much in evidence today.

It may be argued that these recommendations amount to mere organizational expedients, to new insertions into an already excessive government bureaucracy. There are admittedly limits to what government can hope to accomplish in democratic society, especially in the face of complex socioeconomic forces and trends. It should not be forgotten, however, that it is the mandate of government in democratic societies to spotlight critical national priorities, to devise and propose strategies for meeting them, and to assert leadership in the process. That applies particularly to the highest responsibility of government: safeguarding the nation's security.

NOTES

1. U.S. Air Force Association, *The State of the United States Science and Technology Program*.

2. The Mac Group, *The Impact on Defense Industrial Capability of Changes in Procurement and Tax Policy*, 1988.

12

Conclusion: How the Challenges and Dangers of the Post-Containment Era Can Be Mastered

H. Joachim Maitre

This book was written during historic times of great international upheaval, the defeat of this century's most destructive secular utopia, and American promises of a new world order based on the rule of liberal and pluralistic democracy almost everywhere.

The peaceful liberation of the nations of Eastern Europe, the collapse of communist global ambition, and the sudden disintegration and demise of the Soviet Union spelled the end of the Soviet threat that had shaped the defense strategy and posture of the West for four decades. On the first anniversary of the Gulf War, which had seen U.S. military forces at their height of preparedness and performance on the field of battle, a clear signal of dramatic changes to come in defense policy emanated from Washington. In a brisk speech before the Atlantic Council on January 6, 1992, under the heading "Understanding the New Security Environment," chairman Les Aspin of the House Armed Services Committee proclaimed with congressional authority, accompanied by the nation's vehement nodding, that U.S. forces must now be reshaped to meet the (yet undefined) threats of the new post-Soviet epoch. "We are experiencing a profound shift in the bedrock of our national security requirements. The demise of the Soviet Union means the old basis for sizing and shaping our defenses is simply gone."[1]

The authors of this book, all of them undisputed authorities in their respective fields of military and strategic studies, do not challenge Congressman Aspin's basic assessment. Rather, their thoughts aim at his claim that "the new American force must be created from the bottom up, not just by subtracting 25 or 30 or 50 percent from the old Cold War structure."[2]

It was that very "old Cold War structure" that enabled U.S. forces to fight in the Gulf War, and win with the lightest possible loss of life and gear. The U.S. force structure, equipment, and fighting doctrine reflected and vindicated the planning for war in Europe, against the massive Warsaw Pact forces led by the Soviet army. That design did not prove disadvantageous or ill-advised in the war against Iraq. In the coming debate over the size and face of the future U.S. armed forces, one of the key questions may well be, Will these down-sized forces be capable of fighting and winning another Gulf war? In the absence of such capability, which includes the ready availability of rapid air- and sealift, the strategic concept of armed power projection and global reach will prove merely hypothetical.

Desert Storm, the swiftest campaign in modern times, was a triumph of military prowess. "The victory won in the desert is not only historic," wrote John Keegan, the British analyst and defense editor of the London *Daily Telegraph* in the *Washington Post* on March 3, 1991, but "it is also a classic. It will be written about for decades to come. More important, it will be studied in military academies and staff colleges throughout the world as an example of a perfect military operation."

The "perfect military operation," to be sure, fell short of producing perfect victory. It left Saddam Hussein in the driver's seat in Baghdad and Iraq's minority Shiites in the south and Kurds in the north under wholesale oppression, their lands occupied by the very Republican Guard units that U.S. forces had failed to destroy in the final hours of Desert Storm. Historians will not ask, however, if our forces could have defeated Iraq and forced Saddam Hussein to unconditionally surrender. About this there can be no doubt. A few more days of war would have been sufficient. It was not Saddam's army that halted the allied armored advance. It was not his air force that stopped the aerial assault. It was the U.S. president's order, given under a self-imposed commitment to restraint and abiding by the United Nations mandate: to drive Iraqi forces out of Kuwait. That objective had been achieved with mind-numbing speed and stunning precision.

Technology provided only one of the decisive factors. F-117A stealth fighters and more conventional F-111F tactical bombers, with their laser-guided precision weapons, and F-15E and F/A-18C dual-role fighters made success in the one-sided air war total. The Tomahawk cruise missiles performed beyond expectations. AWACS and JSTARS airborne radar platforms passed their tests in battle. The Army's M1A1 tank, M-2/3 infantry and cavalry fighting vehicles, and AH-64A attack helicopters proved their worth, as well as the worth of U.S. arms manufacturers. If any doubt remained about the quality of the manpower and training of the All-Volunteer Force, it evaporated in the desert.

In political terms, victory in the Gulf represents a vindication of the U.S. defense build-up during the 1980s. Yet the lessons to be drawn for the future are not nearly so clear-cut. They are overshadowed by the inevitable and massive U.S. build-down, determined as much by domestic policy rearrangements as by the Cold War's end. In the simplest of terms, the defense policy and posture

How the Post-Containment Era Can Be Mastered 187

for the coming decade will be budget-deficit-driven and debated with scant regard for the military necessities and strategic obligations of a superpower.

In an effort to inform that debate, our military contributors have tried to take the opposite tack: to start with an assessment of the types of threats out there, to factor in our strategic obligations, and then to recommend the shape of the forces, all the while keeping an eye on the current budget constraints.

In doing so, from their collective wisdom has emerged the shape of what we have called an "insurance policy" for peace and freedom. As General Starry argued so persuasively in Chapter 2, against a range of unpredictable threats, this is the most prudent approach the United States can take. The author of Chapter 3, General Woodmansee, was one of the first to advocate such an approach in the post–Cold War era. While certain details of the collective insurance policy might be considered too ambitious or too timid, it is a starting point—and a serious one.

Based on the analysis that has preceded, the United States Army would be cut from a force of 746,000 to a force of 535,000. According to General Woodmansee, after a 30 percent cut the Army would have to place a premium on maintaining the high-quality soldiers that were so central to the recent victory over Iraq. He would distribute those forces as follows:

- One corps, three divisions, and three brigade-sized organizations, plus supporting forces, for a total of 125,000 troops, would be forward deployed in Europe, Korea, Turkey, and Panama (or an alternate location suitable for jungle training).
- Four light divisions, four heavy divisions, three corps headquarters, three separate brigade organizations, and the equivalent of three brigades of Rangers, Special Forces, and Special Operations Forces, for a total of 275,000 personnel, would constitute the contingency forces based in the United States.

General Woodmansee advocates that priority in the reserve components be given to "round-up" brigades, which would train with active divisions as a fourth brigade. As for overall strength of the reserve forces, he calculates that about 640,000 personnel would be required, down from the 776,000 soldiers currently serving.

As the Army is reduced, a premium will need to be placed on recruiting high-quality personnel and continuing to modernize the force. President Bush's decision to cancel the Comanche helicopter program, which represented a "leap-ahead" technology, is not a good first step, if the goal is to maintain a slimmer force with a technological edge over future enemies.

In the naval arena, in Chapter 4 Admiral Train sketches out a force of 490,000 personnel and 450 ships. In what he dubs "an exercise in the art of the possible," he lists the following major combat elements:

- 11 aircraft carriers
- 820 carrier-based fighter/attack aircraft

- 160 surface combatants
- 75 attack submarines
- 18 ballistic missile submarines
- 50 amphibious ships

Train makes a case for a balanced force for deterrence and war fighting. The weak spot in the current and projected naval force is in carrier-based airpower. As the A-6 attack aircraft reaches the end of its already extended life, will it be replaced by the AX, under consideration, or will the F/A-18E and F be used to fill that role of medium-range attack?

As for the Marine Corps, in Chapter 6 General Crist painfully concludes that the corps is headed down to a force of less than 160,000 by the mid–1990s, from a force of 199,000 in 1987. He advocates maintaining the structure of three divisions and three associated air wings, which dates back to a 1952 law signed by President Truman. The strengths of these divisions would have to be reduced, however. In effect, the Marine Corps would have the equivalent of two divisions and two air wings, with a structure that could be expanded under the force reconstitution element of the post–Cold War strategy to three full-strength divisions.

One way to prevent too much combat power from being cut from the Marines would be to reconsider providing the two battalions of Marines used for State Department security guard detachments. According to Crist, Marine detachments aboard capital ships, "a relic of tradition," could also be eliminated, making the surviving force as combat oriented as possible.

In the area of tactical airpower, in Chapter 8 General Piotrowski advocates a larger force than the twenty-six tactical fighter wings planned under the base force concept. From the thirty-six wings recently on the books, Piotrowski believes that the lowest the Air Force should go is thirty wings, which would be divided as follows:

- ten forward-based wings (including one in Alaska)
- twenty wings based in the continental United States

In the area of strategic forces, in Chapter 7 General Welch argues for a balanced triad of ICBMs, bombers, and SLBMs, based on a potential adversary's capabilities, not his announced intentions. Under that formula, cuts could be made in ICBMs if Russia, Kazakhstan, Belarus, and Ukraine come through with some of the cuts proposed by both President Bush and President Yeltsin. In the bomber leg of the triad, Welch suggests that the reduced number of B-2 bombers could be offset by using a combination of B-52H bombers in the cruise missile carrier role and B-1B bombers in the penetrating role. Once again, depending on changes in the Russian SLBM force, U.S. D-5 SLBMs could be downloaded to five warheads each.

How the Post-Containment Era Can Be Mastered

With regard to strategic defense, in Chapter 8 General Piotrowski has endorsed the reconfigured version of SDI known as Global Protection Against Limited Strikes (GPALS). Given the proliferation of ballistic missiles, this defensive component of both strategic and tactical forces makes more sense than ever.

A dominant theme among many of the contributors was the importance of airlift and sealift. These components are at the very heart of power projection, and the Gulf War experience suggests a need to expand and improve them, as outlined in Chapter 9 by General Cassidy and Admiral Herberger. Forward prepositioning also proved critical in the Gulf War, especially in the early stages of Desert Shield. In Chapter 10, General Went makes a persuasive case for maintaining a "triad of strategic mobility," which includes airlift, sealift, and pre-positioning.

Under all of these elements of force structure lies the foundation of the U.S. industrial base, the future of which is uncertain. As General Hansen suggests in Chapter 11, the National Security Council and the Department of Defense should devote more attention to industrial preparedness planning and the health of the defense industries.

These are the essential elements of a comprehensive approach to insuring U.S. national security. While the predictable Soviet threat has disappeared, there are many potential threats out there in what continues to be a dangerous, unpredictable world. In the frenzy to cut the U.S. force, it should be remembered that the vaunted Cold War structure, which many today believe is bloated, was taxed by the Gulf War. Reshaping that structure into a slimmer but adequate force can be done, but it must be done judiciously.

In the end, the proposals made by our contributors represent an insurance policy we can readily afford, if we invest prudently by paying the premiums over time.

NOTES

1. Les Aspin, Statement issued by Office, January 6, 1992.
2. Ibid.

Index

Acheson, Dean, 5–6
Aegis. *See* Weapons, ships
Afghanistan, 20, 73, 77
Air Force Reserve, 144, 152
Air National Guard, 143–44, 152
Airland Battle: doctrine, 35; Gulf War, 33–38
Alaska, 86, 89
APF, 164
Arab-Israeli Wars, effect on U.S. doctrine, 34
Argentina, nuclear weapons, 19
Arleigh Burke class. *See* Weapons, ships
Arms Control, reductions, nuclear weapons, 29–30
Arms Control Treaties: ABM Treaty, 138; CFE, 15–16; INF, 16–17; SALT, 119; START, 29, 115–20, 122, 130, 135
A–6 Intruder. *See* Weapons, aircraft
Aspin, Les, 185
AWACS. *See* Weapons, aircraft

Ballistic missiles: Afghanistan, 20; Algeria, 20; China, 19; Cuba, 19–20; Egypt, 20; India, 19; Indonesia, 19; Iran, 19; Iraq, 19–20, 126; Israel, 19; Japan, 19; Korea, North, 19; Korea, South, 19; Levant, 19; Libya, 19; North Africa, 19; Northeast Asia, 19; Pakistan, 19; Saudi Arabia, 19; South Asia, 19; Syria, 19; Taiwan, 19; Yemen, 19
Base Force, 41–42, 89; Atlantic Force, 59; Contingency Force, 59; Pacific Force, 59; Strategic Force, 59
Battleship, 64
BCTP, 44
Belarus, nuclear weapons, 134
Belgrano, sunk by submarine, 63
Bengazi, target of Libya raid in 1986, 71–72
Biological weapons, in Iran, Iraq, North Korea, Syria, 20
Bradley. *See* Weapons, land
Bradley, Gen. Omar, 94
Brazil, nuclear weapons, 19
Brown, Harold, 163
Bush, George H. W., 163; arms control, 29; disarmament initiative, 16–17; National Security Sealift policy, 157; 1991 cuts, 117–18; 1991 cuts in

strategic weapons, 116; redirects SDI, 124, 129

Camp Pendleton, 101
Capital ships, 57
Carrier battle groups, 61–62
Cassidy, Gen. Duane, 159, 189
Cates, Gen. Clifton B., 99
CENTAF. *See* Units, air
Central Command, 97
Chemical weapons, 20
Cheney, Dick, 99–100
China, 86; and ballistic missile, 19
CIS. *See* Commonwealth of Independent States
Civil Reserve Air Fleet, 143–44, 146
Cold War: engagement, 6; lessons, 5; mobilization, 5–6
Commonwealth of Independent States, 24
Crist, Gen. George, 188
Crowe, Adm. William, 72
Cuba, adventurism, 59
Cuban Missile Crisis, 95, 128

Dailey, Gen. John R., 104
Defense cuts: after wars, 77; force planning, 25; Gulf War does not halt, 7, 39; Marine Corps, 98–100; naval reductions, 60–61
Defense Insurance Policy, 9–10, 17
Defense Planning, 9–10, 39
de Tocqueville, Alexis, 4
Dhahran, missile target, 123
Diego Garcia, 171
Doctrine: definition, 8; of U.S. Army, 13
Dominican Republic, Marines in, in 1963, 95
DSP Satellites, 130
Dulles, John Foster, 112

Egypt, 73, 76; CENTCOM exercises, 74; chemical weapons, 20
Einstein, Albert, 39
Eisenhower, Dwight D., 104
Elat, sunk by Styx missile, 58
EUSC, 149–50

F/A–18 Hornet. *See* Weapons, aircraft
Falklands, Argentine decision to invade, 69–70
FEMA, 178
F–14D Tomcat. *See* Weapons, aircraft
Field Manual 100–5: (1976), 13; (1982), 35; (1986), 35, 37–38
F–111. *See* Weapons, aircraft
Force structure: definition, 7; U.S. forces in Europe, 16
Forrestal, James, 5
Fort Bliss, 52
Fort Hood, 52
Fort Irwin. *See* NTC
F–16. *See* Weapons, aircraft

Gabriel, Gen. Charles A., 74
General Dynamics, 176
General Electric, 176
Germany: economic strength, 23; unification, 17–18, 23
Global Positioning System, 126
GLONASS, 126
Gorbachev, Mikhail, 114; economic reforms, 22; modernized forces, 16; out of power, 118; reciprocates cuts, 117; reforms, 22–23; weapons sales, 18–19
GPALS, 125, 136
Greenland-Iceland-UK Gap, 63
Grenada, 95–96, 144
GSTS, 136
Gulf War, 74–75, 186; air campaign, 38, 57, 73; airland battle, 37–38; command, 60–61; criteria, 6–7; defense planning, effect on, 9–11; demanding contingency, 157; doctrine, example of, 14; lessons, 6, 26–28, 34, 42, 56–57, 75–76, 97, 129, 155; lessons, tactical air, 79, 81; mine warfare, 66; missile use, 128–29; mobilization, 123; results, 7; sealift, 153–54; tactical air, 71; transportation, 143; victory, 53; weapons inventories, 18–19; weapons suppliers, 18

Haifa, missile target, 123
Hansen, Gen. Alfred G., 189

Index

Harpoon. *See* Weapons, missiles
Herberger, Vice Adm. Albert, 159, 189
Hitler, Adolf, 123
Holder, Col. Don, 35
Horner, Lt. Gen. Charles A., 38, 72–73
Hussein, Saddam, 4, 56, 166; attack on Kuwait, 21; invasion of Kuwait, 17; microcosm of Third World, 21; timing of attack, 18

IMIP, 174
Inchon, Gulf War compared to, 33
India, 86; adventurism, 59; militarization, 18; nuclear weapons, 20
Indonesia, ballistic missile, research, 19
Industrial mobilization, SEMATECH, MANTECH, IMIP, 174
Intelligence, heightened need for, 24
Iran, 73; biological weapons, 20; chemical weapons, 20
Iran-Iraq War, first missile attack, 123
Iraq, 73, 76; adventurism, 29; Air Force not committed to battle, 56; biological weapons, 20; chemical weapons, 20; chemical weapons, vs. Iran and Kurds, 20–21; nuclear weapons, 20
Isolationism, 2, 5
Israel: chemical weapons, 20; nuclear weapons, 20

Jordan, CENTCOM exercises, 74

Kaneohe Bay, 101
Kazakhstan, nuclear weapons, 134
Keegan, John, 186
Kelley, Lt. Gen. P. X., 73
Kenya, 73
Khafji, battle of, 104
Khrushchev, Nikita, 15, 22
Klingsberg, Frank L., 3
Korea, North, 86; adventurism, 59; biological weapons, 20; chemical weapons, 20
Korea, Republic of. *See* Korea, South
Korea, South, 41; chemical weapons, 20; invasion of, 6
Korean War, 92; mobilization, 177; Pacific logistics, 67–68; preparedness, 90–91
Kuwait, 18, 76, 97; invasion of, 142
Kuwait City, Marines liberate, 97
Kuwait International, Battle of, 104

Labour party (UK), 87
Laird, Melvin, 112
Lebanon, Marines in: in 1958, 95; in 1982, 95
Libya: chemical weapons, 20; crisis in 1983, 61; militarization, 18; raid in 1986, 71
Liddell Hart, Sir Basil, 7
Lind, William S., 103
Lipmann, Walter, 4

MacArthur, Gen. Douglas, 33
MacKinder, Halford, 141–42
MAGTF, 164–67
Mahan, Alfred Thayer, 59
Main Battle Force, 59–60
MANTECH, 179
MARAD, 146, 148
Marine Expeditionary Brigade, 162–63, 168
Marshall, George C., 5
McNamara, Robert S., 112–13
Meyer, Gen. Edward C., USA, 34
Military Airlift Command, 143, 151–52
Military Prepositioning Ships, 154
Military Sealift Command, 143, 146–50
Mine Warfare, 66
Minuteman III. *See* Weapons, missiles
Missile proliferation, 19
MLRS. *See* Weapons, land
M1A1. *See* Weapons, land
Montgomery, G. I Bill, 51
Moskin, J. Robert, 103
MPS, 159–60, 163, 167
M–60 tank. *See* Weapons, land
MTMC, 143, 154
Mundy, Gen. Carl, Jr., 99
Mutla Ridge, Battle of, 104

National Defense Reserve Fleet, 148
NATO, 14
Naval posture of mid–1990s, 69

Norfolk, Virginia, 72
Norway, 164
NTC, 26, 41, 52, 74
Nuclear weapons, 17, 20

Ogarkov, Marshal Nikolai, 16
Okinawa, 86
Oman, 76; CENTCOM exercises, 74
Operational Art, definition, 7–8
Operations, definition, 7–8

Pakistan, 73, 86; militarization, 18
Panama, 96, 168; as lower end contingency, 61; Marines in, in 1990, 95
Peacekeeper. *See* Weapons, missiles
Perisan Gulf, Marines in, in 1987–1988, 95
PGU, 178, 199
Philippines, 86
Piotrowski, Gen. John L., 30, 153, 189
Policy, definition, 8
POMCUS, 160–63, 170, 171
Post Stanley, 56
Post-Containment era, 17–18
Post-Containment strategy, 7
Posture, definition, 7–8
Powell, Gen. Colin, 95
P–3 Orion. *See* Weapons, aircraft

Ready Reserve Forces (RRF), 148, 155–56
Reagan, Ronald, 129
Red Flag, 78
Red Sea, 78
Republican Guard, 83
Reserve components, 43–44; Air Force, 144; Marine Corp Reserve, 103, 150–7; Naval, 68
Reykjavik Summit, 120
Riyadh, missile target, 123
Rotational base, 87–88
Rowen, Harry S., 112
RPV. *See* Weapons, aircraft
Russia: historical role, 15; instability, 15; nuclear weapons, 134–35; threat, 15–17; weapons supplier, 18–19
Russian Federation, 135

Saudi Arabia: airbases, 152; asks for Patriots, 139
Schlesinger, Arthur M., 30
Schwarzkopf, Gen. Norman, 37–38, 72, 80
SDI, 121, 124, 129–30, 136, 138
Seawolf SSN–21. *See* Weapons, submarines
SEMATECH, 174
SETAF, 41
Shaposhnikov, Y. I. Marshal, 134
Ships Taken Up From Trade (STUFT), 66
Simulation, 52
Smith, Gen. Norman H., 100
Somalia: CENTCOM exercises, 74; Marines evacuation, 95
South Africa: chemical weapons, 20; nuclear weapons, 20
Soviet Union: cuts under Khrushchev, 15; former, economic factors, 22; successor states and threats to, 10; threat to U.S., 8; unrest, 14
Special Operations Command, submarine support, 63
Spruance class. *See* Weapons, ships
Stalin, Josef, 15, 141
Starry, Gen. Donn, 33, 34, 158, 187
Star Wars. *See* SDI
Stealth Fighter. *See* Weapons, aircraft
Strategic Rocket Forces, 134
Strategy: components of, 7; containment, 9; definition, 7; military definition, 7; national, 8
Syria: adventurism, 59; biological weapons, 21; chemical weapons, 20

Tactics, definition, 8
T-AGOS. *See* Weapons, ships
Taiwan: ballistic missiles, 19; chemical weapons, 20
Tal, Gen. Israel, 51
Tehran, storming of U.S. embassy in 1978, 93
Tel Aviv, missile target, 123, 124
Teller, Edward, 130
Thailand, Marines in, in 1962, 95
Total Quality Management (TQM), 182

Index

TRADOC, 35, 46
Train, Adm. Harry II, 187
Tripoli: F–111 target, 72; Libya raided in 1986, 72
Truman, Harry S, 5–6, 100, 188
Truman Doctrine, 6
Tucker, Robert W., 6
Turkey, 76, 176

Ukraine, nuclear weapons, 134, 135
Unit, military, TDA units, 45
United Kingdom, 87
Units, air: 3rd Marine Air Wing, 102; 4th Marine Air Wing, 105; 9th Air Force, 73–74; Royal Saudi Air Force, 73
Units, military: 1st (British) Armoured Div., 38; 1st Cavalry Division, 168; 1st Marine Division, 104; 1st Marine Expeditionary Force, 97, 104; 2nd Armored Division, 1st Bde, 104; 2nd Marine Division, 38, 104; 4th Force Service Support Grp., 105–6; 4th Marine Division, 105; 6th (French) Light Armored Div., 38; 7th Light Infantry Division, 96; 10th Mountain Division, 96; 24th Mechanized Division, 42, 96, 98, 156, 168; 82nd Airborne Division, 42, 96, 97–98; 101st Airmobile Division, 36, 38, 96; TDA units, reducing, 46; Third Army, 73; Tiger Brigade, 104; VII Corps, 38; XVIII Airborne Corps, 73
Units, naval, Sixth Fleet, 66–67
Unmanned Aerial Vehicle (UAV). *See* Weapons, aircraft
USTRANSCOM, 142–44

Vandenberg, Sen. Arthur, 6
Vietnam, 86; breakdown of consensus, 6; doctrine, effect on, 14; mine warfare, 66; Pacific logistics, 66–67; preparedness, 91; syndrome, 6
Vietnam War, 91–92; mobilization, 175
VLSIC, 130
Vuono, Gen. Carl (USA), 35, 76

Warsaw Pact, 14; disbanded, 15
Warships: Belgrano, sunk by submarine, 62; Curtiss, TAVB, 166; Elat, sunk by Styx missile, 58; Wright, TAVB, 166
Weapons, aircraft, A–10, 82–83; A–12, 177; A–16, 83; A–4, 103; A–6 Intruder, 62; AH–1 Cobra, 102, 103; Apache, 67, 72, 186; AT–28, 91; AV–8 Harrier, 102, 103; AWACS, 74, 80, 186; B–1A, 113; B–1B, 121, 188; B–2, 81, 117, 121, 188; B–26, 91; B–52, 83, 120, 121, 188; B–70, 113; C–130, 145; C–141, 145, 152; C–17, 152, 153; C–21, 145; C–27, 145; C–47, 91; C–5B, 145; C–9, 145; Commanche (LHX), 69, 187; E–3A (AWACS), 123; EF–111, 79, 82, 85; F–111, 72, 86, 89; F–111E, 89; F–111F, 186; F–117, 79, 81–82, 186; F–14D Tomcat, 62; F–15, 74; F–15E, 82, 85, 86, 89; F–16, 78, 85; F–16 Falcon, 78, 176; F–22, 81; F–4G, 79, 82; F/A–16, 83, 84, 86; F/A–18 Hornet, 62, 103, 186; Guardrail, 36; JSTARS, 36, 37, 186; KC–135R, 113; MiG–15, 90; P–3, 64, 65, 68; P–7, 64; RPV, 37; YAK–9, 90
Weapons, anti-missile: Arrow, 137; Brilliant Pebbles, 130–34, 136–37, 138; ERINT, 137; Patriot, 36, 47, 123–24, 139; THAAD, 307
Weapons, ballistic missiles: CSS–2, 20; Scud, 19, 36; Third World proliferation, 19
Weapons, electronic, LANTIRN, 85
Weapons, land: AASW-M, 50; Abrams, (M1, M1A1, M1A2), 50, 51; Bradley, 38–39, 162, 186; Firefinder radar, 38–39, 67; FOG-M, 50; Gepard, 66; Ground Based Sensor (GBS), 48; Leopard, 51; LOSAT, 50; M–109, 104; M–110, 104; M–60 tank, 38; M1989, 16; M1A1 Abrams, 38, 47, 104, 186; Masked Target Sensor (MTS), 48; Merkava, 51; MLRA/ATACMS battalion, 41; MLRS 34, 47, 104; OH–58D Scout, 68; SADARM, 50; T–72, 18; T–80, 16, 51; Wide Area Mine (WAM), 50
Weapons, mines, CAPTOR, 66
Weapons, missiles: ATACMS, 36, 47,

48; D-5 SLBM, 113; Exocet, 56–57; Harpoon, 63, 64; Hellfire, 52, 73; Maverick, 83; Minuteman III, 118, 121; MX, 113; Patriot, 129; Peacekeeper, 117, 121; Scud, 123, 125, 137; SS-18, 115, 118, 125; SS-24, 118, 125; SS-25, 125; SS-N-21, 125; Styx, 58; TLAM, 65; Tomahawk, 65–66, 79, 126, 186; Trident II, 113; V-2, 123
Weapons, RPV: Pioneer, 39; Pointer, 39
Weapons, ships: Aegis, 60, 62; AE Refrig. ship, 67; Afloat Prepositioning Ships, 148; AFS, 67; Ammunition Ship, 60, 62; AOF, 67; AO Fleet oiler, 67; APF, 159, 160; Arleigh Burke class, 60; Aviation Logistic Support Ship, 148; Fast Sealift Ships FSS, 146, 154, 159, 168; Forrestal class, 60; Hospital ships (TAH), 148, 167; Kirov class, 58; LASH, 156; LCAC, 64; Maritime Prepositioning Ships, 147, 154; MPS, 159–60, 163, 165, 166, 167; OPDS, 148; RO/RO (Roll on/Roll off), 155, 164; Spruance class, 60, 62; T-AGOS, 63; TAVB, 167; Victory ships, 148
Weapons, submarines; Charlie-class, 58; Echo-class, 58; Juliet-class, 58; Los Angeles class, 65; Oscar-class, 58; Seawolf class, 63; Seawolf SSN-21, 63
Welch, Gen. Larry D. USAF, 188
Went, Gen. Joseph, 189
Wood, Lowell, 130
Woodmansee, Lt. Gen. John W., 187
World War I: mobilization, 174; Russia in, 15; ships, 57
World War II: demobilization, 90; mobilization, 173, 182; naval warfare, 67; Russia in, 15; U-Boats, 67; U.S. in, 5

Yeltsin, Boris, 118, 135, 138, 188; modernized forces, 16; reforms, 23; uncertain control, 134
Yemen, ballistic missiles, 19
Yom Kippur War, 163

About the Editors and Contributors

GENERAL DUANE CASSIDY served thirty-six years in the U.S. Air Force, retiring in October 1989. He was, among other positions, commander-in-chief of U.S. Transportation Command and Military Airlift Command (responsible for global land, air, and sea transportation for all U.S. fighting forces), Air Force deputy chief of staff, manpower and personnel commander of MAC's 21st Air Force at McGuire Air Force Base in New Jersey, and MAC's deputy chief of staff for operations. He is a command pilot and senior navigator with over 8,000 flying hours and assignments at Strategic Air Command at McCoy, Little Rock, and Lincoln Air Force bases. General Cassidy served in Vietnam, first with the 7th Air Force's Tactical Air Control Center and then with the Military Assistance Command Vietnam Directorate of Public Affairs as an air briefer to the Saigon press corps. He is currently Senior Vice President—Sales and Marketing of CSX Transportation, Inc.

GENERAL GEORGE CRIST was the first Marine to be appointed a four-star unified commander. As Commander in Chief of the United States Central Command, he had military responsibility for nineteen countries in the Middle East and southwest Asia and directed the successful American escort and retaliatory operations in the Persian Gulf during the 1987–88 "tanker war." A veteran of Korea, Grenada, and two tours in Vietnam, General Crist's military career of more than thirty-six years encompassed diverse assignments in Washington,

Europe, the Caribbean, the Middle East, and the Far East. He was a military consultant for CBS during the Gulf War, appearing on national television and radio.

WALTER HAHN has commuted professionally between think-tank analysis of defense and foreign policy issues—including tenures in the Institute for Defense Analyses (Washington), Foreign Policy Research Institute (Philadelphia), and Institute for Foreign Policy Analysis (Cambridge, MA)—and editing and publishing in those fields, notably as Editor-in-Chief of *Strategic Review* from 1977 to 1990. The author or editor of a half-dozen previous books and numerous other publications on topics of military strategy and international relations, he is a member of the Board of Advisors of the Center for Defense Journalism and an Adjunct Professor of International Relations at Boston University.

GENERAL ALFRED G. HANSEN retired from the Air Force in October 1989 as the Commander of the Air Force Logistic Command. His responsibilities included providing the worldwide logistic resources necessary to maintain Air Force units and weapon systems in a state of readiness and combat sustainment. Under his command were seventeen major repair/manufacture centers with over 100,000 people. He started the first total quality effort in the Air Force and was awarded the Eugene M. Zuckert Award for Management Excellence. His command later received the federal equivalent of the Malcolm Baldrige Award. He joined Lockheed in 1990 and is presently the vice-president of Airlift Programs.

STANLEY E. HARRISON is the Chairman of the Board of Directors and President of The Potomac Foundation, located in McLean, Virginia. He is recognized as a leading authority in areas such as high technology business, national security, and higher education. A professional manager and problem solver, he has turned his talents easily from business to public policy to education, energy, and other areas. He was a member of the U.S. Air Force from 1948 to 1952, and he has worked with the Martin Marietta Corporation, has been employed as a working scientist with the Sandia Laboratory in Albuquerque, New Mexico, and recently served as president of the BDM Corporation.

VICE ADMIRAL ALBERT HERBERGER served in the merchant marine in his early career years and was a Surface Welfare Officer in the United States Navy for thirty-two years. He retired from active duty in the Navy in April 1990. He has been Vice-President, Maritime Affairs, of IPAC, Inc. (International Planning and Analysis Center) since August 1990. Among the positions he held during his naval service were Deputy Commander-in-Chief of the U.S. Transportation Command and Director of Logistics on Staff for the Atlantic Fleet Commander-in-Chief. He is a graduate of the U.S. Merchant Marine Academy and the Naval Postgraduate School.

H. JOACHIM MAITRE, a professor at Boston University, is the Center for Defense Journalism's founder and its director. He also holds a dual faculty appointment in the School of Journalism in the College of Communication and

About the Editors and Contributors

the Department of International Relations in the Graduate School. Previously, Maitre served as the dean of the College of Communication. Before coming to Boston University, he was editor-in-chief of Axel Springer Publishing and general manager of Ullstein/Propylaeen Books in Berlin, Germany. He has also held a number of academic positions, including faculty appointments at the University of Nigeria and McGill University (Montreal, Canada), department chairman at McGill, and national fellow at the Hoover Institution. In the field of journalism, Maitre has served as editor of *Die Welt* and *Die Welt der Literatur* (Hamburg, Germany) and as editor-in-chief of *Welt am Sonntag* (also in Hamburg). He currently serves as editor-in-chief of the center's monthly newsletter, *Defense Media Review*.

GENERAL JOHN L. PIOTROWSKI held the positions of Commander-in-Chief North American Aerospace Defense Command (NORAD) and Commander-in-Chief United States Space Command when he retired from the U.S. Air Force in April 1990. During his thirty-eight-year service General Piotrowski rose from the enlisted ranks to a variety of key positions. He created the E–3A Wing and brought it to operational status; commanded Air Defense TAC, now 1st Air Force; served as Tactical Air Command Director of Operations and Vice Commander; commanded 9th Air Force; stood up Central Air Forces of Desert Storm fame; and served as USAF Vice Chief of Staff prior to moving to NORAD and USSPACECOM in 1987.

GENERAL DONN STARRY is the originator of the Army doctrine, now called AirLand Battle, so successfully employed by coalition forces in Operation Desert Storm in 1991. A former chief of armor, he later commanded, in turn, the Fifth U.S. Corpsin Europe, the Army Training and Doctrine Command, and U.S. Readiness Command. Following his military retirement, he became vice-president and general manager of Space Missions Group and later executive vice-president of Ford Aerospace Corporation. He is a two-term member of the Defense Science Board and adviser to the military, industry, and government in the United States and several foreign countries.

ADMIRAL HARRY TRAIN II served as NATO's Supreme Allied Commander, Atlantic; as Commander-in-Chief, U.S. Atlantic Command; as Commander-in-Chief, U.S. Atlantic Fleet; and as Commander U.S. Sixth Fleet. Admiral Train is currently Manager of Strategic Research and Management Services, Science Applications International Corporation.

GENERAL LARRY D. WELCH served thirty-seven years in the United States Air Force, retiring in 1990. He served as Air Force Chief of Staff from July 1986 to July 1990. Before becoming Chief of Staff, he served as Commander-in-Chief, Strategic Air Command; Vice Chief of Staff, U.S. Air Force; and Commander, 9th Air Force. His earlier service was in a variety of operational and staff assignments with the tactical forces. He is currently President of The Institute for Defense Analyses, a Washington-based federally funded research and development center serving the Department of Defense.

GENERAL JOSEPH WENT retired from active duty in the U.S. Marine Corps in July 1990 after nearly thirty-eight years of active service. He has experience flying transport, reconnaissance, and fighter-attack aircraft as well as extensive experience in logistics, including supply, transportation, and maintenance management. He served as the Director of Logistics for the Marine Corps and then as the Assistant Commandant. General Went currently holds a number of advisory positions and is a self-employed consultant.

LIEUTENANT GENERAL JOHN W. WOODMANSEE, JR. has for the past seventeen years served in a variety of assignments alternating between command of tactical units of combat development and force development functions. Through his assignments he has developed a broad-based knowledge of land power and the interaction with air power, and he has had extensive experience in training soldiers and staff to execute doctrine, as well as with "black" programs. In 1986, he directed a study for Chief of Staff, Army, on the feasibility of defending NATO conventionally and the cost effectiveness of "smart" conventional weaponry over short-range tactical nuclear weapons. In 1978, he was a key player in developing the emerging doctrine of "2nd echelon attack" and reorganizing the Army's heavy division. Lieutenant General Woodmansee served as a White House Fellow to Secretaries of State Dean Rusk and Edward Rogers in 1968–69 and participated frequently on Army Science Board and Defense Science Board deliberations. He also has served as an Associate Professor of Military History at the United States Military Academy, commanded units in Vietnam during two tours as a Captain and a Lieutenant Colonel, and flew over 1,500 combat hours.